10^{00}

HANNIBAL'S CAMPAIGNS

HANNIBAL'S CAMPAIGNS

The story of one of the greatest military commanders of all time

Tony Bath

BARNES
&NOBLE
BOOKS
NEW YORK

This edition published by Barnes & Noble Inc.,
by arrangement with Patrick Stephens Limited.

1992 Barnes & Noble Books

ISBN 0-88029-817-0

Printed and bound in the United States of America

M 9 8 7 6 5 4 3 2

Contents

Introduction

I was first introduced to Hannibal at quite an early age; when in Infants' School, I was taught to sing a song entitled 'Hannibal Crossed the Alps'. Whether this made an indelible impression upon me I cannot say, but certainly when I first became interested in military history he was one of the first ancient Generals I studied, and similarly, when I became interested in wargaming as a means of studying the practical aspects of ancient warfare, the first campaign I ever organised was based on the Second Punic War.

Hannibal has not, in my opinion, had a completely fair Press over the years; too many writers have looked merely at his three brilliant victories and his one decisive defeat and virtually ignored the greater part of his career—the part in fact which is probably of the greatest interest. In this book, therefore, I have tried to set the record straight to some degree and present a balanced picture of the great Carthaginian. I will undoubtedly be accused by some of being biased in Hannibal's favour; to this accusation I freely plead guilty. It is my humble opinion that no worthwhile historian is free of a measure of bias. You write about a period or a man because you are genuinely interested in it or him, and through this interest you inevitably tend to favour one side or the other. A writer who shows no bias at all is one who lacks enthusiasm for his subject, with the result that the book he produces is usually dull. I hope that I have restrained my bias within reasonable grounds and that my readers will not find the account lacking in interest, but I am certainly not ashamed of my belief that Hannibal ranked with the highest for military ability.

Since I have no claims to being a scholar, I have not attempted to search out the correct names for people or places in their ancient Greek or Latin forms but have used throughout those which tend to have become common usage, in the hope that this will make things easier for the reader. I would also mention that there tends to be a good deal of confusion because, particularly with regard to Carthage, the same names tend to crop up over and over again, not only from period to period but often within the same time span. Thus the Carthaginian ranks are overflowing with Himilcos, Hasdrubals, Hannos and even a few Hannibals, while even among the Romans names can be confusing. I have tried wherever possible to qualify the bearer of these names by adding some other reference to make it clearer to whom I am referring.

There is no lack of books on the period, but most of them are derived from the same original sources. One would expect this to make things easier and that most accounts of events would tally. In fact the reverse is the case; on almost every important point throughout the period there are disagreements on geography, numbers and many other things. Even when original sources are available, they cannot always be taken on trust. As already stated, most historians are liable to bias of some sort, and very often those writing nearer the events are more biased than others, since they are often trying to put their own country or countrymen in a better light. The modern historian thus has to chart his course through a good number of reefs, balancing one source against another and adding a good dose of common-sense plus a feeling of what is militarily likely. Where I have followed other writers I have said so, where not, if I am in error, the fault is mine alone. All the opinions expressed are mine, but I do not claim to have thrown any particularly new light on the subject.

Although this book is essentially about Hannibal's campaigns, to understand these properly, it is necessary to know something of the background to the Second Punic War. In the first two chapters, therefore, I have sketched in the general history of Carthage and the events which led, almost inevitably, to the greatest challenge Rome was ever to face in her rise to world dominance.

I would like to express my gratitude to my wife, who throughout has been a great support and has borne with my irritability when things would not go well, in addition to typing the manuscript for me; and also to Phil Barker and Bruce Quarrie for their confidence in my ability to write this book—I hope they will not think it misplaced.

Chapter 1

The rise of Carthage

Among the early civilisations of the eastern Mediterranean basin, the cities of Phoenicia, and principally those of Sidon and Tyre, produced the hardiest and most daring seafarers and traders. From earliest times their fragile ships pushed steadily west into unknown waters, trading with the natives, fighting when necessary, and founding trading stations and occasionally small colonies on promising sites. It was, in fact, the Phoenicians who first penetrated the Pillars of Hercules, as the Straits of Gibraltar were then called, braved the waters of the Atlantic and opened up the tin trade with Britain. Carthage itself seems to have been founded in 814 BC, either direct from Tyre or as a sub-colony of the earlier Utica. It was, in fact, known to its inhabitants as Kirjath-Hadeschath, or New Town; the Greeks knew it as Karchedon; the Romans in their turn called it Carthago; and we today speak of it as Carthage.

The site of the New Town was well chosen, a small bay within the great natural harbour now called the Bay of Tunis. The surrounding area was fertile and well-watered, the river Bagradas (modern day Mejerda) being nearby. The original foundation was probably what became later the Byrsa or Citadel, built on a rocky promontory overlooking the harbour; this latter area was soon built up into what became known as the Cothon, and as the city prospered it expanded north and west to form the Megara, or suburbs, until the whole city finally covered an area some 23 miles in circumference and containing, so we are told, over 700,000 souls.

If we are to believe Virgil, the fates of Rome and Carthage were linked from their earliest days. According to *The Aenead*, the Trojan hero Aeneas, fleeing from the destruction of Troy, was welcomed at Carthage by its Queen, Dido, who fell in love with the handsome Trojan and offered him permanent sanctuary. The gods, however, had scheduled Aeneas as the founder of Rome and ordered him to quit his dalliance and get on with the job in hand; he duly obeyed, and Dido, heartbroken, committed suicide. Alas for legend! It seems that Virgil discovered an earlier tale of how Carthage was founded by a Queen Elissa or Dido, herself fleeing from Tyre, and used poetic licence to embroider this into his story; and indeed it would seem that Dido, if she existed at all, was two hundred years in her grave at the time of the foundation of Rome. It would be nice to believe Virgil; we could point to the strange coincidence that the founder of Rome destroyed the Queen of Carthage, just as his city was later to destroy the Queen City of Carthage; and modern psychiatrists could no doubt propound the theory that Rome's enmity for Carthage was built on a sub-

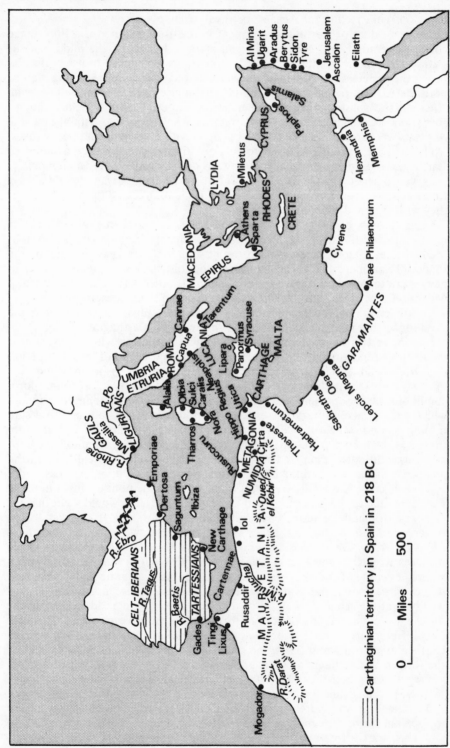

Al Mina
Ugarit
Aradus
Berytus
Sidon
Tyre
Jerusalem
Ascalon
Eilath

Salamis
CYPRUS
Paphos

Memphis
Alexandria

LYDIA
Miletus
RHODES
CRETE

Athens
Sparta

MACEDONIA
EPIRUS

Cyrene
Arae Philaenorum
GARAMANTES

Cannae
Tarentum
Capua
LUCANIA
Syracuse
ROME
Panormus
Lipera
MALTA
UMBRIA
ETRURIA
Aleria
R.Po
Nola
Neapolis
LIGURIANS
Olbia
Sulci
Hippo
Utica
CARTHAGE
Caralis
Regius
Oea
GAULS
Massilia
Tharros
Rusicurru
METAGONIA
Sabratha
Lepcis Magna
R.Rhône
Emporiae
NUMIDIA
Hadrumetum
Dertosa
Iol
Cirta
Theveste
Saguntum
Olbiza
Oued
el Kebir
CELT-IBERIANS
New
Carthage
M A U R E T A N I A
R.Ebro
Cartennae
Baetis
Rusaddir
R.Tagus
TARTESSIANS
Tingi
Gades
Lixus
R.Darat
Mogador

Carthaginian territory in Spain in 218 BC

0   Miles   500

conscious guilt feeling for Aeneas' betrayal of Dido's love!

The early days of Carthage were spent in the usual manner of a Phoenician colony, in trading and occasional small affrays; but about the middle of the sixth century BC the pattern changed. Under a leader named Malchus the city began the systematic conquest of the surrounding area and the subjugation of both the African peoples who inhabited the interior and the small Phoenician cities on the coast and along the Bagradas valley. Under Malchus and his successors Carthaginian hegemony over the whole area was established; the Africans were treated as a conquered people, with few rights and heavy taxes, while the cities, though allowed to retain a titular independence as allies of Carthage, were forced to destroy their walls and surrender their foreign policy. This was to cost Carthage dear in the future, as a foreign invader could always find a certain amount of support from the local populace and the towns, even if they wished, could offer no resistance.

Carthage now began to turn its attention overseas, and to establish itself as master also of the far-flung Phoenician settlements throughout the Western Mediterranean, along the North African littoral, in Southern Spain, and on the islands of Sardinia and Corsica. In order to do this, she had to create a powerful navy, both to deal with pirates and to discourage other nations from competing with her traders. It is about this time that we hear of the first established contact with Rome; a treaty which effectually debarred Roman shipping from the Western Mediterranean and established the area as a Carthaginian lake.

It is interesting to compare this Carthaginian expansion with the growth of the British Empire in the 18th and 19th centuries. It was said of the latter period that 'trade follows the flag' which meant in fact just the opposite: the traders led the way, got themselves into difficulties with the natives or found local conditions too chaotic, and practically forced the hand of the home government which had to take military possession of the area in order to establish a safe trading ground. Much of the same policy may well have applied in Carthage; trade was the lifeline of the city, and though the ruling body seem to have been more agriculturalists than traders themselves, they must have realised that the prosperity of the city, and therefore of their estates, relied upon overseas trade.

There is considerable difference of opinion about the political institutions of Carthage, due to the lack of written evidence available. It would seem that the city was originally a monarchy, but that at some stage it changed to an oligarchy. Most authorities agree that there were two officials known as *Shophets* or *Suffetes*, a legislative body of some three hundred members which has been likened to the Roman Senate, and a Council of One Hundred which was either elected from the Senate, or was an entirely separate body; what they do not agree upon is the relative powers and duties of these institutions. It may well be that they changed from time to time. It would seem, however, that the families who formed the backbone of the administrative power of Carthage were different from those who provided the Generals and Admirals who led the Carthaginian armies and fleets, the latter being very much under the control of the former. A Carthaginian commander who failed in the field had to explain himself to the Council of One Hundred, and if his explanation was not satisfactory, the punishment was often crucifixion. A too-successful General might end up the same way, purely because the Council feared he might use his success to supplant them, though there is no evidence that any General ever tried to do so. This harsh treatment of their military commanders was, however, accompanied by a freedom of action while in command which was not given to Roman Generals and there is no real evidence that the penalties for failure had much influence on Carthaginian leadership.

While the armies of Carthage were of a mercenary character, her navy was very much a native affair, as was to be expected from such a seafaring nation. The Carthaginian navy which reigned supreme in the Western Mediterranean was a highly skilled professional force which, at the time of the struggle with Rome, was built around the quinquereme as the standard fighting ship of the day. The quinquereme was the product of a gradual evolution in oared fighting vessels from the days of the original hollow, undecked galley which transported the Greek army to Troy. As maritime trade increased, piracy followed in its wake, and the need became obvious for a fast, manoeuvrable vessel which could outrun and outfight the fat, clumsy trading ships. Through the penteconter and the bireme this evolved into the trireme which was the standard fighting ship of the Peloponnesian War. In the Alexandrian and post-Alexandrian period in the Eastern Mediterranean naval architects thought big, and they produced not only quadriremes and quinqueremes but huge crafts rated at as much as fifteens and sixteens. It is probable, however, that these bigger ships proved of more prestige value than actual battleworthiness, and certainly they do not appear to have spread to the western basin. Here evolution stopped at the quinquereme, which was a much larger vessel than the trireme, carrying some two hundred oarsmen and a hundred and twenty marines, armed with a vicious ram which was the chief weapon in a seafight. Carthaginian quinqueremes tended to be light and manoeuvrable, just as had been the Athenian triremes of their day, and Carthaginian seamen were well practised at the intricate manoeuvres called for in a sea battle.

North from Carthage, across ninety miles of water, lay the fertile island of Sicily. From early times Sicily had beckoned to both Greeks and Phoenicians, and its shores were littered with Phoenician trading stations and Greek colonies; intermittent fighting between these went on for centuries, but in 480 BC Sicily became the stage for the first large-scale Carthaginian attempt at imperial expansion. Gelon, Tyrant of Syracuse, was making an attempt to unite the island's cities under his leadership, and in so doing was menacing the Phoenicians of the south and west. Carthage therefore sent out an expedition under a leader named Hanno to meet this threat. It is possible that in fact the expedition was planned in concert with Xerxes' invasion of Greece, since the Greeks certainly applied to Gelon for help against the Persians, and it would have been good strategy to keep the Syracusans out of the main conflict. At all event, Hanno sailed with what must have been the largest force Carthage had yet fielded: though accounts of 300,000 men are obvious exaggerations it was still a formidable force. Hanno landed at Panormus, having apparently suffered some loss from bad weather en route, only to be decisively defeated by Gelon at Himera on, it is said, the same day as the Persians were defeated at Salamis. The first major Carthaginian attempt on Sicily thus ended in disaster. So great was the loss that Carthage seems to have gone into a decline over the next few decades, but in 410 BC she had recovered enough to intervene in Sicily once more; this time a smaller expedition under Hannibal, grandson of Hanno, was successful in capturing the cities of Selinus and Himera before returning home with much booty. The main enemy, Syracuse, was however still untouched, and four years later, a second Carthaginian expedition was sent out; this was said to consist of a thousand transports escorted by a hundred and twenty warships and was certainly a formidable force. The Carthaginians, however, were dogged by ill-fortune; plague ravaged their forces, killing Hannibal during the siege of Agrigentum, and though his successor, Himilco, succeeded in capturing both that city and Gela and defeating a relief attempt by Dionysius, the new ruler of Syracuse, a return of the plague left him so weak that in 405 BC he signed a peace with Dionysius and sailed back to Carthage.

Eight years later Dionysius felt strong enough to renew the war and marched on the Carthaginian stronghold of Motya. The city duly fell, but this sparked off a new Carthaginian effort, in which Himilco not only retook Motya but sacked Messina and finally, after a decisive naval victory, layed siege to Syracuse itself. This expedition, however, also finally ended in complete disaster and the loss of the entire expeditionary force, which in turn sparked off a revolt by Carthage's African subjects which was only put down with much difficulty and grave loss. But by now Sicily was an obsession; a third major attempt at its conquest was made in 339 BC and yet again ended in disaster and defeat. Yet despite this, the lack of unity among the opposition enabled Carthage to hold on to the south-western corner of the island.

In 311 BC Agathocies, Tyrant of Syracuse, invaded these last Carthaginian possessions, but was heavily defeated and driven back into Syracuse itself, most of the island falling into Carthaginian hands. In desperation the Syracusan commander lòaded fourteen thousand men on to sixty ships and sailed for Africa, hoping by this counterstroke to save the situation. In this he was successful; having defeated a Carthaginian army which opposed him, he was able to move at will through the fertile countryside and the undefended town-ships, and Carthage had to recall troops from Sicily to deal with him. Peace was made in 307 BC, leaving Carthage in control of most of the southern half of Sicily.

Carthage had one more enemy to face before the curtain went up on the struggle with Rome. In 281 BC the Italian Greek city of Tarentum, under attack by the expanding Roman state, had called in Pyrrhus of Epirus, an outstanding mercenary soldier, to assist them. Pyrrhus succeeded in defeating the Romans in two battles, but at such heavy loss that the phrase 'a Pyrrhic victory' was coined. He also succeeded in antagonising the citizens of Tarentum by expecting them to assist in the fighting, so in 278 BC he transferred his operations to Sicily, fighting for the Greek cities against Carthage. For a time he carried all before him, but eventually his Sicilian supporters, suspicious of his motives, turned against him, and in 275 BC he sailed back to Italy, being soundly trounced by the Carthaginian fleet en route. The status quo in Sicily was thus restored: meanwhile Rome succeeded in defeating Pyrrhus and capturing Tarentum and her power thus lapped down into the toe of Italy. At last the rival powers of Rome and Carthage were face to face.

Chapter 2

The First Punic War

After the death of Agathocles, a great part of his Campanian mercenaries found themselves without employment. Rather than return home, in 259 BC they seized the prosperous town of Messana, facing across the straits to the toe of Italy, and set themselves up as brigands, terrorising the surrounding countryside. Not long afterwards, however, the new ruler of Syracuse, Hiero, determined to take action against them, and in a strange reversal of history concerted measures with the Carthaginians. The Brigands who by now were calling themselves the Mamertines or 'children of Mars', were divided in counsel: one party favoured surrendering to the Carthaginians, the other asking for the protection of Rome, and embassies were sent to both the great powers.

For Carthage, action was obvious: for centuries she had fought for control of Sicily, and a forward policy in the island was second nature to her. Rome, on the other hand, had a grave decision to take. Intervention in Sicily must inevitably lead to war with Carthage, with all that was entailed in a struggle between a land and a sea power; but dare she let Carthage gain control of what might easily be a stepping stone to Italy? In the event, Rome decided on intervention, and though no formal declaration of war was issued at that time, the First Punic War was set in train.

By the time that the Roman Senate had decided on action and directed the Consul Appius Claudius to cross into Sicily, the Carthaginian party in Messana had gained the ascendancy, helped by the spectacle of two armies, one Carthaginian and one Syracusan, outside their walls. A Carthaginian fleet accordingly sailed into the harbour and a garrison was admitted to the citadel. The Romans, it appeared, were too late; but the Carthaginian commander, Hanno, seems to have been a man of little sense or resolution; Claudius succeeded in seizing him by trickery and persuading him to evacuate the town, the garrison being replaced by a Roman one. How twenty thousand Roman troops were ferried across the straits in face of the Carthaginian fleet we do not know, but the whole episode was a disgrace for Carthage. Hanno was accordingly crucified, and a second Hanno took his place. He fared little better; Claudius, sallying out from Messana, defeated both the Carthaginian and Syracusan armies, and operated so successfully that Hiero of Syracuse, with great wisdom, made peace and became an ally of Rome.

Rome now proceeded to the conquest of Sicily, and in 262 BC the Consuls Posthumus and Mamilius advanced to lay siege to the city of Agrigentum, on the south coast: the second city of Sicily and an important Carthaginian base.

Carthage meanwhile had been hastily raising mercenary troops, and the city was well fortified and garrisoned, under command of an excellent soldier, Hannibal Gisco. The siege dragged on for five months with neither side apparently gaining any ground; but in fact Hannibal was running short of provisions and had appealed to Carthage for relief. This relief now appeared in the shape of a new Carthaginian army under Hanno; but in the ensuing action he was utterly defeated, so that Hannibal, whose troops were now starving, was forced to cut his way out with his garrison and retire across the Halycus river, leaving Agrigentum to the mercy of the Romans.

The war thus far had been a series of Roman successes and Carthaginian disasters, and this pattern was not yet to be interrupted. Rome had by now realised that, in order to complete the conquest of Sicily, she must challenge Carthage at sea, for the Carthaginian fleet was already making itself felt along the coasts of both Sicily and Italy, besides providing the shield under which fresh Carthaginian forces were transported to Sicily. The problem was, how? Rome at this time possessed no fleet; one therefore had to be created and manned, a task of no small difficulty. Fortunately a model was at hand in the shape of a Carthaginian quinquereme which had run ashore and been captured, and accordingly the Italian shipyards were soon turning out copies. Rowers and sailors were more of a problem; had the standard fighting ship still been the trireme, with its one man per oar, it might have proved insuperable, but the quinquereme could, at a pinch, be manned by one trained oarsman and four novices to each oar, and enough trained men could be scraped up from the Italian cities on the coast to provide this nucleus.

The first effort of the new Roman navy was not a resounding success. In the spring of 260 BC a fleet of a hundred ships was despatched to Sicily. Unfortunately, the Consul, Cornelius Scipio, pushed on ahead with only seventeen ships and while at anchor in the Lipari Islands, was surprised by twenty Carthaginians. The raw Roman crews panicked, ran their ships ashore and fled, the Consul himself being captured with his ships. This bad beginning, however, was somewhat offset when the Carthaginian commander, similarly reconnoitring in careless fashion, blundered full into the main Roman fleet, and, outnumbered some two to one, lost half of his 50 ships before he could extricate himself.

Before the main fleets engaged, however, the Romans produced a secret weapon. This was invented, it would seem, while the raw Roman fleet lay at anchor in Syracuse harbour, and it seems probable that the idea came from a native of the city and may, indeed, even have been the brainchild of the great Archimedes, the local genius. The Roman problem was in effect a simple one: they were first class soldiers on land, but at sea could not hope to match the manoeuvring power of the experienced Carthaginian seamen. The answer was just as simple: the *corvus*, or crow, which was designed to turn the sea battle into a very close imitation of a land battle. The device itself consisted of a gangplank thirty-six feet long and four feet wide, with a heavy spike at the outboard end and a long slot at the inboard end. This latter fitted around a pole set up like a mast in the ship's bows; when raised it lay against the pole, and when lowered it projected out over the bows. One tackle between the outer end and the head of the pole controlled the raising and lowering, and two more on the deck made it possible to swivel the device from side to side. Thus, as an enemy ship approached to ram, the *corvus* was dropped, the spike embedded itself in the enemy deck, and with the two ships thus locked together the Roman marines could pour across the improvised boarding bridge and overcome the enemy crew.

The fleets clashed at Mylae in August 260 BC. The Carthaginian commander was that same Hannibal Gisco who had held Agrigentum; the fleets were about equal in strength, and Hannibal, overconfident and contemptuous of his adversary, attacked at once without waiting to put his ships in order of battle. The entire vanguard of thirty-one ships fell victim to the *corvus*; Hannibal, shocked and furious, drew off, regrouped and attacked again in grim earnest, his ships sweeping through the Roman lines in beautiful manoeuvres; but the Roman Admiral, Duilius, had anticipated just such a move, and had a reserve squadron deployed in his rear. As the Carthaginians broke through, these ships moved forward and again the *corvus* was used to deadly effect. Hannibal lost another fourteen ships, broke off the action and fled. From now on, Carthage could no longer count on mastery of the sea.

For the next two years the war went steadily in favour of Rome. Not only did she prevail in Sicily, where Carthage was now confined to a handful of fortresses on the western coast, but Roman expeditions invaded Corsica and Sardinia, and a Roman fleet even raided the African coast. But the war seemed no closer to an end, so the Senate decided to carry it into Africa itself. Possibly the capture and destruction of Carthage was not envisaged, but by threatening the heartland to force concession of the outlying possessions. At all events, by the summer of 256 BC Rome had assembled a large fleet and a force of forty thousand troops under the Consuls Manlius and Regulus. This expedition, probably the largest up till then of ancient times, set sail from Messana; the Carthaginian fleet, well aware of both the expedition and its objective, intercepted it off the promontory of Ecnomus.

The Roman fleet, encumbered as it was by its transports, was drawn up in a huge triangle or wedge, with two divisions advancing in echelon in converging columns forming the sides, a third division the base (this latter with the horse transports in tow) and a fourth division in reserve. The Carthaginians under Hanno and Hamilcar, in contrast, were formed in a long, concave line abreast, well overlapping the Roman flanks. As the Romans advanced, the Carthaginian centre gave way before them, with the idea of separating the first two divisions from the rearward two; when this had occurred, Hamilcar, who commanded the centre, turned his ships about and engaged, while the two uncommitted wings wheeled in on the rear Roman divisions. All this tactical skill, however, proved useless in face of superior Roman fighting power, for Hamilcar's squadron, though fighting hard, was soon overcome by the two divisions under the personal command of the Consuls. Leaving Manlius to finish things off, Regulus with his freshest ships then turned back to the aid of the rear divisions, which till then were having rather the worst of it. His intervention was decisive, and the action ended in a complete Roman victory, thirty enemy ships being sunk and sixty-four captured for a loss of twenty-four Roman vessels sunk.

Encouraged by their victory, the two Consuls now pressed on across the Mediterranean and disembarked their army unopposed in Africa. Once again, as in the case of Agathocles, Carthaginian distrust of their native subjects and neighbouring towns became an advantage to the invaders, who met with little or no resistance and ravaged the rich countryside as they wished. Carthage had in fact been warned, Hanno having hurried home from Ecnomus with the bad

news, but no field army was available to face the invaders. Fortunately for
Carthage, the Roman Senate now made a bad blunder, ordering Manlius to
return home with his half of the army while Regulus and the other half wintered
in Africa. Thus not only was Carthage given time to raise fresh forces, but the
army she faced in the following spring was only twenty thousand strong instead
of forty thousand. At last, too, the Carthaginians had found a skilful leader in
the form of the Spartan mercenary, Xanthippus. Even so, a better General than
Regulus might well have carried the day, but the Roman Consul adopted an
almost suicidal formation of his army, abandoning the usual open order of his
legionary units and cramming them into a solid mass with which to face the
elephants Xanthippus had posted in advance of his centre. Why Regulus chose
this formation is a mystery; the Romans had already, after some early disasters,
dealt successfully with the elephants of Pyrrhus and had similarly defeated
Carthaginian elephants in Sicily, so they had no lack of experience of the
strengths and weaknesses of this weapon. As it was, the legionaries were first
trampled and disarrayed by the elephants, which did great execution in their
packed ranks, and then held frontally by the Carthaginian infantry while
assailed in flank by the cavalry, which had easily disposed of the small Roman
mounted force. Only some two thousand Romans escaped from the field, and
these, embarking on a Roman squadron, also perished when their ships were
overwhelmed in a sudden storm.

Regulus himself was taken prisoner, and the Carthaginian Senate took
advantage of this fact to use him as a messenger to the Roman Senate, bearing
offers of peace. If we are to believe the noble words of Horace, Regulus was
allowed on the embassy on the understanding that he would work for its success
but if it failed he would return to Carthage and be put to death. Arrived in
Rome, he in fact advised the Senate to continue the war since Carthage was
weak, and then honourably returned to Carthage where he was tortured to
death. The facts would appear to be that having broken his promise to promote
the peace he very wisely also broke his knightly word to return, dying of old age
in Rome!

Despite the African disaster, Rome continued to prosecute the war with
vigour. Fresh troops were raised and fresh fleets built. In 254 BC the important
Carthaginian fortress of Panormus in Sicily was captured, almost without
resistance, and the Romans pressed on to attack what was almost the last enemy
stronghold in the island, Lilybaeum. Here, at last, they met a determined
resistance from the Carthaginian garrison under Himilco, which counter-
attacked with such vehemence that the Romans were at length forced to convert
the siege into a blockade. In 251 BC, however, they won yet another victory
when the main Carthaginian army was heavily defeated at Drepanum.

By now the Carthaginian hold on Sicily had been reduced to the two coastal
fortresses of Lilybaeum and Drepanum, both under siege by the Romans. At
sea, the position was once more even, both sides having built fresh ships to
replace those lost in the earlier disasters. The difficulties of blockade in the days
of oarpower were exhibited well at this period when the Carthaginian fleet had
little difficulty in throwing ten thousand reinforcements into Lilybaeum in
despite of the Romans. Stung by this success, the new Roman commander,
Publius Claudius, resolved to attack the Carthaginian fleet under Adherbal
while it lay at anchor in Drepanum harbour. His officers attempted in vain to
dissuade him from so desperate an enterprise, and the sacred chickens, so the

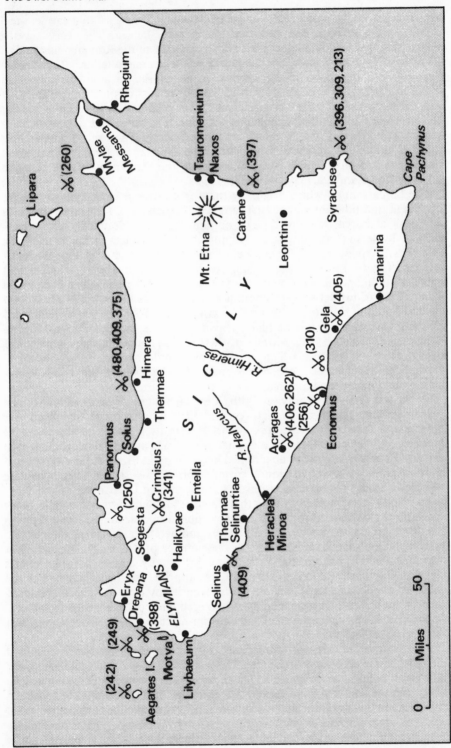

Rhegium

Messana

Mylae ✗ (260)

Lipara

Tauromenium

Naxos

✗ (397)

Catane

✗ (396, 309, 213) Syracuse

Cape Pachynus

Leontini

Mt. Etna

S I C I L Y

Camarina

Gela ✗ (405)

Himera

Thermae

✗ (480, 409, 375) Solus

R. Himeras

✗ (310)

Acragas ✗ (406, 262)

✗ (256)

Ecnomus

Panormus

Solus

Crimisus? ✗ (341)

Entella

R. Halycus

✗ (250) Segesta

Halikyae

ELYMIANS

Thermae Selinuntiae

Heraclea Minoa

Eryx

Drepana ✗ (398)

Selinus

Thermae Selinuntiae ✗ (409)

✗ (249)

Motya

Aegates I.

Lilybaeum

✗ (242)

0 50 Miles

augurs reported, refused to eat—a sign of disaster. 'If they will not eat, let them drink', said Claudius, and had them flung into the sea. The story may be apocryphal, but is in accordance with the arrogance of the Roman commander. Disaster did indeed follow, for the attack was a complete failure. The Roman fleet fell into confusion in the narrow waters of the harbour entrance, and Adherbal, attacking with spirit, routed it with the loss of ninety-three ships.

A further naval disaster soon followed when a large Roman supply convoy for the troops blockading Lilybaeum was driven ashore, and destroyed by a sudden gale, leaving the Romans once more without a fleet. It was at this moment that there appeared upon the scene the first member of that great Carthaginian family which was to dominate the remainder of the struggle between Rome and Carthage—Hamilcar Barca.

The Barca family, which originally came from Cyrene, was a powerful one but not at that time among the first families of Carthage. Of the earlier exploits of Hamilcar Barca we know little or nothing, but he undoubtedly had experience of leadership and a gift of gaining the trust and even the love of his followers. Arriving in Sicily in command of a fleet in 247 BC he at once made his presence felt by ravaging the Italian coast and then proceeded to seize and fortify a commanding position on the Sicilian coast at a place called Ercte (now Monte Pellegrino) between Lilybaeum and Panormus. This hill is about two thousand feet in height, two of its sides rising sheer from the sea while a third similarly thrusts up from the plain, leaving only the fourth side, that facing Panormus, at all accessible. Moreover, there was an abundant water supply and a sheltered cove where his light raiding ships could anchor. Here, for three years, Hamilcar Barca defied every Roman effort to dislodge him, while carrying on his raids by land and sea.

So the war dragged wearily on, both sides reluctant to invest more wealth in a supreme effort. Hamilcar, in fact, received virtually no support from his home government, and it is a measure of his stature as a leader of men that he managed to keep control of his mercenaries as their pay grew more and more in arrears. Finally in 244 BC he abandoned his position at Ercte and moved instead to one equally as strong, although cut off from the sea, at Mt Eryx, where he was closer to the besieged garrisons at Lilybaeum and Drepanum.

Two years later Rome, realising that the Carthaginian fortresses would never succumb to blockade while they could be supplied by sea, decided once more to put her trust on the waters and build yet another fleet. By great efforts two hundred ships were launched, and in the summer of 242 BC the Roman fleet appeared off Lilybaeum and Drepanum, effectually cutting off Hamilcar's supplies. Carthage was taken completely by surprise; in an effort to reduce the expenses of the war, and lulled into false security by Rome's virtual abandonment of the sea, the Carthaginian fleet had been laid up and allowed to fall into decay, and it was not until the following spring that a relief force was at last despatched to Sicily.

The position at sea was thus practically reversed from that which had prevailed in the early days of the war. The Roman fleet, well built and equipped, had had a full season in which to shake down, learn to work as a unit and to bring its rowers up to a good standard of training; the Carthaginian consisted in the main of converted merchantmen, was poorly equipped, manned in the main with raw recruits and heavily laden with stores. Hanno, the Carthaginian Admiral, therefore made for the Aegates Islands to get into communication with Hamilcar, land his supplies and take on board some of Hamilcar's veteran troops before engaging the enemy. Lutatius Catulus, the Roman commander, naturally wished to prevent such a manoeuvre, and in this he was successful. The two fleets met off Aegusae, and the lighter, better handled Roman ships proved far more than a match for their heavier, clumsier opponents. Nothing is said in accounts of the battle of the use of the *corvus*; it would appear that as their training and seamanship improved the Romans placed less faith in this weapon. At all events fifty Carthaginian vessels were sunk and a further seventy taken, and all prospect of relief for Hamilcar vanished.

The defeat of Aegusae virtually ended the war, for Carthage was no longer capable of further effort, either in men, money or ships. Accordingly she once again proposed peace, pressing into service the talents of Hamilcar Barca as chief negotiator. Fortunately Rome, though militarily victorious, was economically in little better condition than Carthage, and Hamilcar was therefore able to wring from her better terms than might have been expected. Nevertheless, the peace settlement represented a heavy blow to Carthage: by its terms she renounced all claims to Sicily, recognised the claims of Hiero to Syracuse and its surrounding territory, and agreed to pay a war indemnity of twenty-two hundred talents over the next ten years. It was a chastening blow, and the future of Carthage seemed reduced to that of a second-rate power. But Rome had reckoned without the genius of Hamilcar Barca.

Chapter 3

A new empire

With the end of the First Punic War the Carthaginian garrisons in Sicily were gradually shipped back to Africa. Carthage no longer needed a large mercenary army, but before the mercenaries could be discharged they had to receive the arrears of pay they were owed. This, the Carthaginian Senate was not prepared to pay, and as the time dragged on the mercenaries, encamped outside the city, became more and more impatient at their treatment. Finally, they rose in revolt under two leaders, Spendius and Matho, and called upon the Africans and the smaller townships to join them in overthrowing Carthage.

Even at this stage the Senate mishandled affairs, giving charge of operations against the mercenaries and their allies to the incompetent Hanno; under his direction things went from bad to worse until at last, in despair, the rulers of Carthage turned to the only man who could save them—Hamilcar Barca. Raising some ten thousand men from among the citizens, and gathering to his standard those of the mercenaries who were still prepared to follow him, plus hordes of Numidian horse, Hamilcar marched out and defeated Spendius, breaking the blockade of Carthage; but the war was far from over. The Senate, thinking they were now safe, reinstated their favourite Hanno in joint command, whereupon the towns of Utica and Hippo Zarytus, which had until now been loyal to Carthage, promptly went over to the enemy.

Reinstated in sole command, Hamilcar was now forced to employ total war. Both sides committed the most appalling barbarities, and though things went steadily in favour of Carthage, it was not until 238 BC that the last embers of revolt were stamped out in Africa. Meanwhile the revolt had spread to Sardinia, and with Africa safe Carthage began fitting out an expedition to recover the island. At this stage Rome sudddenly stepped in with a typical act of duplicity. The treaty of peace specified that Carthage ceded to Rome Sicily and all the islands between it and Africa. Sardinia, the Romans claimed, lay between Sicily and Africa—a palpable falsehood—and Carthage was breaking the treaty. Rome therefore declared war. Carthage was in no position to renew hostilities, being bankrupt of both men and money; and, smarting under the indignity, she was forced to accept the loss of Sardinia and pay a further indemnity of twelve hundred talents for her 'crime'.

Unfortunately our sources are not clear on the political position in Carthage at this time. Some authors state that, after his victory over the rebels, Hamilcar and his followers were supreme and remained so for many years; others that he in fact led only a minority party and was strongly opposed by the senators who supported Hanno and his policies. Judging by events, it seems more likely that the latter is the truer picture, though it may well be that Hamilcar was able to sway events while he was in Carthage, but that once he left the city he was unable to retain much political support. There can be no doubt, however, that at this point in time Hamilcar, with great vision, saw that Carthage had entirely to change her policy. With Sicily and Sardinia now closed to her, if she was to survive as a major power, she had to turn her attention westwards, to the coasts of what are now Algeria and Morocco, and above all to Spain. Here, he felt, she could find alternative markets and sources of men and money to replace those she had lost in the Central Mediterranean. With this purpose in mind, he obtained from the Senate command of an army which was to subdue the tribes along the North African littoral; no mention was made of Spain, but there can be no doubt that secretly his plans were already laid. With Sir Winston Churchill, he could say that he was calling in a new world to redress the balance of the old.

Undoubtedly Hamilcar Barca expected his stay in Spain to be a long one, because he took his entire family with him. This consisted of his son-in-law, Hasdrubal the Splendid, and his three sons, Hannibal, Hasdrubal and Mago. Hannibal at this time was nine years old; according to Harold Lamb's biography, he had been with his father in Sicily at the age of five, but we have no certain knowledge of this. Most authorities agree that before the expedition left Carthage, Hamilcar assembled its leaders in the temple of Melcart and that oaths were there sworn, but stories differ as to just what they were. Hannibal apparently told the story later to Antiochus of Syria, and there seems no reason to doubt that an oath was indeed sworn. However, the popular concept as given to us by Livy and the Victorian authors, of the child swearing on the altars of the gods undying vengeance against Rome is probably a distortion. It would seem that all the leading officers swore the oath, not just Hannibal and his brothers; and the oath they swore was not vengeance on Rome but a promise never to be 'a friend to Rome'. This is important phraseology: in those days the term 'a friend of Rome' implied a vassal state of Rome, such as Hiero of Syracuse, and it would make sense for Hamilcar Barca, well aware that eventually, if Carthage was to regain her place as a great power, a second clash with Rome was inevitable, to wish to make it clear to his family and followers that when the clash came there would be no tame submission. The oath has been interpreted as an act of aggression against Rome: I prefer to see it as a defensive assurance against the day when Rome thrust herself across the path of Carthage and denied her a place in the sun.

From Carthage Hamilcar with his army—we have no knowledge of its exact size, but it would appear to have been fairly small and in the main of Carthaginians and Africans, mercenaries being in short supply—marched along the North African coast, accompanied by a squadron of warships, until the Pillars of Hercules were reached. En route the local African tribes were pacified, but it does not appear that any large-scale fighting took place. Now at last the real objective, Spain, lay before the expedition.

Carthage had for long maintained trading colonies in Spain, and had founded a flourishing city at Gades, the modern Cadiz. Spain—or Iberia to give it its ancient name—could at that time be divided roughly into three. First there was the area along the southern and eastern coasts, which had been colonised and civilised and contained a number of towns and a rather mixed Phoenician-

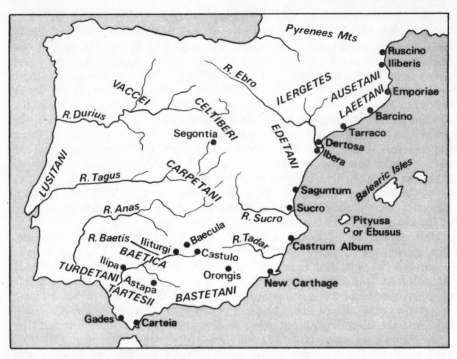

Greek-Iberian population; the second part comprises mid-Spain, where an early influx of Gauls had mingled with the original Iberian inhabitants to form an essentially tribal society of natural horsemen and warriors, moody, emotional, quick to see an insult, friends one moment and enemies the next. Of these, the most important tribes were the Turdetani who controlled the area between the Guadiana and the Guadalquivir, the Carpetanii in central Spain around present-day Toledo, and the Vaccaei around the headwaters of the Douro. Finally, to the north-east lay the third section, the most recent Gallic invasion, hardly as yet assimilated; here the main tribal divisions were the Sedetani, Seussetani and Ausetani along the coast, and the Celtiberes and Ilergetes further inland.

Up till now Gades had been the chief Carthaginian settlement in Spain. Well situated on the Betis (Guadalquivir), inland the country was fertile and flourishing, while at the headwaters of the river lay the Sierra Morena or Silver Mountains with their rich gold and silver mines. Hamilcar, pausing only a short while in Gades, pushed on up the river and established his headquarters in the mountains, taking the citadel of Castulo for his own. From here he began the conquest of the central plateau, bringing the tribes under control by force of arms in the main. For nine long years he laboured to complete the Carthaginian conquest of central Spain, but it would appear that his methods may not have been well-chosen; seizure and crucifixion of their kings was not likely to endear Carthage to the tribes, even if it implanted a healthy fear.

Then in 228 BC Hamilcar Barca was slain. We do not know all the details, but it would appear that he was tricked into meeting a delegation from the tribes and ambushed; Lamb has a story of how Hamilcar, who was accompanied by his sons, deliberately led the tribesmen in one direction while the boys escaped in another, and in doing so was killed. It would certainly be in keeping with his character. Be that as it may, on the news of his death his officers met in council and elected his son-in-law, Hasdrubal the Splendid, to succeed him in command. Hasdrubal swept into the mountains with fire and sword to avenge his dead chief, but this once accomplished, Carthaginian policy under the new leader changed abruptly. Hasdrubal was a different character from Hamilcar, a diplomat rather than a soldier; he replaced conquest by force of arms with conquest by friendship and peaceful penetration.

Hasdrubal ruled for eight years, and under his able administration Carthaginian Spain prospered. Headquarters was switched from Gades to a new site further up the coast, where he founded the city of New Carthage—present day Cartagena—which was to all intents and purposes a copy of the original. The rise of New Carthage, however, drew the attention of the trading city of Massilia—present day Marseilles—who, fearing competition, reported on Carthaginian progress to Rome, to whom it was an ally or vassal. The Roman Senate, having debated the matter, despatched an embassy to Spain, requesting from Hasdrubal a pledge that he would keep his operations within certain bounds.Here we come to a fairly vital point: Hasdrubal pledged that the Carthaginian army would not cross the line of a certain river—but which river? Polybius calls it the Iber, and most historians have deduced that it was in fact the present-day Ebro; this makes sense in that it was a reasonable request, the Carthaginians still being a long way to the south of that river and Massilia having a number of trading colonies north of it. On the other hand, one of the planks of the Roman case for showing that Hannibal alone was responsible for the Second Punic War is that he broke this agreement by attacking Saguntum—yet Saguntum was situated forty miles south of the Ebro. Was, in fact, the river in question one of the smaller ones further south, or is this simply a suggestion made by pro-Roman historians attempting to bolster up the Roman case? The question is academic only, since a clash between the two powers was in any case inevitable, but it does show the lengths to which the Roman historians went in their endeavours to place the blame for aggression on Hannibal rather than where it truly belonged.

Hasdrubal has been rated by historians for accepting this restriction on his activities, but it is difficult to see how he had any alternative. At that time Carthaginian power in Spain was still not fully established, and Carthage herself was by no means ready for a renewal of hostilities with Rome. Had Hasdrubal dug in his heels and refused to meet the Roman request, a declaration of war might well have followed, and this could only have one of two results; a second humiliating climb-down by Carthage leading to a virtual abandonment of the Spanish empire before it was even in being, or a war which Carthage was in no way capable of winning. By giving this pledge, Hasdrubal gained time to consolidate the Carthaginian hold on central Spain and averted a war, which as diplomat rather than soldier would have been his natural inclination; while at the same time he no doubt foresaw that when the time came the pledge could be disowned by either his successor or the home government.

For a further five years Hasdrubal the Splendid continued his policy of welding the tribes into alliances and gradually extending Carthaginian power into the interior. These years of peaceful penetration established a solid-seeming base, yet the moody, fickle nature of the Spanish tribes was such that the strength of the Carthaginian position was never more than a facade, maintained by personal charisma and skilled diplomacy. It could not survive the removal of skilled leadership, as Scipio was later to show. Then, in 221 BC Hasdrubal was assassinated; the story goes that he had a Spanish chieftain executed and was in turn murdered by one of the victim's slaves or retainers. How he died is not of great importance: what followed is, for the Carthaginian officers, meeting in council, elected as his successor Hannibal Barca.

Hannibal was at this time twenty-six years of age, in his prime. He had spent most of his adult life in Spain, and had grown to love the country and to know its inhabitants probably better than he knew the citizens of Carthage. Indeed he seems to have adopted the dress and manner of a Spaniard, wearing simple and durable clothes rather than the splendour of his predecessor, showing his rank only in the excellence of his weapons and horse trappings, and about this time he married a Spanish princess named Imilce. Though the marriage may well have been politic, since her tribe was strategically placed to be of use to him, it may well also have been a love match. Hannibal was a man easy to love, gifted with an ironic sense of humour and the ability to bring out the best in others. Physically he was strong, able to endure extremes of heat and cold, a bold and skilful horseman, abstemious with food and drink and able, apparently, to exist on little sleep. Even the Romans were forced to admit that not only was he a great commander, infinite in resource and skill, but also a superb warrior who shared the hardships of his men. Being Roman, however, Livy hastened to add that with these strengths he combined inhuman cruelty and a total disregard of truth, honour and religion; an accusation which has no basis at all other than the hysterical hatred of the man who, almost alone, brought Rome to the brink of defeat. Hannibal's physical appearance is known from coins and two marble busts, one in Copenhagen and one in Madrid, and a bronze bust excavated in 1944. A clean shaven young man with round head, high, jutting eyebrow ridges, a long arched nose pointed at the end with well defined nostrils, a small mouth turned down at the corners, full lips with the lower drawn in, and a strong chin. Both Hellenic and African characteristics, showing the Phoenician-African heritage of his ancestors plus a Greek admixture.

Once in command, Hannibal set about completing the work begun by Hamilcar and Hasdrubal. Where one had operated by force of arms and the other by diplomacy, Hannibal combined the two, defeating the tribes in battle where necessary and then consolidating his position by skilled diplomacy. He began operations by thoroughly subduing the Olkades, and then in the following spring pushed inland through the Sierra Guadarama, making allies and recruiting men, until he reached the territory of the Vaccaei. Here he met a determined resistance, and was forced to storm their principal towns of Hermandica and Arbocala. The Vaccaeans, still unsubdued, succeeded in arousing the neighbouring Carpetani, nominally at peace with Hannibal, and their combined forces attacked Hannibal near the Tagus river. Livy talks of a hundred thousand tribesmen, a ridiculous figure, but no doubt Hannibal was heavily outnumbered. With sound tactical sense he fell back across the Tagus; the tribesmen, attributing his withdrawal to fear, rushed after him throwing themselves into the strongly flowing river in great disorder. Hannibal had drawn up his heavy infantry on the far bank to receive the charge, backed by forty elephants; as soon as the tribesmen were committed he then launched his cavalry into the water on their flanks, and slaughtered them in droves. Once they began to give way, the Carthaginian infantry and elephants in their turn crossed the river in good order and completed the victory. Within days the Carpetani had sued for peace; Hannibal at once turned diplomat, asking only a nominal tribute, provisions for his army, and the enlistment of large numbers of tribal warriors in his ranks.

Carthaginian power in Spain was now at its apex, with virtually the whole country south of the Douro and the Ebro under some sort of control. Though only the coastal area could be regarded as solidly Carthaginian the inland tribes now acknowledged a loose vassalship, paying tribute of sorts and sending their young men to serve in the army. Yet Hannibal with his shrewd knowledge of the Spanish character, must have realised that the imposing edifice of the Barca Hegemony rested on unstable foundations, held together only by his own charismatic personality and that of his brothers. It must have been with grave forebodings as well as great hopes that he contemplated the future.

Chapter 4

The Carthaginian army

The Carthaginian army is generally regarded as having been a heterogenous collection of mercenaries; while this was certainly true in the earlier period of Carthage's history, it is not strictly so at the period of the Second Punic War. While her armies at this stage could in no way be described as citizen forces such as those of her great opponent, they were to a large degree now drawn from the territories she either ruled or dominated, these troops therefore only being mercenaries to the extent that they fought for pay rather than patriotism. An analogy can in fact be drawn with the sepoy troops of the British East India Company and later of the Indian Army. Mercenaries as such—ie, soldiers from outside Carthage's dominions—were still employed, but to a much lesser degree since very much larger sources of manpower were now available within the empire.

The early armies of Carthage usually had a nucleus of citizen troops, but as Carthage grew in size and strength these tended to dwindle away, the citizens having better things to do with their time than the coarse and dangerous business of fighting. Nevertheless the organisation for a citizen militia remained in being and could be called out in times of emergency, as was to happen in the late stages of the war. Unfortunately, by then it would seem that the courage and training of the average citizen had declined and the citizen levies were not to prove a great asset to Hannibal. It is not clear whether at that stage there still remained in being the elite unit of citizens which was compared by the Romans to the Sacred Band of Thebes; it is last reported overseas in 339 BC and by our period was probably no more than a largely ornamental guard unit.

The Carthaginian citizen militia was armed and organised in the Greek style as hoplite infantry, armed with a heavy spear and a sword, probably by this time the Spanish variety which was to become so popular. They wore Greek style helmets, either Thracian or Corinthian, greaves covering the leg from ankle to knee, and carried a large shield. So far authorities are agreed, but at this point they tend to differ. The shield is described as both circular and oval, though the balance seems to be in favour of a circular of three feet diameter with a spiked metal boss. It is on the main dress, however, that the foremost contemporary authorities disagree. Phil Barker in his excellent *Armies of the Macedonian and Punic Wars* describes the citizens as wearing a long red tunic without belt, whereas Peter Connolly in his beautifully illustrated but somewhat superficial *Hannibal and the enemies of Rome* states that they wore typical Greek cuirasses —though he does qualify this somewhat since he appears to be dealing more

1 *Carthaginian citizen spearman.* 2 *Carthaginian noble cavalryman.* 3 *South Gaul cavalryman.*

with the African levies than the citizens, and alludes also to spoils captured in Italy. The balance therefore seems to be in favour of the unarmoured infantryman.

If the Carthaginians disliked serving as infantry, there is evidence that the nobility still formed the nucleus of the heavy cavalry, though in relatively small numbers. They wore tunics and high open-toed boots and were protected by the Greek style corselet and helmet, crested in black or white, and a two-foot diameter round shield. Arms were a short stabbing spear, or possibly a pair of javelins, and the Spanish sword. The balance of the African heavy cavalry was made up by Libyan-Phoenician levies who would have been armed and equipped in much the same pattern though probably less ornately. They formed in the Greek style in troops of sixty-four, on a frontage of eight files.

The Libyan or African infantry formed the backbone of the original Carthaginian entry into Spain, but became proportionally less numerous as the Spanish contingent grew in numbers. Those used as close order infantry were equipped in much the same style as the citizen militia—here again we have the divergence of opinion as to whether they wore the simple tunic or the cuirass, and it is certain that after his early successes Hannibal re-equipped the majority of them in the Roman style. Their original organisation was as a phalanx, but it would have been the hoplite rather than Macedonian version, eight ranks deep with each file having a three-foot frontage and each rank a three-foot depth on the move, but halving this in defensive formation. The Libyans also supplied light infantry mainly in the form of javelinmen, wearing a short sleeved tunic and carrying a small hide shield. They were notable mostly for their hairstyles, the different tribes partially shaving their heads in differing ways, some of them wearing ostrich feathers in addition.

The most important African contingent to a Carthaginian army, however,

1 *Numidian javelinman or light cavalryman.* **2** *Libyan javelinman.* **3** *Libyan spearman.*

was undoubtedly provided by Numidia, which is the area of latter-day Algeria: the Numidians were in fact the predecessors of the Moors. The Numidian cavalry were the finest light horse of their day, accustomed to being on horseback almost from infancy. They wore only a light, short tunic, sagging baggily over a belt, and carried a small round hide shield. Their main weapon was the javelin, though they carried a dagger or light axe for close-quarters work. Their mounts were ponies or small horses, which usually looked scrawny but were capable of enduring where the heavier mounts of the medium and heavy cavalry could not. Though outclassed by the Roman cavalry in close order fighting, they were brilliant skirmishers and on campaign were ideal for foraging, reconnaissance and ambush. According to Denison they were organised in squadrons of sixty-four in the same manner as the regular cavalry, but fought in loose groups. They were an integral and essential part of a Carthaginian army, and it was to be their defection which, more than any other factor, turned the scale against Hannibal on the fatal field of Zama.

In addition to the cavalry, there was also a contingent of Numidian foot, equipped in much the same style as the horse. These were useful light troops but by no means as essential as their mounted brethren.

Spain was to prove a fertile recruiting ground for the Carthaginians, but using Spanish troops in their own country could be dangerous; while there are no reports of Hannibal's Spaniards being anything but loyal in Italy, there are several instances of Spanish troops deserting both Carthaginian and Roman armies in Spain. Probably, however, under a leader they liked and trusted they were reliable enough. Spanish troops all wore a white tunic—dazzling white, according to Livy—with apparently a purple or crimson border, the tunic being V-necked instead of the more usual square neck. The infantry were divided into three types. First came the light infantry, or *Caetratus*, who carried a small round shield, several light javelins and a short sword; they were excellent skirmishers and were in fact used later by the Romans as well as the Carthaginians. The heavy close order infantry carried a larger, oval, spined shield, probably of Gallic origin, and usually wore black cloaks. They were armed with heavy iron javelins—believed to have inspired the Roman *pilum*— and the short cut and thrust sword. Spain was well advanced in the production of iron, and many Spanish troops wore iron helmets instead of the more common bronze. Finally came the slingers, drawn in the main from the Balearic Isles. They were few in number, averaging only a few hundred to an army, but were deadly accurate, using different slings for long- and close-range work.

The Spanish cavalry were similarly divided into light and medium types. The lighter carried javelins in addition to a sword, with a small round shield for protection, while the heavier carried a large shield of three lime planks, slightly rounded off, and a longish thrusting spear in addition to his sword.

After Hannibal's march into Italy his army contained a large Gallic element, recruited from southern France and northern Italy. Though brave and hardy, the Gauls were never so important a part of the army as the Spaniards or Africans, since they were individual tribal fighters who failed to respond readily to discipline and organisation. As we shall see at Cannae, Hannibal tended to use them as expendable elements, reserving his better quality troops for the more important tasks. In the main they were infantry, fighting stripped to the waist in just trousers, usually plaid, though they might retain a loose cloak. They carried javelins, but the main weapon was the long, blunt pointed iron sword, useful only for cutting, and usually of such poor quality that it bent easily. As is obvious a cutting sword needs a good deal of room if it is to be employed efficiently, and Gallic infantry could be rendered helpless if it was compressed into a solid mass—a fact which tends to explain the disparity in casualties during the Roman conquest of Gaul and Britain. Gallic shields were similarly large and clumsy-looking. The first Gallic charge was an awesome thing, but if this could be held they tended to discourage easily; their general reputation was for fickleness and unreliability.

Gallic nobles rode to battle in the main, but were equipped much as the foot, though the southern Gauls favoured knee breeches rather than trousers, with the addition of a long, broad-bladed spear which could be thrown or used as a thrusting weapon.

Yet another late addition was that of a large numbers of Italians who were dissatisfied with Roman rule. These were largely Bruttians and Campanians, plus Greeks from the many colonies scattered along the coast of southern Italy. The Bruttians in particular were a backward people with little resource in the way of armour or weapons, but by that time Hannibal had no lack of captured Roman equipment, so they were undoubtedly fitted out in the Roman style. They seem to have fought well and become an integral part of the army, unlike the Gauls.

Hannibal also made use of another Spanish asset—their light, well made ox wagons, drawn by small, quick-paced teams, which he used exclusively for his supply train.

Which brings us to the last, and possibly the most fascinating element of the Carthaginian army—the war elephant. Military authorities today tend to dismiss the war elephant as a weapon which was more often dangerous to its owner than its enemy; yet elephants formed an important part of armies in the Middle

1 *Balearic slinger.* **2** *Spanish medium cavalryman.* **3** *Spanish caetratus or light cavalryman.* **4** *Spanish scutarius.*

and Far East and India for hundreds of years. The soldiers of these times were not fools; therefore it would seem that perhaps the elephant was a more worthwhile weapon than modern authorities give credit for.

The use of elephants seems to have originated in India, where they were in plentiful supply. The Indian elephant is in any case a milder and more easily domesticated beast than its African cousin, besides being somewhat smaller; the average Indian elephant stands some eleven feet at the shoulder, while the African bush elephant averages thirteen. The Western world had its first real experience with elephants when Alexander invaded India and fought the Indian king, Porus, at the Hydaspes—though there is some evidence that the Persians employed an elephant corps and that some beasts may have been present at Arbela, though they played no part in the battle. Alexander's experiences do not seem to have impressed him with the value of elephants—though they caused him considerable trouble at Hydaspes—for we have no evidence that he ever considered forming an elephant corps. It was under the Diadochi—Alexander's successors—that the elephant came into its own. Seleucus who controlled the eastern part of the Empire, is credited with their introduction, but they had already appeared on several battlefields, notably between Antigonus and Eumenes. Seleucus, however, was the first to use them decisively. He purchased no less than five hundred of the great beasts from India in exchange for giving up the area north of the Indus. With this mass of elephants he met Antigonus, till then the leading contender for Alexander's crown, at Ipsus. Antigonus was roughly equal in number of infantry, but had a huge advantage in cavalry; his mounted men under his son Demetrius easily routed the enemy horsemen but, having chased them off the field, found a long line of elephants barring their return to the central, crucial area. To his dismay, Demetrius found that his horses would not go near the elephants, and his attempts to ride round them were foiled by the sheer length of the line. The elephants thus took him out of the conflict; Antigonus died among the pikes, crying till the last that Demetrius would come to save him: and the elephant was established. No Greek army henceforth was complete without them.

Asclepiodatus, who wrote a book on tactics dealing with this period, had a lot to say about elephants, going into detail on their organisation into brigades or phalanxes of sixty-four, divided into a keratarchy of thirty-two, an elephantarchy of sixteen, an ilarchy of eight, an epitherarchy of four, a therarchy of two, and even a zoarchy of one. Whether these organisations existed in more than name is unclear; they may well have been mere administrative titles, since few rulers outside India would muster such large numbers of beasts. We do know however that the officer in command of an elephant corps had the title of Elephantarch, and that elephants all had individual names. It would seem, moreover, that it was common practice for a mahout to be with his beast almost from childhood, so that a good deal of rapport would exist between man and beast.

The Romans, as we have seen, had already encountered elephants before the First Punic War in their conflict with Pyrrhus of Epirus. Carthage employed elephants from an early date, but it would appear that only a minority of hers were Indian. Geographically speaking she was a long way from India, even if the rulers of India and the states between were willing to effect the transfer; elephants were always in demand, and at the far end of the queue, so to speak, Carthage would find them scarce and expensive. The Carthaginians therefore turned to their own native supply, the African forest elephant—now largely extinct. This poor relation of the bush elephant was to be found at the foot of the Atlas Mountains and on the Moroccan littoral. It stood a mere eight to nine feet at the shoulder and was altogether less powerful than its larger African and Indian cousins, but was still an impressive beast.

When we think of war elephants today we are conditioned by films and such like to see them carrying ornate howdahs or towers crammed with warriors; certainly towers were used at times, but much less commonly than is imagined. The Indian elephants Alexander faced at Hydaspes were ridden, apart from the mahout, by men who sat astride the bare backs, possibly with some form of harness for balance. It is probable that those of Seleucus followed the same custom. Certainly the smaller forest elephants carried no towers into battle, as the weight would have been altogether too much for them. We have no real evidence as to whether they carried any soldiers apart from the mahout; without a howdah the usual complement was two, often a bowman and a spearman. We have some pictorial evidence regarding Hannibal's elephants, though it is true that the most famous one, on a coin found in the Chiana valley, depicts what is undoubtedly an Indian elephant and was probably his own favourite beast called Surus. This shows the elephant without a tower, and if the larger Indian elephants were used without them, there is at least the assumption that the smaller African ones were equipped in similar fashion. Towers may have been used on ceremonial occasions, however, to impress onlookers. There is, however, an interesting engraved gem in the *Cabinet de France* which depicts an elephant carrying, not a tower, but a flat platform, possibly attached to a framework round its body. This might well have been used to give the men a better support than simply straddling the elephant's back, but we have no other real evidence for its use.

Tactically, elephants were usually deployed in a single line across the front of the army, and used to open the attack. Occasionally they might be massed on one wing, or, if they were few in number, might be concentrated at one part of the line. The tactic of using them against enemy cavalry was only viable when the enemy horses were untrained to act with or against elephants—which disposes at once of the commonest criticism of Hannibal's use of them at Zama. One hundred feet between beasts was about the normal distance, but would depend a great deal on circumstances. When intervals were large and elephants few, special light units were often placed in the intervals to work with the elephants and cover them against opposing missile men; such units were usually specially trained for their work and may have been permanently assigned to a particular animal, so that they knew its peculiarities. The elephant's best weapon, however, was the terror it inspired in troops who had never faced it before; once this had been overcome it could be seen that elephants in fact panicked easily, being frightened by sudden loud noises—it is suggested that some at least of the elephants at Zama were turned back merely by the shrill sound of the Roman trumpets—and very vulnerable to fire weapons. Certainly it was recognised by all that elephants were an uncertain weapon which could be dangerous in use, and we know that at the Metaurus Hasdrubal's mahouts were said to be equipped with a hammer and spike with which to kill their beasts if they ran the wrong way; there is, however, little evidence of this being common practice, and my own feeling is that a mahout who had spent a large proportion of his life with an individual elephant would be most reluctant to adopt such measures.

Summing up, it must be agreed that elephants were always something of a gamble, and more so against experienced troops and commanders. But, nevertheless, even for experienced troops the charge of trumpeting war elephants in full career must have been a most impressive sight and one to be faced with a certain amount of reluctance and heart-searching.

Chapter 5

The Roman army and military system

The basic tactical unit of the Roman army, right from the beginning of the city of Rome, was the Legion. The meaning of 'Legion' is selection, and in fact the men to make up this unit were selected; on the day on which the army was levied every Roman citizen aged between seventeen and forty-six, who owned property and thus qualified, was assembled on the Capitoline Hill. They were first sorted out by height and age, and the tribunes of the legions then selected the men they required. Naturally as Rome grew in size and number of citizens the process underwent changes, but the basic system remained unchanged. The army was thus a citizen army, serving for patriotism rather than pay, and enrolled for one season. At first two Legions were raised each year, but again as time went on and crises occurred the number was increased.

The original Roman Legion was armed, equipped and organised very much on the Greek style in phalanx formation. This organisation, however, with its close order and solid formations, was found to have grave disadvantages during Rome's early wars against both Pyrrhus and the Gauls, and somewhere about the time of the Punic Wars the Legion underwent drastic changes. We cannot therefore be too precise about legionary equipment and organisation of this period, since it was one of change and experiment. It would seem, however, that by the time of the Second Punic War the new Legion had been more or less established—though equipment still continued to change, mostly as a result of experience in Spain, from whence the new pattern legionary sword, among other items, was derived.

The legionary infantry fell into four classes. The first of these was the *Hastatus*, made up of the youngest age group. The poorer class citizens had to make do with issue equipment, a bronze chest protector over a knee-length tunic; the richer often replaced this with a mail shirt of iron rings. All, however, wore the Attic style helmet with a tall crest of three feathers and carried a large oval or semi-cylindrical shield, two feet six inches wide and four feet in length, made of laminated wood covered with hide and bound with iron; it had a vertical raised strip down the centre. There is some dispute as to whether greaves were worn, and it has been suggested that only one was worn, on the leading or left leg. The main weapon was the short thrusting sword—we are not certain at what date the Spanish sword was adopted as standard issue, but the earlier one was of the same general type—supplemented by two heavy javelins or *pila*. These may have been of different weights for different ranges, but were in any case close range weapons designed to be thrown immediately before the opposing lines closed. Again, there has been considerable controversy over the use of these weapons; two assertions, that they could penetrate virtually any armour and that they were of such soft metal that they bent on contact with the victim's shield, thus making the shield unusable, seem contradictory. The answer would appear to be that the javelin head was of needle sharpness and may even had been specially tempered, but the weight of the haft was such that when the weapon lodged in a shield the haft bent and made it difficult to remove.

Next came the *Princeps*, drawn from the middle age groups. His equipment was in all essentials the same as that of the Hastatus, but certainly at the beginning of our period he was armed with a long thrusting spear in place of the *pilum*. This may have been given up during the war, in which case there would have been little difference between the two classes; it seems unlikely that the Princeps wore greaves, and it is possible that his helmet plumes differed.

The third class was the *Triarius*; this was drawn from the older age groups and would therefore consist of veteran soldiers who had served in earlier campaigns. Again the equipment was almost identical, but here there is no doubt that throughout the war the Triarii retained the long thrusting spear in preference to the *pilum*.

Finally came the *Velite* or light infantry. Rome never took to the bow, and her light infantry, drawn from the poorer class citizen, relied on the javelin as its missile weapon. The Velite wore only a light tunic and carried a large round shield for defence. He was armed with a number of light javelins but carried also the standard short sword.

The Italian cities allied to Rome were obliged to supply an equal number of soldiers to those fielded by Rome itself, and they were equipped in the same style. Though always treated as being slightly inferior troops, they seem to have fought, on the whole, just as well and to have been completely reliable on the battlefield.

At the outset of the war and, in fact, throughout the fighting in Italy, the Roman cavalry were few in number and of poor quality. The cavalry of Rome itself was drawn from the richer citizens, which would tend to disprove Fuller's statement that they had no armour, carried only leather shields and had indifferent swords and javelins. It seems more likely that they wore a metal cuirass and carried a flat, round shield; their weapons would be javelin or throwing spear and the long cavalry sword, although Phil Barker states that they carried the Spanish sword and I bow to his greater knowledge. The numerical weakness of the Roman cavalry was somewhat compensated for by the allies, who were required to supply three times as many mounted men.

In Spain, however, Scipio very early on devoted himself to a reform of the cavalry service. According to Denison, he equipped his men in the Greek style with a cuirass, oblong buckler and boots, and armed them with a curved sabre in addition to their missile weapons. He was very particular over their training, and under him Roman cavalry was exceptionally manoeuvrable. The horses were equipped with bridle and reins, but at this time the saddle had not been invented. Instead a double cloth covering was worn, sometimes hide being used instead, held in place by girth, crupper and breast strap. There were of course no stirrups at this period. Horses were apparently unshod, though it does seem that the idea of an artificial protection for hooves had been invented, mules and other such burden carrying beasts being fitted for long journeys with an

1 *Roman princeps or triarius.* 2 *Hastatus.* 3 *Velite.* 4 *Heavy cavalryman.*

artificial shoe held in place by leather thongs. It is doubtful whether Roman cavalry used these in battle, but there is a case for suggesting that they may have adopted them for long marches.

The smallest tactical unit in the Legion was a century, commanded by a centurion. These officers were the backbone of the Legions throughout history, just as the NCO was said to be the mainstay of the German Army in the nineteenth and twentieth centuries. It is, however, a mistake to think of a century as mustering one hundred men; even their paper strength was not always that, and in the field it would necessarily often be below strength. Two centuries formed a Maniple, but whereas both Hastati and Principes normally had a hundred and twenty men to a Maniple, the Triarii mustered only sixty. Normally the Legion was drawn up in three lines, Hastati in the first, Principes in the second, and Triarii in the third. The Maniples would be deployed six deep —except for the Triarii who would be three deep—and in order to give each man room to use his weapons each file would have a frontage of six feet, giving a Maniple a frontage of forty yards; a Legion would cover about half a mile. The Maniples would normally be drawn up in chequer board fashion, so that each Maniple of the second line covered the interval between Maniples of the first.

The cavalry was formed into *Turmae*, each of thirty horsemen in three smaller units, and ten Turmae were attached to each Legion. The Legion itself was commanded by a *Legate*, who was assisted by a number of *Tribunes* who formed his staff. These Tribunes were young men of good birth who thus gained military experience which would be useful to them in later life; as with all classes there were good and bad among them but it is a mistake to dismiss them as gilded youths knowing nothing of war and caring less. The field strength of a Legion at this time would be around 4,500.

The Roman command system was simple. Each year the Senate elected two

Consuls who in effect were the executive officers of the Republic. In times of war, they would each command, if necessary, a consular army which normally comprised two Legions. If the war was widespread and more than two armies were required, the Consuls of the preceding year could be pressed into office for the minor commands. This system has been laughed at on the grounds that it was completely unprofessional and provided Rome with a series of untrained civilians in command of her armies. To believe this is to take a much too simplistic view; to become a Consul a citizen had first to put in service as a Tribune, so that no Roman commander came to his post as a complete novice. Moreover, the Roman Legion was such an excellent war machine that all it needed, in most cases, was a commander of reasonable competence; Rome was perhaps fortunate that throughout her reign she rarely faced a worthy enemy, so that the odds were usually stacked in her favour from the beginning.

The system did, of course, have disadvantages. A change of commander every year meant that in a long war there was no continuity of command and that a General had small opportunity to learn and gain experience. This, in Roman eyes, was compensated for by the fact that, similarly, he had no opportunity to gain the devotion and loyalty of his men and then use them to overthrow the Republic—a fear always foremost in the minds of the Senate. While the system threw up few commanders of real genius, it must be admitted that it also threw up very few real incompetents, and that most Roman commanders under the Republic were sound enough, if uninspired. We have in fact no real proof that the employment of professional soldiers in command would have improved the efficiency of the Roman war machine.

In times of grave emergency, as was to happen in the Second Punic War, the system could be overridden. The best known variation was that the Senate could elect a Dictator, who took sole command for a limited period, subject only to the Senate deciding to revoke his office if he was considered to have failed or when the emergency ceased. He was provided with a lieutenant entitled a Master of Horse. The less well-known variation was that a successful commander could be retained in command beyond a one year period, as Publius Scipio was in Spain and Africa. The Roman Senate was thus a fairly flexible body, not as hide-bound as it has sometimes been portrayed.

To sum up, it must be concluded that the Roman Legion was the finest fighting instrument of its day, flexible, well trained and capable of manoeuvring and fighting in any kind of country. Its men were brave, patriotic and used to victory; its commanders were competent at giving it the limited commands which were all it usually required. As will be seen, however, though this was enough to carry it to victory ninety-five per cent of the time against barbarian tribes or even civilised opponents led by merely competent Generals, it was to prove unequal to the task of facing what must be admitted was an inferior style army led by a commander of genius. Even a Roman General of the calibre of Scipio Africanus needed the odds stacked in his favour to beat Hannibal.

Chapter 6

The war begins

When Hannibal returned to his capital at New Carthage in the winter of 220-219 BC he found awaiting him there an embassy from Rome. This embassy delivered to him a message from the Roman Senate, instructing him not to interfere in the affairs of Saguntum—which was a smallish town on the sea-coast between the rivers of Jucar and Ebro. Some time previously this town had placed itself under the protection of Rome, and it is by virtue of this fact that Roman historians have attempted to place the whole blame for the war on Hannibal. It would seem that there had been, as so often in towns of Greek extraction, an internal struggle for power within the town, and that the pro-Roman party had triumphed, promptly executing their opponents. It is also a fact that the new rulers of Saguntum were soon quarrelling with the surrounding tribes, who were vassals of Carthage. Who started the quarrel depends on whether your authority is pro-Roman or Carthaginian, and matters little: the fact remains that by lending support to Saguntum, Rome herself was breaking the treaty of 226 BC which, by inference if not in words, gave Carthage a free hand south of the Ebro. The attempts of a few writers such as Picard to suggest that the treaty named the River Jucar and not the Ebro are not born out by earlier authorities; even Livy, whose story of these events is otherwise a tissue of fabrications and half-truths, admits that the Ebro was the river in question though he claims, with no apparent justification, that Saguntum was excepted from the treaty.

Hannibal answered the envoys coolly and calmly, pointing out that they had no right to interfere in his sphere of influence, and telling them that it had always been Carthage's policy to aid oppressed peoples—ie, the tribes around Saguntum. In view of Carthage's treatment of the African tribesmen in her own neighbourhood this can only be taken as tongue in cheek diplomacy; but he went on to inform the envoys that he had no authority to act in the matter and to pass them on to the home government. In Carthage there was considerable debate, with Hanno calling for conciliation; but in the end the Barcid faction was able to win the decision, and a reply was sent to Hannibal authorising him to act as he saw fit.

The ball was now well and truly in Hannibal's court. Obviously if he disregarded Rome's warning and attacked Saguntum, there was a virtual certainty of war between the two great powers. The alternative was to turn aside and further consolidate his hold on central and southern Spain. At first sight it may appear that the second course might have been wiser; war might be averted and time gained to turn Spain into a more stable Carthaginian state. It has been

asserted that Hannibal's youthful eagerness for a forward policy, plus the oath
he swore before the altar seventeen years previously, swayed the decision;
certainly these factors must be borne in mind, but a far more potent reason was
doubtless that by accepting Rome's right to interfere south of the Ebro he would
have been clearing the road for any little town or chieftain within his empire to
call on Rome's protection in the future. Even had Rome had no inclination to
thwart Carthaginian progress—and we cannot doubt that there was always a
party in the Senate which wished to—a further intervention became inevitable.
By temporising now Hannibal might on the face of it buy time; but he would
inevitably lose face before the Spanish tribes, who would be encouraged to
transfer their allegiance to what they would see as the stronger power. It was a
clear case of stand or go under; in Hannibal's mind it must have seemed very
much the same situation as Britain was to face in September 1939—appeasing
an aggressor, as Chamberlain had done in Munich and Hasdrubal the Splendid
had done in 226 BC, only encouraged him to make further demands. To a man
of Hannibal's stature, there could only be one answer: in the spring of 219 BC he
marched on Saguntum.

The town, though of no great size, was well fortified; the Saguntines, of
course, could not hope to face Hannibal in the open field, but they manned their
walls with grim determination, possibly inspired by hopes of Roman support—
in which case they were doomed to disappointment. Our knowledge of the
course of the siege is limited, and comes very largely from Livy, who clearly tries
to show the defenders as paragons. According to his version, Hannibal selected
a weak point in the walls and made a breach by use of mining and battering
rams, but was unable to force a way into the town. A period of skirmishing
followed, in which the besieged often sallied out, and in the course of one of
these encounters Hannibal himself was severely wounded in the thigh by a
javelin. When he recovered, he transferred operations to a new point, threw
down the walls and ordered a general assault which, after some very heavy
fighting, was finally repulsed. Our other sources agree that Hannibal's first
attempt to storm Saguntum was repulsed, but state that after this the siege was
converted into a blockade for lack of siege weapons. We know indeed that the
siege operations lasted for a full eight months, which supports this latter view.
During this time Hannibal had to leave the scene for a while to deal with a small-
scale revolt in his rear; he took advantage of the interlude to visit his family, and
there is a possibility that at this time his wife Imilce gave birth to a son. If so, he
was not fated to make his mark on history, and we have no knowledge of his
subsequent fate.

Finally, in the autumn, Hannibal launched a second general assault. This time
his troops were successful in breaking into the town and holding on to their
gains, but the Saguntines were not yet finished; indomitably they built inner
walls to contain the invaders, and resistance continued. Finally, however, as
supplies dwindled and hopes of Roman support ebbed away, Hannibal offered
terms. The lives of the citizens would be spared, and they could depart in peace,
each of them with two garments; all other property to be left behind. Whether
the pride of the city's rulers was too high, or whether they distrusted Hannibal's
word, when they saw that the city was ready to accept the terms, they set fire to
the central area and committed suicide in the flames. In the confusion the
Carthaginian army broke in, and Saguntum perished in the fire and slaughter.
The booty was considerable, but so had been the losses among the besiegers; it

has been said, and probably with considerable truth, that it was the resistance of Saguntum which convinced Hannibal that laying siege to Rome would be a hopeless task.

Why, then, had Rome let its ally perish without lifting a finger to help? There are three possible reasons: the first, a totally cynical one, that Saguntum had given Rome the *casus belli* she required, and was of no further interest or use; the second, that Rome was still too pre-occupied with the Gauls to be able to despatch a large enough force to Spain at that time; and the third, that the war party in the Senate was not yet strong enough to force an open breach. None of the three is totally convincing by itself, and it is probable that it was a combination of all three. The period immediately prior to the attack on Saguntum had seen Roman armies steadily in action against the Gallic tribes of the Po valley, and when these had been at least temporarily brought under control, attention had turned east into Illyria, where the Consuls of 219 were engaged. Though it would have been possible to have despatched a force of sorts west in the same year, it seems unlikely that it would have been large enough to face the whole might of Barcid Spain. Moreover, there were still factions within the Senate opposed to war with Carthage. Livy claims that a second embassy was sent by the Senate during the siege to bring pressure to bear in support of Saguntum, but he is almost certainly confusing this with the mission which failed to secure any agreement before the actual operations began. In this matter it seems much safer to follow Polybius' version of events than Livy's, so we can discount the oratory described by Livy as no more than his usual poetic licence.

The news of the fall of Saguntum seems to have reached Rome soon after the return of the unsuccessful first embassy, and to have come as something of a shock—though why it should have done so is unexplained. Did the Roman Senate have so little knowledge of the state of affairs in Spain that they really expected a small town like Saguntum to hold out indefinitely against the full strength of Carthaginian Spain? Even now, however, there was no unanimity of opinion in the Senate: though the news gave strength to the war party and possibly swayed the election as Consuls for 218 BC of Publius Cornelius Scipio and Sempronius Longus, two prominent 'hawks'. But, even so, the Fabian faction, who favoured peace with Carthage while Rome dealt with matters in Illyria and the incipient hostility of Philip V of Macedon, debated the issue fiercely; and though the Senate made preparations for war, they agreed to despatch a final delegation to Carthage. This delegation was to demand the surrender of Hannibal and his officers for punishment of their crimes, and the payment of reparations and the evacuation of Saguntum. But though the Fabii had secured this much, they were not strong enough to prevent the five-man party having a three to two majority of 'hawks'.

The scene in the Carthaginian council chambers is a famous one, and though we cannot be absolutely sure of the speeches made, the course of events is clear. To follow the generally accepted version, after Fabius Buto had presented the Roman demands, a Carthaginian spokesman pointed out the various legal points and rebutted any guilt of treaty-breaking on the part of Carthage. Fabius, ignoring this speech, pointed to his toga and said, 'I carry here peace or war; choose which you will have'. The Carthaginians, with unusual unanimity, then cried out, 'Give us whichever you please', and Fabius, shaking out his toga, said, 'War then'. And so the Second Punic War was finally launched.

After the fall of Saguntum, Hannibal had returned to New Carthage, dispersing his army into winter quarters. Though he had no certain knowledge of how Rome would react to events, he must have been fairly sure in his heart that war would follow. There can be no doubt that he had been preparing for such an event since he took command in Spain, and to this extent there is some truth in the accusations made against him; but it is only stupid rulers who do not take pains to prepare for eventualities, and to make preparations for action if war is thrust upon you is a different matter from deliberately forcing war upon an unwilling opponent—a policy more in line with the actions of Rome. Hannibal was determined that, if war came, Carthage would not make the mistake she had in the First Punic War, of acting almost entirely on the defensive and letting Rome seize the initiative. This time, Hannibal would dictate events, and he determined to do this by carrying the war into the heartland of Roman power and invading Italy itself.

To make such a decision was simple; to carry it out another matter entirely. Once arrived in Italy, Hannibal could count on support from the still incompletely subdued Gauls of the north, and in particular the large tribes of the Boii and the Insubres. He had already been in touch with their chiefs and had received promises of men and supplies; Roman actions over the past year or so in planting new colonies within the tribal areas had not endeared them to the Gauls, and though the latter were as fickle and unstable as their Spanish counterparts, Hannibal could be reasonably sure of a firm base of operations. By invading Italy, he was bound to make it the main seat of war, and thus draw Roman attention away from Spain and Africa; his plan was thus strategically sound militarily, and it contained the germ of his great diplomatic plan. This was no less than, by striking at the roots of Rome's Italian confederacy, to break it apart and replace it by a new power base, a widespread federation of southern Italy and the Gauls of the north, Gaul itself, and Spain. We will discuss this at rather more length in a later chapter; suffice to say here that if the concept was a dream, it was based on solid enough foundations.

But first Hannibal had to reach Italy, and his first and most basic decision had to be by which route: sea or land? It has been suggested that he had, in fact, little choice, since Rome now enjoyed control of the western Mediterranean, but this is not strictly true. It is true that the fleet at Hannibal's immediate disposal totalled no more than fifty galleys, while we know that Rome in 218 BC had 220 at least in commission. It is equally true that, had Carthage itself wished to make the effort, she could have equipped a fleet of at least a further one hundred ships, though she could not, at this time, in all probability have matched Rome's full complement. But it was terribly difficult in ancient times to practise complete control of the sea even with a superior fleet; we have numerous instances of such fleets failing to prevent the passage of hostile armies. Moreover, there was the certainty that the Roman fleet would be split between two or three different areas, so that, by concentrating her own fleet, Carthage could probably have attained parity or even local supremacy. There can be little doubt that, had the warships been provided and had Hannibal decided to go by sea, he would have had no difficulty in finding sufficient transports to embark at least as many troops as he eventually reached Italy with.

But—and it was a large but—the Carthaginian navy had not exactly covered itself with glory during the First Punic War, and we have no indication that anyone had devoted much attention to it in the interim period. Certainly, the army had not fared a great deal better, but it could point to some victories and stubborn defences, and in any case Hannibal would feel that he and his father before him had transformed it into a far superior fighting instrument. We can only proceed by inference, since we have no detailed knowledge, but it does not seem that the Barcas were greatly sea-oriented. It is true that Hamilcar Barca had commanded a squadron of galleys, but his main training had been in land fighting, and it seems likely that his sons had followed this trend. The navy had taken small part in the conquest of Spain other than a ferry service across the straits from Africa. We can, then, conclude that Hannibal did not have great faith in the ability of the fleet to carry him safely to Italy.

The alternative, though, was no easy one: a march of some eight hundred miles as the crow flies, much more in reality, crossing one major river—the Rhône—a number of smaller ones, and two formidable mountain ranges, the Pyrenees and the Alps. Though it is certain that Hannibal's agents had been in touch with at least some of the tribes along the route, and that he had questioned merchants and traders, much of the route would lie through unknown territory; even the merchants would not have known a great deal, since much of their travel would have been by sea rather than land. To us today, travelling by good, well-kept roads, the journey is no great effort; but in 218 BC to carry an army over the route was a major undertaking and one which had to be planned with great forethought. Though obviously a good deal of supplies could be obtained en route, by foraging, purchase or fighting as the case might be, the army must carry supplies with it, involving numbers of supply wagons, pack horses, mules, etc; water supplies would be vital for such a multitude. In particular, thought must be given to the elephants which would form a vital part of the army. We know, from the experience of the British army in India, a good deal about elephants on the march. Their speed would only have been around three miles an hour, and their daily distance from fifteen to twenty miles. We do not know whether war elephants could be used as baggage animals on the march, but if so the Indian elephant could certainly manage a load in excess of twelve hundred pounds; probably his smaller African companion would carry rather less. An elephant needs to be watered twice a day, at least, and their daily capacity would have been from thirty to fifty gallons, while the daily food ration would have been in the region of fifteen pounds of grain and two hundred pounds of dry fodder. Elephants have very sensitive skin, and cannot stand extremes of hot or cold, and if cold and wet they easily catch chills; while their feet cannot stand up to prolonged marches on wet or rocky ground. Similar problems would have applied to the unshod cavalry horses, while the foot soldiers would have needed extra footwear. The more one looks at this march, the more one realises just what an achievement it was.

During the winter, besides making all the necessary preparations for his own operations, Hannibal had to set things in order in the areas he was soon to leave behind. His first concern was to provide both Spain and Africa with trustworthy garrisons: though he hoped and expected that his march would draw off the main Roman forces, there remained a strong possibility that Rome would invade Spain and a lesser one that she might still be able to send an expedition direct to Africa as a counter to his own invasion of Italy. Native troops in their own country were always subject to certain tensions—desertion among others— and with this in mind, Hannibal transferred large drafts of Spanish troops to Africa and summoned equal strength of African troops to Spain to replace them. The numbers sent to Africa amounted to 13,850 foot, 1,200 horse and 870

Balearic slingers; they were to be distributed among the African garrisons, but 4,000 picked troops were to hold Carthage itself. The security of Spain was entrusted to his brother Hasdrubal, who was given 11,580 African infantry, three hundred Ligurians, five hundred Balearic slingers, 2,550 horse, mostly African though with a small Spanish contingent, and twenty-one elephants. Hasdrubal was also to retain the naval squadron of fifty quinqueremes, though it is a mark of either Barcid lack of interest in seapower or the decline of Carthaginian seapower generally that only thirty-two of these were actually in commission, the remainder being laid up. In addition to these forces, of course, Hasdrubal had at his disposal the ample Spanish recruiting grounds should he need extra troops.

Hannibal prepared his own army for its journey by giving all his Spanish troops winter leave to visit their families, thus putting them in good heart for the long absence which stretched before them. With the spring, they reported back to camp, and Hannibal began slowly to put his plans into motion. All the various troop movements would have taken time, and though the orders would have gone out during the winter, the sea crossings at least may well have been delayed until the spring when sailing weather would be better. Some writers have assumed that time was of the essence and that Hannibal made a hurried departure in the early spring, but these writers have not been military men; a little thought shows that an early departure would have benefited Hannibal little. In the spring the Spanish rivers would be at spate and thus more of an obstacle to cross, while the question of forage for his animals—a matter of vital importance in lands beyond his immediate control—urged delay until the grass was ripe. Thus it would seem that it was not until May that he himself departed from New Carthage, though parts of his army would doubtless already be on the march north for the Ebro. There are unconfirmed stories that at this time he placed his wife Imilce—and her child, if there was indeed one—on board a galley and sent her to Carthage for safekeeping. I find this difficult to believe, since it would imply a grave distrust in his brother's ability to hold Carthaginian Spain. Some writers have accused Hannibal of writing off Spain the moment he crossed the Pyrenees, and of having no further interest in it. This is ridiculous, for in his grand plan, which these writers seem to have completely overlooked, Spain had a vital part to play. If Spain was of no further interest, why then did he leave it so well garrisoned with troops who could have been taken with him to Italy?

Hannibal's army at the outset numbered ninety thousand foot, twelve thousand horse and thirty-seven elephants. Its march north to the Ebro was uneventful, and it would appear to have crossed that river about mid-July. Hannibal was now in new territory, among tribes which owed him no allegiance and whose chiefs had already been approached by Roman envoys. Moreover, on the coast were two small towns, Emporiae and Rhode, which owed allegiance to Massilia, itself a Roman ally. Here again we are at variance with those writers who believed that Hannibal's only thought was the destruction of Rome, and that he had already dismissed Spain from his mind. Had that been the case, with the force at his disposal he could undoubtedly have overawed the local tribes and marched swiftly to the Pyrenees, giving the locals assurances that he was only passing through. But to do so would have left a dangerous power vacuum between the Ebro and the mountains, of which a Roman expedition could easily take advantage. So, far from hurrying his march and soothing the local tribes with fair words, Hannibal spent a minimum of six weeks in the area dealing with the Ilergetes, Bargusii and Ausetani tribes and teaching them the full might of Carthage. Unfortunately we have no great details of his movements, and extremely conflicting reports of the losses he suffered in subduing the area. It seems likely that he left the two Massiliot towns untaken when they offered resistance, having the siege of Saguntum in mind, but there appears to have been fighting with the tribes and storming of tribal capitals at heavy expense. We are told by Polybius that when about the end of August he began the crossing of the Pyrenees his army had been reduced to fifty thousand foot and nine thousand horse; this represents a huge reduction in numbers, of which we can only account in part. We know that he left a General named Hanno—said by some to have been his brother or brother-in-law, though this is doubtful—in charge of the trans-Ebro province (another sign of his concern for Spain) with ten thousand foot and a thousand horse; and we know that a similar amount of troops left him at this point to return to Spain. Livy declares that these men were Spaniards who deserted or refused to travel further into unknown territory, while friendlier writers contend that Hannibal gave them free leave to return to Spain and carry the news of his conquests to their fellow tribesmen. Reluctant though one may be to accept Livy where there is any doubt, since he always takes the pro-Roman line and has no hesitation in inventing what suits him, his story here does seem more plausible. It would appear unlikely that Hannibal would march ten per cent of his army all that way only to send it back voluntarily at this stage, and one must conclude that some at least of his Spanish troops shrank from the venture. Certainly there would be little point in compelling them to remain with the army, where they would only be a source of discontent, and the wisest course would therefore be to allow those who wished to turn back to do so. Even accounting for these, however, we are still left with a deficit of twenty thousand foot and a thousand horse, which seems on the face of it an excessive number to have been lost in six weeks fighting against local tribes. Polybius does not in fact mention his authority for the figure of fifty thousand foot and nine thousand horse, and it is possible that he was mistaken; we can only be certain that it was with greatly reduced forces that Hannibal prepared to cross into Gaul.

Unfortunately again we have little detail concerning the crossing of the Pyrenees and the subsequent march to the Rhône river, which took him about three weeks of steady marching. It does not appear that the army met any serious resistance during this time; Hannibal's emissaries had been busy among the Gallic tribes, and he seems to have been welcomed rather than opposed. This was all part of his overall plan for an Iberian-Gallic-Italian alliance, which is supported by the fact that he dropped off garrisons at various points along the way, notably to guard Pyrenean passes; by this means more than by losses in battle his numbers were further reduced, so that by the time he reached the banks of the Rhône he probably disposed of no more than thirty-eight thousand foot and eight thousand horse, with an undetermined number of elephants.

There is some dispute as to exactly where Hannibal crossed the Rhône. After entering Gaul he seems to have kept parallel to the coast for some distance, but on approaching the Rhône he turned inland, probably in the vicinity of Aigues-Mortes. Polybius tells us that the crossing point was where the river was a single stream, four days march from the sea, and Livy follows Polybius in his account. If we assume that Polybius was consistent in his measurements, and there is no reason to doubt this, four days' march would be approximately thirty-five miles; this would appear to dispose of those who have put the crossing points as far north as Avignon or Roquemaure. Two possible crossing points are left: both are today bridged by *Routes Nationales*, one between Fourques and Arles, the other between Beaucaire and Tarascon. De Beer, whose work on Hannibal's crossing of the Alps is the definitive one, believes that the crossing of the Rhône was made at the former; he says, the Rhône is eight hundred metres wide, shallow and slow, the only spot which corresponds with the description given by Polybius. A more recent writer, Lazenby, prefers the Beaucaire-Tarascon site, basing his claim perhaps on Strabo and the *Roman Itineraries* which described the main routes crossing Gaul. Which of these is correct does not seem to me to be of great importance; they are only some ten miles apart and neither has any more tactical or strategical significance than the other.

The important fact is that here, at last, Hannibal was faced with strong resistance. The Volcae, who were the largest tribe in the area, had succumbed to the blandishments of the Massiliots, and while Hannibal was collecting boats and building rafts with which to make his crossing, the tribesmen gathered in great strength to oppose him. A river crossing in face of determined resistance could be a fairly desperate enterprise, but history has shown that river lines have seldom deterred great Captains for long; it is too easy to find a weak spot, and too difficult to defend a whole length of river in strength. Hannibal kept the attention of the Gauls by massing at the main crossing point and making great show of his raft building and boat assembly; meanwhile a strong detachment of Spanish horse under Hanno, son of Bomilcar, was despatched upstream, possibly to the area of Avignon, to a point of which Hannibal's Gallic guides had told him, where an island divided the stream into two main branches. Here he constructed rafts and proceeded to pass his force across the river. Hannibal waited until a smoke signal from Hanno indicated that he was in position, and then ordered the main army to commence crossing. The largest boats took the upstream station to break the force of the current, and rafts and smaller craft, often with horses tied in strings behind, crossed lower down. The Gauls pressed down to the water's edge to receive them, and with perfect timing Hanno's detachment charged down on the enemy's rear. The Gauls, taken completely by surprise, gave way at once and fled in all directions, and that was the end of resistance.

With the tribesmen dispersed, Hannibal could now set about the proper business of getting his army and all its baggage, supplies and impedimenta across the Rhône. All went swiftly and well, and by nightfall the whole army was across, with one exception—the elephants. These needed some complex preparations, since they greatly distrusted the water; Hannibal's men first built piers leading out into the river, and then fastened them to large rafts, the whole being covered with earth and grass to deceive the elephants into believing they were a mere extension of the road. Two female elephants were then put in the lead and led the unsuspecting male elephants on board (a possible explanation of the old proverb of 'being led up the garden path'?) and the rafts were then cast loose. The journey across was not without hazards, since the dismayed elephants tended to jostle and bump each other as they tried to press away from the edge of the raft, with the result that one or two lost their footing and fell overboard. Fortunately the river being of fairly shallow depth none of these suffered more than a wetting, and by dusk all were safely assembled on the further bank. Meanwhile grave news had reached Hannibal: a Roman fleet was anchored at the mouth of the Rhône, and a Roman army was encamped alongside it.

It is now time to turn to the Roman preparations for war. There is some confusion over these as, not for the first time, Livy and Polybius are in disagreement on several basic points. It seems fairly clear, however, that initially the Senate had authorised the raising of four Legions for 218 BC with the intention of operating principally in Africa and Spain. The two Consuls for the year were Publius Cornelius Scipio and Sempronius Longus; lots were drawn, and Scipio was assigned to Spain and Sempronius Longus to Africa. It is clear that at this point Rome, with a natural arrogance based upon her run of successes in the First Punic War, expected the new conflict to follow much the same script, with Carthage standing on the defensive and Rome dictating the course of events. It is extremely unlikely that anyone in Rome had any inkling of the calibre of their new opponent or that he planned to carry the war into their own territory.

Accordingly Scipio was given two Roman Legions, fourteen thousand allied foot and fifteen hundred horse, and sixty quinqueremes, with instructions to proceed by sea to Spain; while his colleague Sempronius was to take two Legions, sixteen thousand allied infantry, eighteen hundred allied horse and a hundred and sixty quinqueremes to Sicily, where he would prepare for the invasion of Africa. However, although Sempronius left to take up his consular command in the spring, before Scipio could embark the Roman plans were thrown into initial confusion by events in the Po valley. Orders had been given for the planting of two new Roman colonies at Placentia and Cremona, in territory recently taken from the Gauls. This, plus the urging of Hannibal's envoys, roused the Boii and the Insubrii into open revolt, and their warriors attacked both colonies, driving them to take refuge within the walls of Mutina. The Praetor, Manlius Valso, marched to relieve Mutina but en route was ambushed; after suffering considerable loss he in turn was forced to take up a defensive position at Tannetum.

It is not clear whether Manlius at this time had any regular troops at his disposal or not. Polybius states that he had the 4th Legion, but this should have been part of Scipio's command; subsequently he states that both of Scipio's Legions were ordered to Cisalpine Gaul, while Livy only mentions one being sent. Since we later find Manlius in command of two Legions, it seems possible that the 4th Legion was in fact detached from Scipio originally, and that he was ordered to send his other Legion under the second Praetor, Gaius Attilius Seranus, after the revolt had begun. What is virtually certain is that Scipio had to raise two entirely fresh Legions, and that this greatly delayed his departure for Spain. When at last he did embark, his warships and transports took the coastal route—a common practice still, ancient fleets preferring to remain in sight of land whenever possible—and, naturally, he called in at Massilia to take on supplies and allow his men to stretch their legs ashore. It seems likely that it was at this point that he first received news that Hannibal, far from waiting passively in Spain to be attacked, was across the Pyrenees and marching for Italy.

Even now, the Consul was not unduly alarmed. He still judged by Roman experiences with the Gauls, and, assuming that Hannibal would have to fight his way across Gaul, felt that he had plenty of time to intercept the march of the Carthaginian army. He did, however, despatch a scouting party up river, and it was a clash between these cavalry and Hannibal's Numidian scouts which informed both sides of the other's position. Scipio, it would seem, took some convincing that this was indeed the Carthaginian army on the Rhône: but, once convinced, he called his own army to arms and pushed north up the river to give battle. He was too late; on arriving at the crossing place he found that the Carthaginians were three days ahead of him. A difficult decision now faced the Roman Consul: he could follow the Carthaginians; he could carry out his original mission by continuing on to Spain; or he could return by sea to Italy ready to oppose Hannibal if he succeeded in crossing the Alps. The first possibility was not attractive; it meant pressing into completely unknown territory in pursuit of an army whose objective he knew only vaguely. In the end he reached a decision which made sound strategical sense and was to have a decisive effect on the war: he sent the bulk of his army on to Rome under his elder brother while he himself, with an escort, returned to Italy to organise the northern defences.

The question which no-one seems to have asked is, why did Hannibal not turn and destroy Scipio's army before continuing his march toward Italy? A comparison of the strengths involved shows that the Romans were fairly heavily outnumbered—though it seems probable that Hannibal at this stage had no such knowledge of Scipio's strength, his own scouts having been defeated in the encounter with the enemy. He could, however, have drawn a fairly shrewd assumption that it would be a normal-sized consular army. This being so, at first sight it would appear good strategy to turn back and destroy this Roman force, thus removing a possible threat to both his Spanish base and his line of communications. On the other hand, such a move would further delay his march—with the possibility of finding the Alpine passes impassable—and he may well have felt the unwisdom at this stage of taking any risks with his own army. If things should go wrong—and no wise General ever discounted such a risk in battle—it would have been the end of his venture before it was properly begun. Once across the Alps and into Italy, he could count on reinforcements from his Gallic allies to replace battle losses, but here he was in a no-man's-land with neither base nor reinforcements readily available. Why take a risk, he may well have reasoned, when by pressing on he would draw Scipio's army after his to Italy and destroy it at his leisure, on a field of his own choosing? It is unlikely that he anticipated Scipio's decision to send his army on to Spain. As it happened, it was a strategic error which was to mar an otherwise exceptional performance.

From the crossing point on the Rhône, the most direct route to Italy would have been by the valley of the Durance and the Col de Mont Genèvre; we know for sure, however, that this was not the route Hannibal followed, and there seems little doubt that he never had any intention of using it. To march by this route would have kept him uncomfortably near the coast, dominated by a hostile Massilia and the Roman fleet, and would, moreover, have led him out into Italy at a point well covered by Roman garrisons and far from the lands of his friends the Boii and Insubrii. We can therefore assume that he intended all along to take the more northerly route. At the Rhône crossing he was met by Magil, king of the Boii, who was to be his guide; and it seems likely that at this time both Hannibal and Magil made reassuring speeches to the army about the Alpine crossing, which by then may have been beginning to prey on the minds of Africans and Spaniards alike.

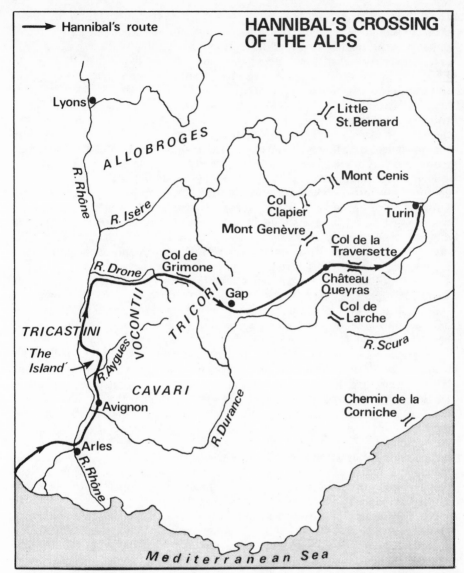

Hannibal's route

HANNIBAL'S CROSSING OF THE ALPS

Lyons

Little St. Bernard

ALLOBROGES

Mont Cenis

R. Rhône

R. Isère

Col Clapier

Turin

Mont Genèvre

Col de la Traversette

Col de Grimone

R. Drone

VOCONTII

TRICORII

Gap

Château Queyras

Col de Larche

TRICASTINI

R. Aygues

'The Island'

R. Scura

CAVARI

Avignon

R. Durance

Chemin de la Corniche

Arles

R. Rhône

Mediterranean Sea

The Carthaginian army, therefore, turned left up the Rhône valley, crossed the Durance—at this point an obstacle of no importance—and continued their march to an area called by both Livy and Polybius 'the Island' formed by the junction of the Rhône with another river called by Polybius the Skaras and by Livy the Arar. This area was inhabited by the Allobroges, who were at this time in a state of civil war caused by the revolt of one of the princes against his father, or possibly elder brother, Brancus. Hannibal settled this dispute in favour of Brancus, and thereby gained his support, with supplies of food and warm clothing. Identification of this area had been the cause of much bickering and in-fighting between antiquarians, many of whom, by tampering with the original Latin and Greek, have managed to identify both names as the River

Isere. This interpretation, however, just will not do if we accept that the Rhône crossing was at either Arles or Tarascon, and none of the alternative crossing places seem to qualify. It would have been wellnigh impossible for Hannibal's army to have reached the Isere in the time of four days which is given by Polybius, and in order to justify this identification historians have been forced to twist the earlier happenings quite needlessly. It seems much more logical to accept that the river forming the Island was not the Isere but a much earlier tributary, the Aygues, which in fact occurs at just about the right distance from the crossing place; and this would seem to be supported by De Beer's assertions that in ancient documents this river was called at different times many different names, several of which can be easily derived from either Skaras or Arar.

Here again Hannibal could have turned right and made a fairly direct Alpine crossing, but instead he continued on up the Rhône to its confluence with the Drome before turning off. Again, some historians have been confused by the passage in Livy which avers that on leaving the Island he turned left, but this quite obviously merely means that he followed the left fork—the Rhône—rather than taking the right fork or Aygues. He was now approaching the Alps themselves, and the most formidable part of his journey was about to begin. The Alps do not form a single but a double chain of mountains in this area, some 125 miles deep from the Rhône to the frontier ridge leading down into Italy, and to cross them it was necessary to first climb the northern slopes, then descend into a central valley and again climb the second line of hills before beginning the final descent.

From this point on we enter a maze of conjecture as to Hannibal's exact route, and I do not propose to devote overmuch space to what must remain largely guesswork. Even his leaving the Rhône at the Drome means following De Beer's route as opposed to Lazenby's who asserts that the turning off point was the Isere, and gives some convincing facts to support his assertion. The main fact, however, is that on approaching the first main Alpine ridge Hannibal encountered his first real opposition, from a branch of the Allobroges unconnected with those of the Island. These wild tribesmen looked on travellers merely as a source of profitable loot, and were not open to persuasion. Instead they manned the defences of the main pass and waited hopefully for the spoils of the Carthaginian wagon train.

Not for the first or indeed the last time, however, an enemy underestimated Hannibal's tactical skill—a skill which was to seem devious and tricky to his less complicated opponents. His scouts informed him that the mountaineers only manned their defences during the day, withdrawing at dusk to the shelter of their town in the valley beyond. Encamping for one night to lull them into false security, on the following night he kept his campfires burning while he personally led a column of infantry up the sides of the gorge to seize the vacated defences. It was a difficult and dangerous climb by torchlight, and casualties were suffered, but finally the crest was reached and secured. A torchlight signal from here set the main body in motion through the gorge, but it proved impossible to pass the whole through before dawn, when the warriors began to stream up from the town to resume their positions. At first bewildered by the sight, they soon began to attack the lumbering train of wagons and animals, doing considerable damage before Hannibal, swooping down from the heights, drove them off with heavy loss, and pursuing, entered their township unopposed.

In the town he found enough supplies to make up for those he had lost in the passage of the gorge, and the army accordingly rested there on the following day before resuming the march. At first it appeared that the salutary lesson had had an effect upon the mountaineers, for the following day's march was uneventful, and it was not until the fourth day after leaving the township that he ran into further trouble. At first it seemed, indeed, the reverse, for he was met by a delegation of tribesmen bearing green branches in token of peace, who offered to guide him safely through the remaining passes. Though he was suspicious of their intention, he was by now without any guides—the Boii delegation having left him to return home and prepare his reception, and the men from the Island having similarly returned once they had reached an area unknown to them—and he therefore accepted their assistance though marching in good order in case of attack. It would seem that, in fact, had he continued along the route he was traversing, he would have passed over the last ridge with little further effort; but in fact the treacherous guides led him off by another route into an ambush.

As the army threaded its way through a narrow gorge, with rock walls on one side and a sheer precipice on the other, the mountaineers launched their attack. It was a situation such as was so often experienced by the British Army on the North-West Frontier; but fortunately Hannibal's dispositions were equal to it. His cavalry were at the head of the column, followed by the convoy of wagons and animals, with his main body of infantry bringing up the rear; when the attack commenced the infantry were therefore able to move forward and take up a blocking position to give cover to the convoy. Even so losses were very heavy, and the attacks continued throughout the following day, though in diminishing strength.

Finally, on the eighth day after leaving the township, the enemy withdrew and the battered, weary army at last approached the highest Alpine pass. The time of year was now growing late, the summit was covered in snow and it was very cold. Climbing the pass was bad enough, but descending the further side was little short of a nightmare; animals and wagons slipped and slithered on the hard-packed, treacherous snow, and at one point the track became absolutely impassable, forcing the army to bivouac while the engineers, with great difficulty, built a new passage. The story of how they removed a huge rock by heating it with fires and then pouring vinegar over it is a familiar one; the difficulties of working at that altitude for men unaccustomed to it are less obvious but must have been formidable, and it is a measure of Hannibal's control over his men that the task was finally accomplished.

From this point it was, as one might say, all downhill; the path became gradually easier, and no further resistance was encountered. But when the Carthaginian army finally stood on Italian soil, it could muster no more than twelve thousand African foot, eight thousand Spaniards, and six thousand horse. The passage of the mountains had been as costly as a severe defeat, and at first sight the army, weary, ragged, weak in numbers and body, might have seemed a pitiful remnant of the proud force which had crossed the Ebro so many months before. But appearances were deceptive. Losses had indeed been heavy, but what remained was the strongest and the best, a hard core which was to prove capable of survival under the most arduous circumstances, and which was borne up by the indomitable will of its young commander. Losses could be replaced by levying troops from the Gauls who now awaited them; and those Romans who were already writing off the invasion army were to have a rude awakening in the following spring.

Chapter 7

The first clash

Hannibal was now safely in Italy: but to his annoyance he found the promises made to him by Magil had not been kept, and that no huge Gallic host was waiting to join him. In defence of the Boii king, it was now much later in the year than warlike operations were usually carried on, and it is probable that the insurgent Gauls had not expected a campaign to be carried on at this season. Hannibal, however, was determined not to waste time. First giving his army a few days' rest to recover from its exertions, he then marched into the land of the Insubrii, where he found that hostilities had broken out between them and their neighbours, the Taurini. Hannibal first tried persuasion to settle their differences, but, when he found the Taurini to be intractable, he swept into their lands and assailed their capital, which probably lay on the site of modern Turin. After a three-day siege he took the place by assault and put its inhabitants to the sword; by this single act of terrorism he completely overawed Cisalpine Gaul and brought the tribes under his sway.

This work was completed none too soon, for a more important foe was now approaching. Scipio, having returned from the mouth of the Rhône, had hastened north to take over command of Manilius' force; it is possible that he had hoped to meet Hannibal as he debouched from the Alps, but thought better of the project when he realised the true situation, for it meant penetrating into rough and unknown country in inclement weather. He also found his new command somewhat weakened and dispirited by its lack of success against the Gauls. Meanwhile the Senate, once apprised of Hannibal's intention to invade Italy, had cancelled its orders to Sempronius to invade Africa, and had ordered him to ferry his Legions back across the straits from Sicily and march north to join Scipio. Thus already Hannibal's strategic threat had saved Carthage itself from direct attack.

Scipio, who at this stage had little or no news of the enemy, crossed the Po at Placentia, and probed cautiously forward to the Ticinus, a stream which owes its source to Lake Maggiore and joins the Po near Pavia. Arrived here, he proceeded to build a bridge over the stream and construct a field work to cover it. This done, the army crossed over and advanced a further five miles before encamping. Hannibal meanwhile had been descending the left bank of the Po with the intention of forcing a battle on the Romans and driving them back across the river, to demonstrate to the Gauls who was the master. By now both sides had some indication of the other's presence, without precise information; and it so happened that on the same day both Generals decided to make a reconnaissance in force with their cavalry. This decision brought on the combat of the Ticinus.

Columns of dust were the first indications to both sides of the presence of the enemy, and both Generals accordingly halted and deployed for action. Scipio drew up his force with his few light infantry in front and his horsemen behind, the latter in apparently a single line of *turmae* with intervals in between, Gallic horse in the centre and Roman on either wing. Hannibal similarly deployed his heavy cavalry, which held the centre, in a single line of sixty-four-man troops, again with intervals in between, the whole extending across the Roman front; on either wing the Numidian light horse therefore outflanked the enemy line. No sooner had the deployment been completed than Hannibal ordered the charge, and the Carthaginian line rolled down on the enemy at a steady pace. The Roman infantry broke at once, possibly without even discharging any missiles, though Polybius does suggest that they threw one volley of javelins, and fled to the rear; but the Roman horse advanced steadily enough to engage the Carthaginians at close quarters. There was a brief but fairly bloody mêlée in which Scipio himself was severely wounded, being saved according to one account by his son, the future victor of Zama; and then the Numidians, who had swept round the flanks and ridden down the light infantry, crashed in on the Roman rear. Nevertheless, though the Romans gave way, they seem to have withdrawn in fair order rather than complete rout.

The Ticinus by itself was a small and relatively unimportant skirmish; its real importance lay in the fact that it was the first meeting on Italian soil and Hannibal had won it easily. None of our authorities quote numbers engaged or casualties inflicted; if we assume that Scipio had all his cavalry with him it would seem that his strength would not exceed two thousand horse and probably five hundred foot. We know that Hannibal had six thousand mounted men available, and there is no reason to believe that he did not have most of them with him, so the Romans were almost certainly heavily outnumbered. Their defeat was therefore no disgrace, but its impact went far beyond the mere tactical scale. Carthaginian morale was raised, the Gauls were suitably impressed, and Hannibal gained an immediate psychological advantage. It would seem that Scipio was most unwise to enagage the enemy in these circumstances; it is possible that he was overconfident and contemptuous of his adversary, in which case the result must have come as a nasty shock.

At all events his reaction was fairly extreme: he at once gave up any hope of operating north of the Po—which in face of Hannibal's cavalry superiority was a wise decision—and pulled his army rapidly back across the Ticinus. Here he left behind a detachment of six hundred men to destroy the bridge he had so painstakingly built, and made a rapid march back to his bridge of boats opposite Placentia and crossed to the southern bank of the Po. Hannibal meanwhile, not expecting so precipitate a retreat, followed up fairly cautiously, anticipating a general action on the Ticinus itself. He was therefore too late to force an action on Scipio's main body, but gratefully gobbled up the detachment which was still engaged in destroying the bridge. We can therefore imagine that Roman losses all told must have reached at least a thousand and the hurried withdrawal across the Po further disillusioned the Gauls, who now began to swarm into the Carthaginian camp.

Having crossed the Ticinus, Hannibal moved on down the left bank of the Po in pursuit of Scipio. What followed after this should have been fairly straightforward, but unfortunately both the ancient writers and their modern followers seem to have got themselves utterly confused over a simple error of direction. According to them, Hannibal pressed on up the Po—eastward—for two days' march until he found a crossing place where he bridged the river with rafts and transferred his army across. He then turned back down the river to find Scipio. The latter, wishing to avoid battle until he was joined by his colleague Sempronius, withdrew from his camp near Placentia in order to put the River Trebbia between the two armies, but almost left it too late, since he was hotly pursued by Hannibal's Numidians who, had they not stopped to plunder the deserted Roman camp, would have caught him in full march and must have done considerable damage to his laden columns. Now if this description had been correct, we would next find the Roman army encamped west of the Trebbia with Hannibal to the east—and, in fact, Dennison seems to accept this, since he criticises Hannibal for not preventing the junction of the two Roman armies when he lay between them—yet all the authorities agree that the battle of the Trebbia was fought west of the river after the Romans had crossed it from their camp on the east. Lazenby attempts to resolve this difference by asserting that Hannibal did indeed move up the Po to cross, but says in the next paragraph that Hannibal approached Scipio's position on the Trebbia from the west; in order to do this the Carthaginian army would have had to march along the Po, cross the Trebbia at its junction with the Po, and then after continuing on along the main river have turned back south-east to approach Scipio from the west. This is just not on; with Hannibal's advantage in superb light cavalry it would be impossible for him to have blundered past Scipio to the north and then turned back to find him. The solution is obvious, if we use the system of Inherent Military Probability invented by Colonel Burne: the direction of Hannibal's march before crossing the Po was not east but west. If we have him crossing the river two days' march *below* Placentia the whole campaign falls immediately into place: Scipio, who was originally encamped west of the Trebbia, then withdrew eastwards across the river, thus retaining his communications with Sempronius, who was approaching from the south-east. Hannibal then drew up his army and offered battle, but Scipio, who had no intention of being drawn, merely constructed a fortified camp near the head-waters of the Trebbia, where the river and the Appenine foothills would protect him from the Carthaginian cavalry, and sat there in safety.

The immediate cause of Scipio's withdrawal across the Trebbia seems to have been the desertion of virtually the whole of his Gallic contingent, a body of two thousand foot and two hundred horse, who mutinied in the night, slew the sentries and, according to one account, their Roman officers, and deserted to Hannibal. The latter received them with gifts and dismissed them to their homes to encourage their friends and relatives to join him, and this was the signal for the majority of the Gauls of the Po valley to throw in their lot with the Carthaginians. This eased Hannibal's supply problems somewhat, and the position was secured for him when the Roman commander of the grain supply depot at Clastidium sold him the settlement for the sum of four hundred gold pieces. It might be noted that this man, Dasius by name, was no native Roman but came from Brundisium in the South of Italy—a welcome indication of anti-Roman feeling in that area, though it is just as likely it was merely a matter of personal greed.

Somewhat similar confusion hangs over the movements of Sempronius before joining Scipio. At the time at which orders from the Senate reached him, he had just completed dealing with a Carthaginian diversionary threat to Sicily. Twenty Carthaginian quadriremes had appeared off the Sicilian coast, apparently threatening the seizure of their old base at Lilybaeum. Unfortunately for them, the squadron was scattered by a storm, and three isolated ships were captured by Hiero of Syracuse, who at once issued warnings. The remaining seventeen were thus engaged off Lilybaeum and defeated with a loss of seven ships and seventeen hundred prisoners, and Sempronius followed this success up by sailing to Malta, then held by a Carthaginian garrison. We do not know what strength Sempronius took with him, but at all events the Carthaginian commander, Hamilcar Gisgo, tamely surrendered with his two thousand men and Sempronius returned victoriously to Sicily to find that he was urgently needed in the north.

It is here that the confusion begins. Livy tells us that Sempronius despatched his army by sea up the Adriatic to Ariminum, following himself, also by sea, some days later after he had made arrangements for the protection of southern Italy from Carthaginian naval attacks. Polybius on the other hand, states that Sempronius dismissed his army with orders to reassemble at Ariminum on a certain day—ie, to make their way there on their own. This may seem improbable to our modern view of military affairs, but it must be remembered that we are dealing with a volunteer citizen army, and that such action would relieve Sempronius of the necessity of arranging for supplies en route. More-over, the season was by now somewhat late for sea travel, though the waters of the Adriatic would likely be more sheltered than the open Mediterranean. Against this, the time given by Polybius of forty days for Sempronius' Legions to march from Lilybaeum to Ariminum seems inadequate, so we are left with two equally doubtful stories; the only certainty being that Sempronius and his army did indeed reach Ariminum early in December. From here he moved directly north-west up what was later the Via Aemilia to join Scipio on the Trebbia about mid-month.

What followed was dictated very largely by the character of Sempronius and Hannibal's skilful handling of him. The new Roman commander was a representative if the Plebeian Party where Scipio was a Patrician; this is not to say that Sempronius was himself of humble origin, though his family may well not have been the equal of the Scipio's, but it did mean that he probably had less military experience and more ambition. The consular elections would soon be held, inevitably meaning a change of command; it was therefore important to fight quickly so that the glory of victory fell upon Sempronius and his party rather than the new Consuls, while Scipio was incapacitated by his wound. Sempronius' only experience so far against the Carthaginians would undoubtedly have lowered his opinion of them and made him feel that victory was inevitable once the armies met in open battle, and Scipio's pleas for caution and inaction until the spring would have appeared the excuses of a wounded failure. Sempronius was therefore resolved on immediate action, and Hannibal proceeded to reinforce this resolve.

Some of the Gallic tribes lying beyond the Roman camp had yet to give up their Roman allegiance, and Hannibal accordingly despatched a force of Numidians to raid the area and teach the local tribesmen the error of their ways. As these horsemen, laden with booty, were returning to the Carthaginian camp, they were intercepted by some Roman horse, and a skirmish ensued. The

Numidians fell back upon some Carthaginian heavy cavalry who were in support, and the whole then withdrew in apparent disorder; there is some question whether Sempronius actually led out his Legions in support of the cavalry, but at all events Hannibal gave the distinct impression of refusing battle and fearing to face the enemy in the open field. Knowing Hannibal's tactical skill and devious mind, it seems extremely likely that his horsemen had orders to behave in exactly this manner in order to encourage the Romans, for the Carthaginian commander had every intention of fighting on ground of his own choosing of he could trick the Romans into attacking him there.

The Trebbia is a typical Italian mountain stream, with a broad gravelly bed over which the river runs shallow in summer, no inconvenience to the traveller who wishes to cross. It was by now, however, almost the end of September and the stream offered an entirely different picture, that of a rushing torrent of icy water, breast-high in most places and thus offering an intimidating obstacle to the passage of an army. Hannibal planned to draw the Roman army across this stream, thus putting it at an immediate disadvantage; and he had selected a position with great care, taking advantage of a small watercourse running between some brush-covered hillocks which he intended to use as an ambush. On the night before he hoped to bring the engagement, he placed a force of a thousand foot and a thousand horse, all picked men, under his young brother Mago, whom he trusted implicitly, in this ambush position where they were totally hidden from view of the Romans. The stage was thus set for the battle of the Trebbia.

At dawn next morning the Carthaginian army stood to arms. The Numidian horsemen mounted and crossed the river to raid the Roman camp and provoke Sempronius into battle, while the main body ate a hearty breakfast and rubbed their bodies with olive oil to keep out the biting cold; flakes of snow hung in the air. The Numidians, skirmishing round the Roman camp, were soon met by the Roman horse, and these were followed by light infantry; at which point the attackers, following their instructions, began to give way and retire toward the river. Sempronius, eager to engage, gave his men no time to eat breakfast; as his cavalry and light infantry pressed forward toward the Trebbia he called the Legions to arms and followed hastily after his vanguard. At the river, the Numidians continued their retreat and the Roman army plunged recklessly into the ice-cold waters, struggling through to the other side where they deployed for battle, cold, wet and hungry; sleet drove in their faces, and suddenly the Numidian horse dissolved to either flank, and in their front they saw the solid battle-line of Hannibal's army.

Hannibal's forces at this time numbered probably 28,000 infantry, ten thousand cavalry and ten elephants, of these some four thousand horse and eight thousand foot being the newly recruited Gauls. He drew up his twenty thousand heavy infantry in a single solid line, with the eight thousand light infantry thrown forward to cover it, and his elephants in two groups of five, one in front of each wing of his infantry line. The cavalry were divided equally on either flank. Sempronius' force consisted of sixteen thousand Romans, twenty thousand Italian allies, and four thousand horse, so that the armies were fairly evenly matched in numbers. The Romans were drawn up in traditional form, the four Legions and the Italian allies alternating along the front in their usual three lines, and the cavalry equally divided between the wings.

It might be well at this point to define what is meant by 'single line'. This has

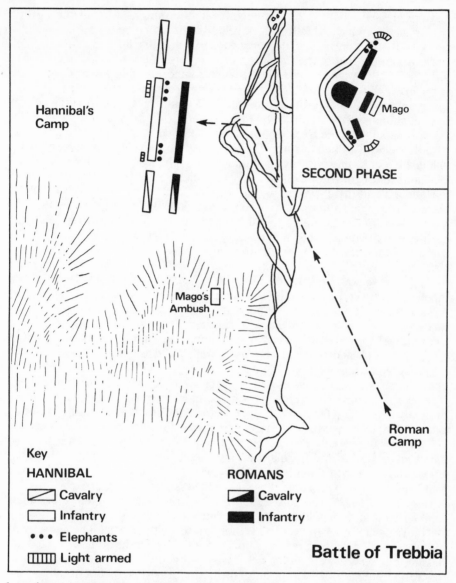

Hannibal's Camp

Mago's Ambush

Mago

SECOND PHASE

Roman Camp

Key

HANNIBAL

◻ Cavalry
◻ Infantry
••• Elephants
▥ Light armed

ROMANS

◼ Cavalry
◼ Infantry

Battle of Trebbia

been interpreted by the uninitiated as a single line of men, whereas in point of fact it is always used in the context of a single line of units. These units might be anything up to eight men deep, but the formation still counted as single line. Single line of men was a virtually unknown formation even among skirmishers, but this misinterpretation has led to some strange ideas.

Deployment completed, the battle was opened by the opposing light infantry, and here the Romans were quickly at a disadvantage; not only were their Velites heavily outnumbered, but they had already been engaged for some time with the Numidian light horse, and had used up most of their supply of missiles. After a short engagement, therefore, they fell back through the intervals of the main line, and Sempronius ordered a general advance of his heavy infantry. As the

Legions pressed forward, the Carthaginian light infantry, rather than following the Roman example and falling back behind their main line, withdrew to either flank of it, thus preventing the longer Roman infantry line from overlapping and outflanking that of the Carthaginians. At this moment both of the Carthaginian cavalry wings charged. These were composed of heavy cavalry in the front line, while the Numidians after rallying from their deceptive flight had taken up a supporting position behind. The Roman cavalry, outnumbered two to one, and already worn down by their pursuit of the Numidians, gave way at the first shock of these fresh troops, broke and fled in utter rout for the river, with the heavy Carthaginian horse in hot pursuit; but the Numidians coming up behind at once swung inwards upon the flanks of the Roman infantry just as the elephants and light troops similarly engaged them.

Hannibal had therefore sprung the classic encircling move, a tactic which he was to repeat again and again with consummate skill. But at this moment the skill and prowess of the Legions showed itself to full effect; held in front and with both flanks collapsing, they nevertheless more than held their own until, at the decisive moment, Mago's two thousand men burst out of their concealment—and fell furiously upon the Roman rear. Then, at last, cohesion and discipline gave way and Sempronius' army began to break up. Even at this moment, however, some ten thousand men in the centre of the first and second lines, refusing to accept defeat, burst their way right through the Gauls who made up Hannibal's centre. Then, seeing that the battle was lost and that a return across the river to their camp was completely cut off, they marched off in good order and made their escape to the walls of Placentia.

Of the remaining thirty thousand men of Sempronius' army, only a minority, and those mostly cavalry, struggled back across the icy Trebbia to rejoin Scipio, who had remained in the camp. Losses must therefore have been heavy, probably at least 25,000, and as a fighting force the army had virtually ceased to exist. Hannibal's own losses were not light, but they had fallen mostly on the Gauls, who were easily replaceable and could thus be spared more than the important Africans and Spaniards. This, again, was a tactic which Hannibal tended to repeat, and though it may have been cold-blooded to thus look upon his Gallic allies as expendable it was nevertheless a realistic approach, since his African and Spanish veterans were virtually irreplaceable, and without their solid core his army would lose its main cutting edge.

The Trebbia was a set-piece battle orchestrated with great skill by a master of the art. Every precaution was taken to ensure that when the armies engaged, all possible advantages were on the one side—the use of the cold water of the river to sap the energies of Sempronius' men, the provision of hot food for the Carthaginians before the battle, the skilful positioning of Mago's ambuscade, and the playing upon the enemy commander's over-confidence, all were spun together so that by the time the armies clashed the result was virtually a foregone conclusion. Yet even so it was a much closer run thing than the eventual result proclaimed, and the fighting qualities of the Roman infantry may well have come as a nasty shock to Hannibal. Certainly he would have filed it away as something to bear in mind, and it is noteworthy that in all his future engagements except the last, where the choice was hardly his, he ensured that these qualities were nullified in one way or another.

As for Sempronius, he trusted too much in the fighting qualities of his men and allowed himself to be deceived by Hannibal's wiles and apparent weaknesses. Yet Scipio's counsel of delay was not necessarily the correct decision; it would seem a display of weakness on the part of Rome and further encourage her enemies and half-hearted allies. The success of the Roman centre shows that Sempronius' confidence was not entirely misplaced, and a victory at this time would have ended the Carthaginian menace once and for all and probably settled the Gallic question as well. It was not necessarily a mistake, therefore, to give battle; but we cannot excuse the rashness which hastened the army out of camp all unprepared and precipitated it into a conflict where all the odds were weighted against it. It must therefore be agreed that Sempronius rates as the type of Roman General who was capable enough to lead an army against an unsophisticated enemy, but out of his depth when faced by a skilled opponent.

Despite all his precautions, however, the wintry weather had taken a heavy toll of his men's energies, and pursuit after the victory was an impossibility for Hannibal. The weather in fact was worsening; the night and the following day were marked by torrential rain and the cold if anything increased. Scipio was, therefore, allowed to break camp unopposed and fall back upon Ariminum while Sempronius, leaving a garrison in Placentia, fell back across the Appenines into Etruria.

So bad did the weather become that the Carthaginians suffered heavy losses among their baggage animals, and even more so among the unfortunate elephants, unused as they were to the cold and wet. At least seven of the ten remaining beasts died, and in fact it seems likely that only one, the almost legendary Indian elephant Surus, survived to go campaigning in the spring.

Hannibal's army now went into winter quarters, feasted and feted by the Gauls who flocked from far and wide to the Carthaginian camp. They were welcomed by Hannibal, feasted in their turn and sent away laden with gifts and inspired by Hannibal's diplomacy. But despite the atmosphere of goodwill on all sides, Hannibal knew full well that he must not overstay his welcome. The next campaign must be fought to the south, on territory outside the tribal sphere, lest his army become an unwelcome burden upon Gallic hospitality, and the present friendship turn into resentment and eventual enmity.

Even though the main fighting was over, it is unlikely that the winter months were entirely quiet. Raiding parties would have been active, and the blockade of Placentia and other such Roman strongholds would have been enforced, though not as completely as might have been wished, since there is evidence that Sempronius himself went south to Rome to preside over the consular elections, and afterwards returned safely to Placentia. Livy tells us at some length of two expeditions which he claims Hannibal made against Roman posts in the Po valley, but we cannot place much faith in either. In the first, if we are to believe him, Hannibal was defeated and wounded by Sempronius, and in the other, eventually successful, Hannibal was opposed by the local inhabitants to the number of 35,000. Polybius is silent on the matter and it would appear that both events are probably no more than figments of Livy's lively imagination.

Thus ended the first of Hannibal's campaigns against Rome. During it he had carried out an approach march of truly gargantuan proportions, bringing his army safely, if greatly reduced in numbers, to the position he desired. He had won one morale-boosting, if tactically insignificant, victory, followed by a decisive defeat of the main Roman field force, and had established a firm base among friendly tribes in the Po valley.

Chapter 8

The Trasimene Campaign

The Roman Senate had received the news of the Trebbia with more anger than consternation; while there was some dissatisfaction with the conduct of the war to date, there was still no apprehension of the final outcome. After all, Roman armies had suffered defeats before, and this particular one was blamed more on the rashness and inefficiency of Sempronius than the genius of Hannibal. It was in this atmosphere that the consular elections for 217 BC were held, the successful candidates being Servilius Geminus and Gaius Flaminius. We know little concerning the former, but quite a bit about the latter, who was to bear much of the blame for later events. He has been described by some authors as a political demagogue lacking in experience of affairs and having no military ability whatsoever, and it has been said that he was elected by the Plebeian party in face of massive opposition from the Patricians. Neither of these accusations seems to have been true. In any consular election of this period there was inevitably opposition to any candidate, but it seems that Flaminius had strong support from sections of the Patrician families, although these were glad enough to disown him after his defeat. As for his abilities, while serving as Tribune of the People he had succeeded in passing a far-sighted bill for agricultural reform; as a Praetor he had governed Sicily, and as Censor he had overseen the building of the great Flaminian Way from Rome to the North—all of these achievements requiring good sense and efficiency. Moreover, as Consul in 223 BC he had commanded in the field in Cisalpine Gaul with considerable success—though we have already seen that success against barbarian tribes was no real preparation for facing a General of Hannibal's calibre. It would seem, therefore, that the Senate generally felt that Flaminius was just the man to put right what had so far gone wrong, and to settle the hash of this upstart Carthaginian.

Nevertheless, though the Senate may have felt confident, it did not neglect to provide its Generals with the tools to do the job. No less than eleven Legions were levied for 217 BC, though these of course included those already in Spain and the wreckage of the armies of Scipio and Sempronius which were to be brought back up to strength, Sempronius himself was out of favour and was quickly relieved of his command—Flaminius hurrying north to take over from him without even waiting to carry out the normal ceremonies in Rome of an incoming Consul. Scipio, however, was apparently absolved of blame since the Trebbia had been fought against his counsel, and accordingly he was despatched to Spain to join his brother Gnaeus and take over command in that area. He presumably took with him reinforcements to replace casualties suffered the previous year by the two Legions of his command. A further two Legions were despatched south to Sicily and a third to Sardinia; Flaminius was taking over two from Sempronius and Geminus two from Scipio, though these, of course, had to be re-recruited. This makes a total of nine Legions, the remaining two being apparently *legiones urbanus* or city Legions which from this time were regularly raised to form a garrison for Rome itself. Thus, despite fairly heavy losses, Rome had nearly doubled the strength of her armies for the coming campaign; but she had made a grave strategic miscalculation in that the numbers actually deployed against Hannibal were only the same—four—as in 218 BC. This proves that, at this stage, the Senate still had no true idea of the danger represented by the young Carthaginian commander, and regarded the previous campaign as a series of regrettable accidents which would soon be corrected by a capable commander such as Flaminius.

Hannibal, no doubt, had spent the winter deciding on a course of action for the next campaign. Obviously he must move south from the Po, but the choice of three routes lay open to him. The first entailed crossing the Ligurian hills and reaching the west coast of Italy near the site of present-day Genoa; the second involved moving south along the flank of the central mountain range, the Appenines, and then crossing these hills to enter Etruria and threaten Rome itself; while the third would take him east to the Adriatic and then a march down the east coast. The only attraction of the first route was that it would possibly put him in touch with the pro-Carthaginian factions in Sardinia; against this it meant operating in the bleak Ligurian hills, and for any expedition to Sardinia he would need the services of the Carthaginian fleet. Though there is evidence that Carthaginian ships were in fact active on the west coast at this time, we know already that Hannibal tended to put little reliance on the navy, and we can therefore assume that this route never figured largely in his calculations.

The third route had the attraction that it avoided an early crossing of the Appenines, an obstacle only less formidable than the Alps themselves, as the Anglo-American armies which slogged through them in 1944-5 were to discover to their cost. But strategically it offered very little unless his intention was to by-pass Rome and head directly for the fertile south; and though this may well have been in his mind, such a move at this stage of the game was likely to sever his communications with the Po valley and Spain and to restore the strategical initiative to Rome. By taking the middle course he retained his communications and he put immediate pressure upon Rome by a fairly direct threat to the capital, while he must have felt that there was a strong possibility of gaining support in Etruria itself, for so long an active opponent of Rome.

The Consuls, naturally, were unable to penetrate Hannibal's plans for the coming campaign, and were, therefore, forced to guard both the eastern and western routes. Accordingly Geminus was stationed at Ariminum while Flaminius positioned himself at Arretium, where he guarded the main route across the Appenines. This was a dangerous strategical decision, since it left their armies separated by a mountain range and in grave danger of being defeated in detail, but it is difficult to see what other decision could have been taken at this stage, given the troops at their disposal. The blame must be laid at the feet of the Senate, which had grossly under-estimated the danger of the situation and the strategical options open to the Carthaginian commander. This

deployment would call for a nicety of judgement and promptness of action on
the part of both Consuls which, in the event, neither of them proved capable of
displaying.

From the outset Hannibal showed his superior skill in out-manoeuvring his
opponents. Having decided on the trans-Appenine route, he ignored the main
crossing guarded by Flaminius and instead chose a less travelled passage further
north. Setting out from his winter quarters around Bonnonia, he followed what
is now Route 64 through the Porretta Pass, having apparently little difficulty
other than inclement weather, and emerging from the hills in the neighbourhood
of modern Pistoia. This was where, in fact, his choice of route led him into
trouble, for he now had to face the swampy, water-soaked plain of the River
Arno. At this time of year the area, soaked by the melting snows of the hills
which had caused the river to burst its banks, was one vast quagmire. So bad
was the going and so wide was the marshy area that it took the Carthaginian
army four days and three nights of utter torment to traverse it, without a single

dry spot on which to encamp. Animals sickened and died in droves, and men, too, exhausted by their exertions, fell prey to the sickening miasmas and white mists which riddled them with malarial fever and other ailments. Hannibal himself, though he rode on the back of his faithful elephant Surus, fell a victim to the general malaise, contracted ophthalmia and lost the sight of one eye permanently. It is once again a measure of the tight control Hannibal was able to maintain over his heterogeneous collection of races that the army did not disintegrate under its sufferings but finally emerged, battered but undaunted, into the relative splendour of the valley of Faesulae. Etruria now lay before them.

If Hannibal had indeed hoped to raise the people of Etruria against their Roman masters, he was to be bitterly disappointed. To date his efforts in this respect had met with considerable success, but this had been among the barbarian Celts and Gauls; here he was dealing with civilised Italians, and indeed by now the Etrurians had become over-civilised, and in doing so, as is often the case, had lost the will to fight. The Roman conquest of Etruria was now well in the past, and the Etruscans had been absorbed by their conquerors, just as the Romans in turn had absorbed much of Etruscan art and culture. The once warlike Etruscans had become peaceful tillers of the soil, artists and artisans; the Roman yoke lay very lightly on their shoulders, and they had no wish to change their status. Hannibal's clarion call of liberty sounded only dully in their ears; they looked with apprehension and distrust as the foreign strange-looking Africans and Spaniards and barbarian Gauls flooded through their towns, and their officials, while giving lip-service to Hannibal, remained loyal to Rome.

Etruria would not rise for Hannibal; very well, then, it would serve him in another fashion. Flaminius still lay in the hills around Arretium, strongly posted, probably awaiting the arrival of his brother Consul. Hannibal had no intention of attacking him there, in a position where the Carthaginian cavalry would be at a disadvantage, so it was necessary to draw him down into the plain where he could be destroyed. The smoke of burning Etruria would be an irresistible lure to a man of Flaminius' character, so the order went out: if Etruria did not want Hannibal's friendship, it could have his enmity instead. As the army advanced south, it was accompanied by the smoke of burning farms and villages as the land was ruthlessly plundered and ravaged. Ignoring Flaminius in his mountain fastness, the Carthaginian army took the road by Cortona for Perusia and Rome, leaving the Roman camp to their left rear and ravaging the countryside with fire and sword as they went. As Hannibal had hoped, the spectacle was too much for Flaminius: ignoring the protests of his staff, he broke camp and hurried in pursuit.

Once assured that Flaminius had gobbled the bait and was following on his heels—watched every step of the way by Numidian scouts—Hannibal was able to select his battlefield. As it happened, an ideal spot lay not far beyond Cortona where the road swung east round the northern shores of Lake Trasimene. Unfortunately, as seems the case throughout this entire period, we at once run into controversy over the actual site of the battlefield Hannibal selected, largely because modern authorities assert that the shores of the lake today are considerably further south than they were in Hannibal's day, due to land reclamation work in the intervening period. For this reason, it has been suggested very strongly that the battlefield was in the region of the village of

Sanguineto; but a study of the descriptions of both Livy and Polybius, though they fail to agree on many points, does not appear to fit this region at all. Livy's account, as usual, is muddled and garbled and fails to make sense in several particulars, but if we follow that of Polybius, it would appear that he sets the battle east of Passignano, near Torricella. For those who wish to study the arguments in detail, I refer them to Lazenby's work, which covers the situation admirably and sums up in favour of Polybius' site. In point of fact, the actual site itself is not of great importance if we bear in mind the physical features which made the battlefield such a perfect site for an ambush.

As it skirts the north-western angle of Lake Trasimene, the road climbs the low ridge of Monte Gualandro and enters the Borghetta defile; leaving the lake on its right, it then descends into a crescent-shape plain, with some broken ground between the road and the lake, and steepish hills on the left. Beyond the modern village of Passignano, which did not then exist, the road climbs a hill, thus forming an amphitheatre bounded on all sides by hills or water—a perfect killing ground for a surprised foe. This fits very well with the description given by Polybius of 'a flat-bottomed valley having on its long sides high and continuous hills, in front a barren, steep crest and in its rear the lake'.

Hannibal set the stage with care. He probably encamped in the little valley which leads up to Magione, and he placed his African and Spanish veterans on the ridge blocking the exit from the killing ground, where they would be in plain view of the advancing Romans. His slingers and other light troops, with the Gallic horse, were hidden from view behind the crest of the hills on his left, the Gallic infantry similarly hidden along the hills leading to the Borghetto defile, and the Carthaginian and Numidian cavalry near the entrance where they could block it off once the Romans had passed through. Dispositions made, the army settled into position for the night,

Flaminius meanwhile was marching hard in pursuit, determined to drive what he possibly regarded as a fleeing enemy into the arms of his brother Consul, whom he believed to be advancing up the Flaminian Way. He reached the western end of the lake just before sunset, and therefore encamped for the night rather than essay the defile in the darkness. He was probably under the impression anyway that Hannibal was encamped in the valley beyond the defile, and would have no desire to bring on a general action at this time of day.

At this time of year—mid-June—it would be normal for a dawn mist to rise over the lake and cover the battlefield for a considerable while until the sun was high enough to burn it away. Doubtless Hannibal counted on this to help the success of his ambuscade and, in fact, as the Romans broke camp the whole area was covered in a clinging white veil which blanketed the low ground and rose to just short of the crests of the hills. Flaminius, eager for action and certain that Hannibal was fleeing before him, wasted no time in reconnaissance but got his men under arms and into column of route and plunged straight into the defile, encouraged by the sight of some of the African and Spanish infantry on the crest of the hill. It seems probable that he assumed they were Hannibal's rearguard and that a rapid advance might enable him to assail the Carthaginian rear with damaging effect. Hannibal on his side watched from his vantage point as the Roman army filed into the defile and almost disappeared in the thick mist. Due to the narrowness of the passage and the length of the Roman column of march, their vanguard was well past the site of Passignano and beginning to climb the far ridge before the tail of the army cleared the Borghetto defile; at which point the main Carthaginian cavalry force moved out from its position of concealment to block the defile, and Hannibal's trumpets screamed out the order to attack.

The six thousand men of the Roman vanguard, who were just climbing out of the mist, halted in alarm as behind them a veritable cacophony of sounds—shouts, screams, the bray of trumpets and the clash of weapons—rang dully through the heavy mist. Down below the mist line, the surprise was complete. The first inkling the Romans had of any danger was when a hail of missiles began to crash into their exposed right flank; the legionaires would have been in normal marching order, carrying full kit, with shields slung on their shoulders, and their losses would have been heavy from this unexpected assault. Then, as the men tried to drop kits and raise shields, out of the mists to the left charged a horde of savage warriors, hurling missiles and swinging long swords. There would have been neither time nor space to form the traditional three lines; even as the Centurions shouted orders to deploy to their left the enemy would have been upon them, and in minutes the column would have dissolved into a score of isolated conflicts, each having little knowledge of what was happening further down the line.

At the rear the position was even worse as the Carthaginian cavalry fell furiously on the Roman rearguard. This part of the column seems to have given way almost at once, the panic-stricken legionaires throwing down their weapons and even taking refuge in the waters of the lake. Burdened by their armour, however, escape by swimming was beyond them; many drowned and others were easily cut down by the horsemen who rode their mounts into the water after the fugitives. In the central area, however, part at least of the Roman army managed to form some sort of line and put up a fight, possibly inspired by the presence of the Consul. Eventually, however, Flaminius himself fell; Livy, as usual, has a circumstantial story of how he was singled out by a Gaul named Ducarius, who recognised him as the man who had defeated his tribe in 223 BC and took his vengeance, driving his spear through the Consul's chest and killing him instantly. Whatever the case, with his fall the heart went out of the remaining Romans, and after three hours of bloody slaughter the mist finally began to lift, revealing to the eyes of a satisfied Hannibal and a horrified Roman vanguard, still halted on the ridge, a scene of utter carnage.

The Roman vanguard, realising that they could do nothing for their comrades below, the bulk of whom were already dead, took discretion as the better part of valour. We cannot be quite certain whether they had in fact already been engaged or whether they had merely stood still until now. It seems a little unlikely that they should have merely halted, but it may well be that their commander was a man of little imagination who, without an order to turn back, feared to act on his own initiative. Some accounts maintain that they had already broken through the troops confronting them, but this seems a little unlikely since they would initially have been opposed by the African and Spanish veterans, and these suffered very few casualties in the action, which indicates that they were not engaged in any hard fighting. It seems more likely that, on realising the position, this Roman force, rather than try and force its way onward, turned half-left and broke its way through that part of the Gauls who would then have been in their front. The only certainty is that, for the moment, the vanguard escaped virtually intact.

The rest of the Roman army had ceased to exist. According to most authors,

Flaminius had begun the battle with thirty thousand men, and both Livy and Polybius state that of these fifteen thousand were killed in the fighting. While we may be suspicious of such exact figures, it would appear that a good half of the Roman strength were slaughtered. In such an engagement loss of life would tend to be very heavy since the opportunities for either flight or surrender would be restricted and quarter would not be given until the end when resistance had virtually ceased. Polybius quotes fifteen thousand prisoners as having been taken, which would neatly eliminate the entire Roman force; we can assume that some few at least must have escaped, though Livy's statement that ten thousand fugitives were scattered over Etruria to make their way back to Rome can, as usual, be taken with a pinch of salt. Whatever the figure of prisoners taken actually reached, it eventually included the six thousand of the Roman vanguard. This force, making off across the hills, was pursued by a strong cavalry force under Maharbal sent after them by Hannibal and, brought to bay next day, destitute of food or water, their commander surrendered at discretion, thus completing a display of ineptitude uncommon in a Roman officer. Carthaginian casualties do not seem to have exceeded 2,500, and once again most of these fell to the Gauls, who indeed did much of the fighting, since the African and Spanish infantry seem hardly to have been engaged.

Even now the tale of Roman disasters was not complete, for scouts indicated to Hannibal that the vanguard of Servilius' army was approaching down the Flaminian Way. Hannibal at once again detached Maharbal with the cavalry and some light infantry, and this force promptly attacked the head of Servilius' column, consisting of some two thousand to four thousand men, and utterly routed it, killing half and taking the other half prisoners. As a result the surviving Roman Consul hastily back-pedalled, leaving the road to the south open.

Back at Trasimene, Hannibal was busily collecting the spoils of his victory. Apart from sorting out the prisoners and stacking up all undamaged Roman weapons and equipment, he also ordered a search through the bodies for the corpse of his opponent, Flaminius; unlike the Roman Nero in his hour of triumph, the magnanimous Carthaginian wished to give his enemy honourable burial, but his men were unable to identify the Roman Consul. This in itself militates against Livy's story since, if he had been slain by Ducarius, the Carthaginians would have known with reasonable accuracy about where he fell.

Once again Hannibal followed his practice of sorting out the prisoners. All Roman citizens were retained, to be sold as slaves; but the Italian allies, as before, were addressed on the perils of Roman tyranny and on Carthage's mission of deliverance, and dismissed to their homes. Obviously, since his whole plan hinged on an eventual break-up of Rome's Italian confederacy, Hannibal could do no less, but it would be interesting to know what percentage of the released prisoners might have been found in the opposing armies of the following year. If Hannibal's policy succeeded, well and good; if it failed, all would fail and presumably a few thousand men more or less would make no great difference to Roman strength, but it was nevertheless a bold step to be taken by the commander of a relatively small force deep in hostile territory.

The Battle of Lake Trasimene must rank in history as one of the most masterly examples ever of the successful ambush. Certainly the countryside lent itself admirably to the scheme, but we can be sure that if Hannibal had not expected to find such a position he would have used a different tactic. Success depended on a number of factors, but Hannibal had weighed up every consideration and turned it to his advantage, from the strong probability of early morning mist to a correct reading of the character of his opponent. The selection of the position, the disposition of his troops and the timing of his attack were all perfection itself, and the result was a foregone conclusion from the moment Flaminius broke camp at dawn. Even the escaping vanguard was promptly rounded up by cavalry pursuit, showing that even in the moment of victory Hannibal still had events fully under control and was not about to lose any of the fruits of success, while the prompt counter-blow against Servilius shows yet again his instinctive feeling for the use of cavalry.

What can we say of Flaminius? Certainly his strategy cannot be faulted in pursuing Hannibal, though it does appear that he was outwitted in his attempt to block the passage of the Appenines; this, however, can probably be put down to his shortage of cavalry, with consequent lack of adequate scouting, rather than to mere inefficiency. His blunder in pursuing the Carthaginians into the defile without adequate reconnaissance in the existing conditions is less easy to excuse, though here again his cavalry shortage would make things difficult for him. Once again, however, as with Sempronius at the Trebbia, it would appear that the Roman Consul was betrayed by a combination of circumstances—lack of experience against an enemy of Hannibal's calibre, for which campaigning against barbarians was no compensation, and general over-confidence amounting to an arrogant assumption of Roman superiority in battle.

Chapter 9

A Fabian policy

The victory of Trasimene and the following bloody nose inflicted on Servilius had left Hannibal in full control of central Italy, free to march in any direction he chose. By any standard it was much too early for a direct attack upon Rome itself—he undoubtedly knew from his intelligence reports that the city was garrisoned by two Legions, which could soon be supprted by Servilius' two—so instead of continuing south, he swung east, crossed the Tiber, and entered Umbria. As usual, we then have two conflicting accounts of the route he took to the Adriatic. Polybius tells us merely that, having traversed Umbria and Picenum, he reached the Adriatic on the tenth day, without saying where. Livy has his usual detailed story, in which Hannibal, having crossed into Umbria, turned south to attack the Latin colony of Spoletium, but was driven off and then turned east into Picenum. Having regard to the nature of the countryside, such a march could hardly have been completed in ten days, and moreover it is unlike Polybius to omit mentioning such an occurrence. On the other hand, it might well have seemed expedient at that point to Hannibal to try the temper of a Latin colony, some of whose citizens could have been among the many prisoners he released. If so, he was disappointed in the response of the town. Probably, in fact, the main body of the Carthaginian army took the more direct route east while a detachment was sent to summon Spoletium—certainly Hannibal's foragers and raiders ravaged the whole area to collect supplies and booty under cover of the shield of the main army.

At all events, having arrived in Picenum Hannibal was able to do two important things: he encamped his army and gave his weary troops, worn out with hard marching and hard fighting, time to rest and recuperate and to change their outworn equipment for the spoils of Trasimene—his horses in particular seem to have been in great need of attention—and he was able to commandeer a ship in one of the Adriatic ports and send despatches home to Carthage to report on his successes and the present position. It may also have been at this time that he first sent messages to Philip of Macedonia suggesting an alliance against Rome.

Meanwhile, how had the news of Trasimene been received in Rome? The news itself, naturally, came first to the Senate, but rumours of disaster were soon sweeping the city and mobs began to assemble asking for news. Finally, about sunset the Praetor Marcus Pomponius came out from the Senate House to address them.

'We have been defeated in a great battle,' he told them 'a Consul is dead'.

The city itself seems to have been in considerable panic and disorder, but to its credit the Senate preserved its usual good sense. Obviously action must be taken; but it would seem that party politics was not forgotten either. Since the position seemed critical, a call went up for the appointment of a Dictator, who would have supreme power for a limited period to control the resources of the State, an action to which Rome had not had recourse for some considerable while. There was, however, a constitutional obstacle: by law, it was necessary for the Dictator to be proposed by a Consul, and of the Consuls for the year, one was dead and the other absent with his army well to the north of Rome. On the face of it, this does not seem to have been an insuperable obstacle; the appointment could surely have been delayed for a day or two while the Consul was summoned to Rome, and though his journey may well have been dangerous because of Carthaginian raiding parties across his route, it would by no means have been impossible. It has been suggested, however, that had he been present his choice of candidate might not have been Quintillius Fabius, who was being pushed for the office. It may well have been that Fabius, recognising this danger, suggested that instead the Dictatorship was elective, and was duly voted into office. If so, his scheme misfired to some extent as, whereas the Dictator usually nominated his own Master of the Horse, under these circumstances Fabius could hardly object to this office also being elective, and he was consequently saddled with Minucius Rufus, a supporter of the Scipio party which was opposed to the Fabians. From the outset, therefore, there was discord between the Dictator and his chief lieutenant. Their term was set at six months; Livy tells us that because of the somewhat unconstitutional appointment the Dictatorship was 'acting' only, but we have no evidence to substantiate this, while inscriptions show that no restrictions were placed on the office.

Once in power, Fabius set to work to restore public morale in Rome by placing the blame for the disasters on the anger of the gods, who were publicly appeased by generous sacrifices. At the same time he gave orders for the raising of two fresh Legions to replace those of Flaminius, and for areas in the path of Hannibal's army to be swept clear of provisions, standing corn to be burnt and the inhabitants to retire into fortified towns. There is strong evidence that this latter policy met with considerable resistance, as is only to be expected: the countrymen would see little point in wasting their own possessions, and would naturally hope that the invading army would pass them by. A scorched earth policy such as this can only be strictly enforced by military supervision, and at this time Rome had not the means to carry it out with more than limited success.

Leaving Minucius to oversee the raising and training of fresh troops, and possibly to call out the urban Legions from their garrison duties, Fabius himself now proceeded north to meet Servilius, who was moving down the Flaminian Way toward Rome. It is noticeable that on their meeting Fabius demanded full constitutional honours and that, taking over the Legions himself, he at once despatched Servilius to take over command of the fleet guarding the shores of Italy against the renascent Punic navy. This is not definite proof of political enmity—the presence of the Consul with the army in the circumstances might be something of an embarrassment, and the fleet obviously needed a commander of high rank—but it is another straw in the wind in support of the theory.

Fabius marched his Legions back to join Minucius and the combined forces then moved east across the Appenines in search of Hannibal. The Carthaginian commander, having restored the health of his army in Picenum, had meanwhile marched slowly south into Apulia, ravaging the countryside as he went; and Fabius accordingly moved down to Arpi in his vicinity. Hannibal at once drew out his army and offered battle, but Fabius was not to be drawn. His policy was to be one of safety and containment, the famous policy now called Fabian and which has given its author the title of *Cunctator* or Delayer. By it Fabius tacitly admitted that a Roman army could not face Hannibal in the field in other than exceptionally favourable circumstances, and that to give battle was to court disaster. His intention, therefore, was to keep his army in being and use it to circumscribe Hannibal's movements as much as possible and to bolster up any waning loyalty on the part of Rome's allies. There can be little doubt, looking at it with the advantage of historical perspective, that at this time Fabius' policy was the correct one, and that his appointment saved Rome from a second large-scale defeat in 217 BC; but it was bound to be unpopular and unspectacular, and it was to prove extremely costly to the Italian countryside. All credit must be given to Fabius for the iron self-control which he exhibited in face of a steadily growing public outcry against his methods; this was courage of the better sort in a situation when it would have been so much easier to play the dasher. As we shall see, these considerations did not apply to his lieutenant Minucius, and the constant bickering, disloyalty and downright disobedience of his Master of Horse made a difficult situation worse.

If Minucius disliked the Fabian policy, Hannibal liked it no better. With no central supply depot, his army had to live off the country and that meant constant foraging—which in its turn meant constant scattering of a good part of his army over a wide area. Fabius, who kept to the high ground, could keep his army fully concentrated and ready for action at any time, and could strike incessantly at the Carthaginian foraging parties, causing constant small skirmishes which, while they were by no means all Roman successes, caused a steady dribble of casualties to the Carthaginians; while there was always the threat that Fabius might choose to take the offensive at a moment when the Carthaginian army was widely dispersed. All the advantages militarily thus lay with Fabius, though the inhabitants of Apulia, seeing their farms burning, their livestock driven off and their crops trampled or burnt, might be pardoned for thinking otherwise.

Since the situation was not to his taste, Hannibal took steps to alter it. Leaving the Apulian plain, he struck north-west up into the Samnite hills and entered the territory of Beneventum. Here he captured an unwalled town, called Venusia by Polybius and Telesia by Livy; but once more he was disappointed by the response from the local inhabitants. Samnium, like Etruria, had once been a fierce enemy of Rome, and therefore might be expected to show sympathy to the Carthaginians; but though it is possible that a few recruits were picked up, there was no large-scale welcome. Two reasons may well have accounted for this: firstly the Samnites were still by no means sure that Rome was losing the war, and secondly the presence of Fabius' army, which was still dogging Hannibal's path and offered a strong threat to any disloyal ally.

Hannibal, therefore, did not halt in Samnium but continued his march into the area north of the river Volturno, crossing that river at Allifae and descending into the Falernian Plain, one of the richest areas of all Italy, where grew the vines which produced the famous Falernian wine. Livy has two stories regarding the march; in the first, he claims that among the prisoners at Trasimene were three Campanian knights who persuaded Hannibal that

Campania was ripe for revolt and encouraged him to move in that direction. This may well have been so, but it is doubtful whether Hannibal needed or would have paid great attention to their stories, since it is obvious that his main campaign was already drawn up in his mind's eye, and that he would pay far more attention to the reports of his spies—his intelligence network being first-class—than the probably biased stories of three prisoners. Moreover, if he was convinced by their stories his route to Campania was an extremely roundabout one. The second story is that Hannibal relied upon three local guides, and told them to take him to Casinum, but in such bad Latin that they thought he said Casilinum and thus led him to the wrong place; when Hannibal discovered their error he was furious and had one of the guides scourged and crucified as an example to the others. Again the story is unlikely; the latter part is obviously one more of Livy's attempts to show Hannibal as a monster of cruelty, while Hannibal's own scouts and outriders would have discovered the error well in advance of the arrival of the main body.

The whole point of this second story of Livy's is that, once descended into the Falernian Plain, which he proceeded to ravage with fire and sword in the usual manner, Hannibal appeared to be in a trap. The plain was bounded on the south by the Volturno, whose crossings were controlled by the Romans, and on the other sides by high hills with few passes. Livy wishes to give the impression that Hannibal thus blundered by mistake into a position of extreme peril, whereas the more likely explanation is that Hannibal intended all along to ruin the Falernian Plain—rich Roman territory which would seriously damage the economy of Rome itself—and had every confidence in his ability to extricate himself from any position of peril; confidence which, as we shall see, was not misplaced. His confidence may at this time have verged on contempt for the skill of his opponents but he was never guilty of such over-confidence or under-estimation of his adversary as had the Roman commanders before Fabius.

Plundering and burning at its leisure, Hannibal's army, by now loaded down with its train of captured cattle and booty-laden wagons, moved slowly north. Fabius meanwhile had taken steps to close the trap upon it; he had strengthened the garrisons of Casilinum, which controlled the Volturno crossing, and Cales, which covered the road leading to Rome; he himself, still keeping cautiously to the hills, made for the pass existing through them, keeping his main force on the slopes of Monte Massico but detaching four hundred cavalry under Hostilius Mancinus to keep in touch with the enemy. Mancinus, it appears, was a disciple of Minucius and thirsted for action with the enemy; he soon abandoned his role of scout to fall upon isolated bodies of Numidian horse which, laden with booty, were returning to the main body. Elated by his apparent successes against these, he pressed on further and further until, too late, he suddenly found himself assailed in front by a strong body of Carthaginian cavalry under Carthalo, while the apparently fleeing Numidians swept round his flanks and rear. The Roman force was cut to pieces, only a few scattered survivors rejoining Fabius; Mancinus himself was among the dead.

Fabius may have privately hoped that this small disaster would crush the importunities of Minucius and his supporters; if so, he was to be disappointed, and this partly by his own actions. Assured that the enemy was withdrawing from the Falernian Plain by the same route he had used to enter it, he proceeded to block the pass with a force of four thousand infantry drawn from his two best Legions, while the main body of the army encamped short of the pass; the

Romans exultantly told themselves that he must either attack them at a disadvantage on the morrow, or resign himself to wintering in an area he had already devastated and swept bare, with the inevitable result that in the spring his army would be reduced and debilitated, easy prey to the avenging armies of Rome. Hannibal, however, had no such thoughts. The idea of an attack on the pass obviously never entered his mind; such rashness was foreign to his nature. The situation was analogous to that which had faced him when he first encountered the Allobroges as he ascended the Alps, with the difference that the Romans could not be depended upon to abandon their position during the night. Very well, they must be induced to do so by deceit. From the hordes of captured cattle in his train he selected two thousand of the strongest, and ordered piles of brushwood to be tied to their horns: as darkness fell, these were assembled and driven up the slopes toward a saddle which he had noticed between his camp and the pass. As they moved up the hill, their drivers ignited the piles of brushwood and headed the now wild and terrified animals toward the saddle, which probably lay between Monte Caievola and Monte St Nicola. Meanwhile the main Carthaginian army, having rested and supped, had formed up quietly in order of march. A body of light Celtiberian foot had been detached to travel with the cattle.

To the Roman force in the pass, the spectacle of hundreds of torches making its way up the hillside, accompanied by the sound of hooves and scattered shouting and the clash of metal, meant only one thing—the Carthaginians were making their escape over the saddle. Here it might well be that Fabius could have done with a commander of the calibre of the man who led the vanguard at Trasimene and refused to do anything positive without orders; for the local commander, not unreasonably, decided to act on his own initiative, and, abandoning the pass, led his troops up toward the saddle. No sooner had they departed, than the main Carthaginian army began to file rapidly through the pass and out on to open ground, completely unmolested. Fabius, whose camp lay west of Monte Caievola, heard the noise and saw the torches, but cautiously refused to be drawn into a night action and held his men within the camp. Hannibal's army thus escaped without hurt, and moreover, on the following morning a detachment sent back to extricate the drivers and light troops who had been with the cattle fell upon the four thousand Romans dispersed across the hills and slaughtered almost a thousand of them.

Under the circumstances, Fabius was probably right to avoid a night action with all its consequent confusion and lack of cohesion: in these conditions the main Roman advantage of disciplined unity and training would have been dissipated and the result might well have been a repeat of Trasimene. We cannot, however, acquit Fabius of extreme negligence in his dispositions for the night, which betray a complete lack of provision against surprise. In common with his predecessors, he had completely underestimated the capabilities of his opponent, assuming quite wrongly that he was helplessly trapped. A Roman army did not move or fight by night; therefore the Carthaginians would not either. Thus no precautions were taken to guard the saddle or other such areas, and no thought seems to have been taken about what to do in the event of a night surprise. This, in fact, is one of the occasions when the comparison of Roman 'amateur' Generalship and Carthaginian 'professionalism' has some truth; Hannibal had been a soldier all his life, while Fabius was only a part-time commander. The difference showed.

Having thus escaped from the Falernian trap, Hannibal moved round the northern edge of a mass of hills which Polybius calls Mount Libirnus, past Aesernia, and then by way of Bovianum to the winter quarters he had selected for his army in the rich country of Campania. The little town of Ferunium, two hundred *stades* from Luceria, having been abandoned by its inhabitants—Livy says part of the walls had collapsed—Hannibal made this his central granary and camped in the vicinity, while Fabius' army, which had as usual followed cautiously in his wake, took position at Larinum. Somewhere along the route, however, Fabius himself had left the army to return to Rome; the reason given was that he was needed there to perform certain sacrifices, but the real one was undoubtedly that his policy of safety-first was under fire in the Senate as well as the army and he was required to defend himself before his critics. He left the army under the command of Minucius, no doubt with grave misgivings, having given him strict instructions that under no account was he to be drawn into a general action.

Naturally enough, Minucius paid little attention to these orders once Fabius was out of the way, and it must be admitted that on the surface he had considerable justification. On arrival at Gerunium, Hannibal had dispersed much of his army to forage; taking advantage of this, Minucius moved his own army down from the hills into a menacing position. Hannibal thereupon assembled about two-thirds of his forces and advanced to protect his skirmishers, occupying with an advanced detachment a small eminence which overlooked the Roman camp. Minucius promptly attacked this forward post with overwhelming strength and drove the Carthaginians from their position with some loss. Hannibal was now in a rather awkward situation: much as he was in favour of a battle, he was not foolish enough to fight one with over a third of his troops absent, and yet in the circumstances his army had to forage for its very existence. So, after a day or two of skirmishing in which the Romans undoubtedly had the advantage, he very sensibly withdrew to his original position at Gerunium.

The news of Hannibal's retreat and Minucius' success was represented in Rome as a famous victory, and no doubt the Senate and the populace, desperate for any good news after months of nothing but tales of defeat and despoliation, were only too ready to be duped into believing the stories. Fabius' position was thus further undermined and his political support was so eroded that he was forced to accept a reduction of his sole control of affairs. The first matter to be dealt with by the Senate was the election of a Consul to replace the dead Flaminius. Livy implies that this was forced upon Fabius as part of the diminution of his powers, but it seems more likely, since the man elected was Atilius Regulus, of the same political party as Fabius, that this was an attempt on the part of the Dictator to throw his enemies a sop to satisfy them. If so, it failed in its purpose—it may well be that Minucius' apparent successes turned the scales at the wrong moment. Polybius says that the Senate thereupon voted to make Minucius a co-Dictator, but it would seem that for once the usually reliable Greek historian is in error; to have two Dictators would obviate the whole point of the office and, in effect, reduce them to the status of Consuls. In this instance Livy tells a more likely story, though as usual he embellishes it with long, windy speeches by the participants which originate only in his fertile imagination. According to his version a Senator called Metellus proposed a motion under which the station of Master of the Horse was raised to equality

with that of the Dictator; although this in effect has the same result as Polybius'
co-Dictator, constitutionally it would sound better. Moreover, Livy's story is
confirmed by Plutarch, though he calls the Tribune Metilius.

At all events, the important result was that, on his return to the army, Fabius
had to take the bitter pill that his erstwhile deputy was now his equal in
command. In fairness to Fabius, it would seem that his main emotion, quite
genuinely, was not anger over his loss of command but fear of what disastrous
results Minucius' anxiety for battle might bring. He offered the Master of Horse
two alternatives; either the army might remain concentrated, with the two
Generals commanding it on alternate days, or it could be split exactly in two
with each commanding one half separately. Minucius, who obviously desired
unfettered command and had no wish to have Fabius breathing down his neck
even on the day he was not himself in command, opted for the second
suggestion, and accordingly the army split in two, each half encamping
separately.

Hannibal, who was quickly informed of the new situation by his scouts and
spies, was naturally delighted by the news. Even had Minucius not been young
and rash, the splitting up of an army in the face of the enemy was a dangerous
move, offering Hannibal opportunities for destroying the enemy in detail. It has
even been suggested that the earlier successes of Minucius were stage-managed
by Hannibal to gain this very result, but I am of the opinion that in this case the
genius of the Carthaginian commander is being over-stretched; Hannibal was a
wiley and devious man, but even he had his limitations.

Hannibal wasted no time in taking advantage of the situation. Between his
camp and that of Minucius lay a small hill which obviously presented a vantage
point for either side—much as in the previous operations. Again, Hannibal
proceeded to occupy it with a detached force, flaunting it in the face of the
Roman General. This time, however, the situation was in fact very different, for
not only was Hannibal's main army waiting to reinforce the hill, but he had
found in the neighbourhood a patch of dead ground which, despite the apparent
flatness of the whole area, was in fact large enough to conceal a force of five
thousand foot and five hundred horse. The trap was thus set, and Minucius
promptly fell into it.

On seeing the Carthaginians in occupation of the hill he at once ordered his
Velites to drive them off it. Hannibal in turn fed on to the hill just enough of his
own troops to keep the Roman light infantry in check, whereupon Minucius
called up his cavalry and added them to the fray. The action remained
undecided, since Hannibal once again sent up reinforcements of his own, so the
Master of Horse finally called out his Legions, and led them, also, up the hill.
Now the teeth of the trap began to close: Hannibal at once ordered his main
infantry force up the hill to receive the Roman attack, and then, when Minucius
was fully committed, the hidden ambushers sprang out of concealment and fell
furiously upon the Roman flank and rear, just as Mago's force had done at the
Trebbia. Fully engaged frontally, the Roman line had no time to turn about and
gave way at once. A complete disaster seemed inevitable, but at the critical
moment Fabius, who had been watching events from his own camp, arrived
with his troops in support. Minucius' fugitives, seeing the solid lines of Fabius'
Legions behind them, began to reform alongside the new troops, while those
Maniples which were still fighting fell back in good order to prolong the line.
Once he saw that Fabius was checking the rout, Hannibal's trumpets sounded

the recall and the Carthaginian army broke off the action and retired to its camp; Hannibal was not prepared at that stage to risk a general action against the combined Roman forces. Minucius thus escaped with a severe mauling—we have no record of his losses, but they were probably fairly high—and moreover seems to have been brought to his senses, since by all accounts after the action he threw himself at the feet of Fabius, thanked him for saving his army and implored him to resume supreme command.

After this both sides seem to have gone into winter quarters, and any further activity was limited to the occasional skirmish between Roman patrols and Carthaginian foraging parties. Some time in December the Dictator and his Master of Horse therefore laid down their commands, their six months of office being about completed, and were replaced in command of the army by the two Consuls, Servilius and Regulus. The Fabian period thus came to a close, and it is interesting at this point to consider just what, in fact, Fabius had achieved. His achievements, in fact, were largely negative—though no less important for all that. He had prevented yet another Roman army being served up to meet its almost inevitable doom at Hannibal's hands, and he had, by keeping his army in the field and in Hannibal's neighbourhood, proved to the wavering allies that Rome still had teeth and thus bolstered their doubtful loyalty. Above all, he had bought time in which Rome could raise fresh troops to replace those lost and to increase her forces to the extent needed if she was to face Hannibal in the field with any hope of success, and to gain ground in other theatres where the conquering genius of Carthage was absent. The cost had been heavy, both material in the territory ravaged so cruelly by Hannibal's army, and morally in the apparent inability of the Romans to prevent him wandering at will about their own heartlands; but the end result shows that in the final analysis the cost was justifiable. Certainly no-one can doubt that Fabius Cunctator, while he may not have been a great tactician or even a great strategist in the Hannibalic mould, was a man of iron moral courage who served his country well at a time when a lesser man might have brought her to her knees.

Chapter 10

Annihilation—the perfect battle

The consular elections for the year 216 BC were held amid scenes of savage bickering and popular demand for strong measures against the invaders. Before the elections themselves took place there was considerable political skirmishing as the opposing parties each attempted to rig the elections in their favour. Constitutionally, one at least of the outgoing Consuls should have been in charge of the elections. Livy says that both Consuls refused to come to Rome on the grounds that it was too dangerous to leave their army in face of Hannibal, and that the senior Consul, Servilius Geminus, asked that they be delayed until the end of the consular year and held under the auspices of an *interrex*. From other sources we learn that this suggestion was refused and that he then nominated Veterius Philo, who had been Consul in 220/19 BC, as Dictator to run the elections. This naturally did not suit Fabius, who was of the opposing party, and he accordingly managed to get the nomination turned down on constitutional grounds. However, Fabius and his policies were by then in poor repute in Rome, and the final appointment to electoral control was another of his opponents P. Cornelius Scipio Asina.

This first round of skirmishing had shown that Rome as a whole was weary of the Fabian policy of containment. Too much weight seems to have been given by most historians to 'popular demand', since the ordinary man in the street in Rome had at that time very little influence on the conduct of affairs; but there can be little doubt that the populace, who were by now suffering from food shortages due to Hannibal's depredations in the previous year, were much in favour of a forward policy, and while they could bring no direct influence to bear on the Senate, the Senators would no doubt take note of their feelings. It is therefore no surprise that when the first consular elections were finally held, the sole candidate to be elected was C. Terentius Varro, a strong advocate of meeting Hannibal in battle.

Varro's subsequent defeat has made him the scapegoat of most writers, who have eagerly seized upon suggestions that he was a common demagogue, a butcher's son and the champion of the people. Such writers have not bothered to investigate either the Roman senatorial system or indeed Varro's previous career. As Lazenby rightly remarks, it would have been impossible for a butcher's son to be elected to the consulate, and the worst that can be said of Varro in this respect is that he probably came from a nouveau riche family rather than an old established gens. He had, in fact, already served in a number of offices such as *Quaestor*, *Aedile* and *Praetor*, and had been active in the

Senate during the previous year, when it was in part due to his support that the bill regarding the elevation of Minucius was passed in despite of Fabius. It is also possible that Varro had seen some military service in Illyria. The picture we are usually given of the vain, arrogant bully who could harangue a meeting but not command an army is therefore very wide of the mark; and it would seem that Varro, while certainly no military genius, was no worse a commander than several of his predecessors, notably Sempronius and Flaminius.

Once elected, Varro then presided over the election of his colleague, who turned out to be L. Aemilius Paulus, who had been Consul in 219/8 BC. Paulus' qualifications were rather more obvious than those of Varro—he had commanded in Illyria during his Consulship (when Varro may well have served under him) which gave him military experience, and he came from the great Aemilian gens, one of the leading Roman families. Moreover, he was a supporter of the Scipio faction. Here again, much has been made regarding the opposition between Varro and Paulus, suggesting that it was the natural antipathy between the aristocrat and the gutter demagogue; but it seems very likely that at the time of the election there was no such opposition, these stories having been spread at a later date when it was necessary to find a scapegoat for the disaster and every effort was being made to hang the responsibility upon Varro and to exculpate the aristocracy.

Of one thing there can be no doubt: once the elections were completed, the mood in Rome became one of almost crusading fervour. All classes were united in the desire to meet the enemy head-on and destroy him, thus purging the shame of the previous year when Roman armies had cowered before the great Carthaginian. More than a hundred Senators left the Senate to serve with the army, virtually the whole of the knightly class volunteered to serve in the cavalry, and the citizens flocked eagerly to the colours. The mood was one almost of euphoria: no-one, with the possible exception of Fabius, seems to have doubted victory now that Rome was prepared to put her full weight in the field, and the Senate formally instructed the new Consuls to seek out Hannibal and bring him to battle.

If we are to believe Polybius—and in general, where we are able to make any check on his assertions, the Greek historian has proved to be the most accurate and reliable of our authorities—the Romans made in this year a truly great effort to field an army which should be more than a match for Hannibai's. According to him the Senate authorised the raising of four fresh Legions in addition to the four already in the field. Moreover, these four were to number five thousand men each, and the four existing Legions were to be raised to a similar strength. This would make the total infantry force, including allies, a remarkable eighty thousand men, probably twice the number Hannibal could field. Some historians have found this figure much too high, and indeed Livy does state that only ten thousand fresh troops were raised; but when you deduct from this total of eighty thousand the garrisons of the Roman camps at Cannae, amounting to fifteen thousand men if you accept the figures given by Polybius and Appian, and compare the result with the figures for casualties and survivors quoted by Livy we find that they balance out almost exactly. To assume that Rome, having decided on decisive combat, would field for it an army hardly larger in numbers than those already decisively defeated by Hannibal, is to assume that the rulers of Rome were stupid men who learned nothing from the past; and while it is true that they had seriously underestimated Hannibal in 217

BC, there can be little doubt that by 216 BC they held him in much higher esteem. In this context Polybius' figures bear the ring of truth.

In addition to the main field army and the forces in Spain, two other Legions were ordered north against the Gauls under the command of the Praetor Posthumus Albinus. These would seem to have been the urban legions which had taken the field after Trasimene, and though we have no definite proof that fresh urban Legions were raised to take their place as the emergency garrison of Rome, it is unlikely that this elementary precaution was omitted. The total Roman strength for 216 BC, was therefore, far in excess of anything ever fielded in the history of the city, yet this did not over-strain her resources.

However, the raising and training of this great mass of new troops would necessarily take time, and the army would not therefore be ready for battle when the spring campaigning season opened. The outgoing Consuls were therefore ordered to retain control of their armies until joined by Varro and Paulus with the new troops, and in the meantime to continue the policy of keeping close to Hannibal but at all costs avoiding a general action. During the spring the Carthaginian General seems to have been content to remain in his camp at Geronium, resting his men and eating the supplies he had garnered the previous year, for only a few small skirmishes are recorded. Undoubtedly Hannibal knew very well just what was going on at Rome and was prepared to bide his time; he was as anxious for a decisive battle as were the new Roman commanders, and had no intention of wearing out his troops by hard marching at this time. He waited, therefore, until his supplies began to run low, and then, breaking up his camp, marched leisurely south past the Roman covering force, crossed the River Aufidus, and seized the great Roman supply depot of Cannae, which would provide him with ample provisions and save him from the necessity of dispersing his men to forage.

Livy has a typical wild story of the circumstances of this march; according to him, Hannibal first failed in an attempt to draw Regulus and Servilius into a general action at a disadvantage, and was then faced with a mutiny by his Gallic and Spanish troops, who were so hungry that they threatened to desert. Hannibal, in despair, at first thought of abandoning his infantry to their fate and taking his cavalry north to the refuge of Cisalpine Gaul, but finally crept cautiously from his camp at dead of night, leaving tents standing and fires burning, and hurried off to the south before he could be attacked by the Romans. This story is so nonsensical that it hardly needs rebutting. That a General of Hannibal's reputation for careful planning and methodical preparation should hang around in one place until he was so short of food that his men were ready to mutiny or desert, when all he had to do at any time was to move south into a fresh area, is in itself ridiculous enough; while that a General who at one point is said to be trying to draw the enemy into battle should, virtually next day, be creeping off like a thief in the night to avoid action is equally unbelievable. As for the story of the despairing withdrawal with the cavalry to Cisalpine Gaul, can anyone believe that Hannibal could seriously consider that he would be received with friendship by the local Gauls after abandoning many thousand of their relatives to be slaughtered by the Romans? It is, of course, true that Hannibal would probably not wish to move until the crops were sufficiently ripe for harvesting and this would delay him, but he would undoubtedly have taken this into consideration in his plans.

The news of Hannibal's move drew the new Consuls hot-foot from Rome with their reinforcements; these by now should have been in fairly good trim, but it may well be that the Consuls would have preferred to delay action a little longer to complete their training. Servilius and Regulus seem to have moved cautiously in Hannibal's wake without waiting for their arrival, and the two armies joined forces in the neighbourhood of Arpi, probably on July 26. The combined forces then continued the advance for a further two days, encamping about six miles from Cannae itself. It is at this point that some slight doubt of Polybius' text creeps in. He tells us that Paulus now began to worry about the terrain in the area, which was flat and treeless, ideal cavalry country, and advocated to Varro that instead of continuing their advance they should turn away and try drawing Hannibal into ground more suitable to their own army. Varro, however, refused to agree and, the next day being his turn for command, continued the eastward movement. During the day the Roman army was attacked by the Carthaginian cavalry and light troops, but no more than general skirmishing occurred and at nightfall Hannibal drew off. Polybius then goes on to say that on the following day Paulus was forced to carry on the forward move and encamp for the night on the banks of the Aufidus, since by then it would have been dangerous to withdraw, and most modern historians agree with this suggestion. On the other hand, Paulus further sent one third of his army across the river, where they were to construct a fortified camp from which to cover his own foragers and harass those of the enemy; a move which, as Lazenby sensibly points out, does not suggest that he was trying to avoid battle.

It must be remembered that the Aemilian family were the patrons of Polybius, and it may well be that the otherwise reliable Greek historian is in this case trying to show Paulus in a rather better light and put the blame for the battle upon the shoulders of his colleague. It would seem much more likely that both Consuls were in full agreement upon the necessity of fighting, and that had Paulus really wished to avoid action he could have withdrawn on his day of command in perfect safety. To be fair, however, to both sides it must be pointed out that the spectacle of the Roman army marching forward one day and back the next like the proverbial yo-yo could hardly have been good for the morale of the troops, and it may well be that, if Paulus had doubts, he allowed himself to be overruled by his more forceful colleague in the interests of general amity.

The town of Cannae lay on a hill on the right bank of the Aufidus some five miles from the sea, the hill being the last spur of generally rising ground in that direction. Below Cannae the river runs through mainly flat ground, but that on the left bank is noticeably more so than that on the right. The left bank, in fact, is perfect cavalry country, never exceeding the twenty metre contour throughout the whole area between Cannae and the sea; whereas on the right bank, though the ground is still mostly level, it rises slowly but steadily from the sea to reach the ridge by Cannae.

After breaking off the earlier engagement, Hannibal had fallen back to his original position near Cannae; but once the Romans encamped with their main body on the left bank of the Aufidus he crossed the river with his whole army, encamped south-west of the larger Roman camp—thus blocking them off from the more broken ground in that direction—and on the following day, July 31, remained in camp while his men put the finishing touches to their equipment and saw to the needs of their horses. The Romans similarly remained quiet in camp which, since it was Varro's day for command, fails to tie in with the later stories of his heedless rushing into action. Next day, Hannibal drew out his army in order of battle facing the Roman camp, but Paulus was not to be drawn; Hannibal therefore pulled his main army back into camp but sent his Numidian light horse across the river, where they began harassing the watering parties from the smaller Roman camp and generally making themselves a nuisance.

August 2 was Varro's turn to command, and soon after sunrise the army was astir, forming up and crossing the Aufidus to the right bank. Most writers have severely criticised Varro for his move, claiming that he made it without consulting his colleague or even against his advice, purely through a reckless lust for battle. No-one, however, with the exception of Lazenby, has bothered to wonder why, if that was the case, he chose to fight on the right bank, which involved getting the bulk of his army across the Aufidus—a time consuming operation even if the stream was easily fordable—instead of fighting where he was on the left bank. In fact, even a short study of the general situation will show that Varro had little alternative to fighting, and that he did in fact do his best to ensure that he fought on the best ground available. To begin with, he and Paulus were in command of nearly ninety thousand men and six thousand horses, plus undoubtedly a number of baggage animals. These numbers require a truly immense amount of daily food, and, more important, water. The area in which the Roman army was encamped was quite incapable of feeding such a multitude, and though the Aufidus offered a plentiful water supply, collecting the necessary amount in face of the Numidians could be a difficult and costly operation. Moreover, camped as they were, the Romans were constantly troubled by the Volturnus, a south-east wind, which blew steady clouds of dust down upon them and contributed greatly to their thirst and discomfort. In these conditions, the Roman army had only two choices: to fight or to retreat in the very near future. In fact the choice was even more limited, since the Consuls had strict orders to fight and a retreat at this stage would have been disastrous to Roman morale. Paulus had refused battle on the previous day because he disliked the terrain on the left bank: there can be little doubt that it was on consultation with him and with his agreement that Varro resolved to cross the river and fight on the slightly more favourable right bank.

While we can be fairly sure that the strength of the Roman army was in the neighbourhood of eighty thousand infantry and six thousand cavalry—ie eight Legions with their counterpart of allied infantry plus the usual cavalry contingents—there is some doubt as to how many of these troops took their place in the battle-line. It must be remembered that the Romans had two fortified camps, one on either side of the river, and it is most unlikely that these would have been left ungarrisoned. Polybius says that ten thousand men (one Legion and its allied troops?) were left in the larger camp, and Appian similarly states that the smaller was held by five thousand men (possibly half a Legion). This does seem rather a large proportion of the army to dispense with in the face of the enemy, but it would still leave the Romans with a three to two advantage in infantry, and there seems a strong probability that the larger number left on the left bank were under orders to carry out a diversionary attack on Hannibal's camp, so that they were to play some part in the action. At most, therefore, it would seem that the Roman battle line numbered seventy thousand infantry and probably rather less, though the full strength of six thousand cavalry was undoubtedly present. It should also be remembered that of the total infantry strength as many as fifteen thousand may have been Velites, so that the main

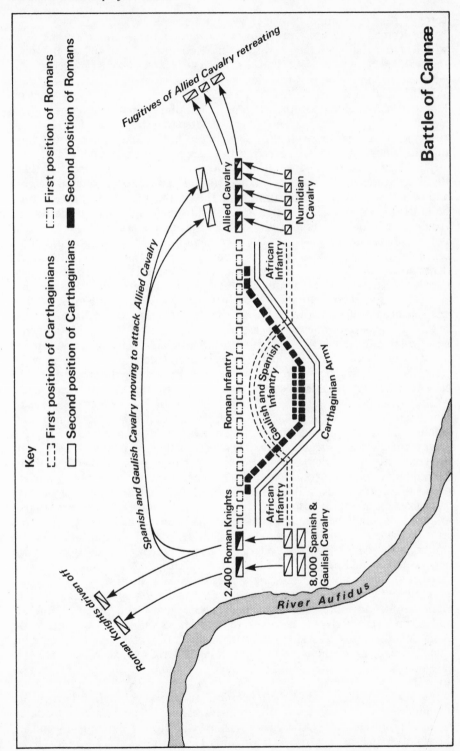

Key

First position of Carthaginians

Second position of Carthaginians

First position of Romans

Second position of Romans

Fugitives of Allied Cavalry retreating

Spanish and Gaulish Cavalry moving to attack Allied Cavalry

Allied Cavalry

Numidian Cavalry

African Infantry

Roman Infantry

Gaulish and Spanish Infantry

Carthaginian Army

2,400 Roman Knights

African Infantry

8,000 Spanish & Gaulish Cavalry

Roman Knights driven off

River Aufidus

Battle of Cannae

force of heavy line infantry probably did not exceed 55,000.

The Roman army was drawn up in conventional formation. On the right, with its flank resting on the river, stood the Roman cavalry, 2,400 strong, under the personal command of Aemilius Paulus. The infantry formed the centre, and were drawn up Legion by Legion each with its allied troops next to it, and the skirmishers thrown out in front; it seems, however, that not only were the Maniples placed closer together than usual but that their frontage was reduced and their depth increased. Lazenby has estimated that this would give a Legion a frontage of eleven hundred men and a depth of nearly fifty, which would mean that the infantry battle-line covered a frontage of about one mile.

The reasons for this change of formation are obscure; it has been suggested that Varro ordered it because he did not trust his new recruits and felt that depth and weight were needed to break through the Carthaginian line by sheer weight of numbers, or alternatively that he realised that if he took up the normal frontage he would not get his full force into the battle-line since it would extend too far. Of the two suggestions, the latter seems more valid, though Varro, who certainly was not a soldier of great experience, may well have felt that extra depth and weight would increase his chances of a breakthrough. The suggestion that he did not trust his recruits, however, seems an unlikely one since they certainly did not constitute more than fifty per cent of his numbers—probably less since the camp garrison would inevitably have been drawn from the least reliable troops—and if he was uneasy about their quality he would hardly have been so eager for battle. We are not even sure that the change of formation was in fact Varro's idea, since, though he was in overall command of the army, he took station on the left with the 3,600 allied cavalry, leaving the centre under the command of the ex-Consul Servilius. Polybius says that Servilius' colleague, Attilius Regulus, shared this command with him, but Livy states categorically that Regulus had been sent back to Rome because of his advanced age—one wonders in that case why he was appointed to his command in the first place—but there is a suggestion that he was actually dispensed with because he disagreed strongly with the policy of giving battle, being a member of the Fabian party. Lazenby considers that his place was probably taken by our old friend Minucius Rufus, Fabius' Master of Horse, and that in effect the two Consuls and their predecessors effectively retained control of their own original armies: thus Aemilius in addition to the cavalry probably had one Legion on the right of the centre, the other being the camp garrison, Minucius and Servilius would have retained their own veteran Legions in the centre, and Varro's two new Legions would have held the left of the infantry line. This may well be the case but we are really only guessing at these particular details.

When he saw the Romans crossing the river and forming in order of battle, Hannibal at once ordered his own light troops across and began leading his main army over the river to accept the challenge. As with the Roman army, we cannot be sure of his exact strength, since he also left a force behind to guard his camp, as many as ten thousand men according to some writers. We can be fairly sure that he had two thousand Numidian horse and eight thousand Gallic and Spanish horse, and that his infantry total was some forty thousand; if he did indeed leave ten thousand of these behind then he was very seriously reducing his numbers, and to me the figure seems excessive. Of his infantry, probably about ten thousand were Africans—re-armed with Roman equipment—and six thousand Spaniards, the rest being mainly Gauls with a small percentage of

Italians. It is therefore clear that he was very heavily outnumbered, almost two to one. His officers appear to have been worried by this fact: one of these, Gisco by name, watching the Romans deploy, commented anxiously, 'It is most amazing to see so many thousands of men'. Hannibal replied lightheartedly, 'I will tell you something more amazing—in all those thousands there is not one called Gisco'. The jest may not have been the bon mot of the year, but it revealed Hannibal's state of complete confidence in victory, and immediately the spirits of his officers lifted. Moreover, messengers carrying deployment orders spread the jest along the lines, and the tonic which it gave can be compared to that of Henry V's supposed speech on the eve of Agincourt.

Hannibal's confidence, moreover, was not founded merely on arrogance, as was that of Sempronius and Flaminius, but upon a carefully considered battle plan which took into account his own superiority in cavalry and that of the Romans in infantry, and made their own superiority work against them. His deployment was very far indeed from matching the conventionality of Varro's. To begin with, instead of distributing his cavalry equally between the wings, he had placed the whole of his heavy horse, eight thousand strong, not on the right opposite the main body of enemy cavalry, but on the left against the river, where they faced only 2,400 enemy horsemen. This gave him a virtual certainty of a breakthrough here, while on the other wing, where his two thousand Numidian light horse faced double their number, there was ample room to manoeuvre and he could rely upon the Numidians' skill to hold the enemy in check for as long as was necessary. It was not in this alone, or even principally, however, that the great Carthaginian showed his genius. When you have ten thousand good cavalry against six thousand of poorer quality even an idiot should be able to gain the advantage; but how to cope with facing seventy thousand good infantry with 35,000 at most, over half of whom were in fact inferior to their adversaries? Hannibal's answer was, as I have already said, to make the Roman advantage in numbers work against them. For this reason he placed his least reliable troops, the Gauls, in his centre, flanked by Spaniards; but instead of drawing them up in a conventional line or, as a merely competent soldier might have done, in a concave formation to refuse his centre, he flung them forward in a convex bow which jutted well forward from his main battle line. On either flank of this bow were stationed his African veterans, drawn up in two deep, solid phalanxes to support the end of the bow. He had, moreover, explained his wishes very carefully to his infantry commanders. He expected the Roman infantry to advance and assail his exposed centre; the Gauls and Spaniards here were not to fight to the death, but to give ground slowly under the Roman onslaught. The one thing they must do was to keep their line intact: if they did so, the weight of the Roman assault and the slow withdrawal of the Carthaginian line would funnel that assault until, as the line became concave instead of convex, the Africans on the flanks would wheel inward to form the shoulders of a huge bag, within which the Romans would be pressed together, hampered by their own mass. Not only was this a beautifully thought out, audacious scheme, but it showed Hannibal's absolute confidence in the fighting powers of all contingents of his army.

As was by now completely normal for this war, we have the usual confusion among authorities on who commanded where. Most agree that the Carthaginian heavy cavalry was commanded by Hasdrubal, who normally served as quarter-master-general, though Chandler's *Guide to the Battlefields of Europe* makes the *faux pas* of calling him Hannibal's brother, who at that moment was commanding the Carthaginian armies in Spain, and one other writer says the left wing commander was Hanno. I think we can take the word of Polybius that Hasdrubal was in command at this point. But Polybius also says that the Numidians on the right were commanded by Hanno, the man who had made the flank crossing at the River Rhône so successfully, whereas in most popular accounts we read of Maharbal being in command. Again, I think we must accept Polybius. Again we have a wild card in that I found one author who put Mago in command on this flank. It seems certain, however, that Hannibal's brother Mago was in immediate command of the centre and that Hannibal himself took post in rear of the centre where he could be in overall control of events. It was, after all, the crucial point: he knew that there was little likelihood of things going amiss on either wing with his cavalry commanders, but if anything went wrong in the centre his presence there could be vital. So the stage was set for the high point of Hannibal's career.

The action began with the usual engagement between the opposing light infantry, who appear to have been drawn up all along the front. This lasted until Servilius, becoming impatient, ordered the Legions forward, whereupon the Roman Velites presumably fell back through the intervals in the main line and seem to have played little further part in the battle. The Carthaginian light infantry, on the other hand, were mainly specialist troops who were trained to fight at close quarters as well as skirmish, and it seems reasonable to suppose that they therefore now retired into a supporting position and fought with the Spaniards and Gauls of the centre. These latter were now the target for the main Roman attack, which was driven in with the usual skill and determination. The Carthaginians in their turn met it with equal gallantry, fighting hard but gradually giving ground under sheer weight of numbers in accordance with their orders. This apparent success, just as Hannibal had planned, played its part in drawing the Romans closer together as they pushed forward; the weather, too, played its part, for although the sun shone obliquely between the armies, favouring neither, the strong Volturnus wind was blowing straight into the faces of the Romans, blinding them with its cargo of dust and thus reducing their awareness of what was happening around them.

Meanwhile the cavalry had also engaged on the flanks. On the Carthaginian left Hasdrubal had charged down on Paulus and his Roman knights. Accounts of the conflict are a little confusing: some say that the Romans, caught almost at the halt, gave way and fled at the first shock, others that they fought hard and gallantly to such effect that, since there was no room to manoeuvre and the two sides met head on, the mêlée became stationary and many of the combatants dismounted and fought on foot. I find this latter a little hard to believe for the Carthaginians, though it may well be that some at least of the Romans, seeing their position to be impossible, preferred to dismount and join the Legions on their flank rather than be borne away in a general *sauve qui peut*. Most accounts agree that Paulus himself died here at the head of his men, though as they also say that he was first wounded by a slingstone it seems likely that he was originally posted with the infantry rather than the cavalry and possibly died while trying to rally the defeated horsemen.

However the mêlée was conducted, it ended in decisive defeat for the Romans, and it is at this point that we see once again the skill and training of the Carthaginian army. Once committed to action, cavalry are notoriously hard to control; many are the times when victorious horsemen have been wasted in pursuit of the flying enemy merely because their commanders were unable to rally them. It may be that Hasdrubal, taking advantage of his superiority in numbers, had drawn his men up in successive lines and had held back uncommitted squadrons who were thus under full control when the Roman horse broke: of this we have no real knowledge. What we do know is that at this point in the battle, far from being dissipated in useless pursuit, Hasdrubal's cavalry, in perfect order, swung right-handed right round the rear of the Roman infantry centre to appear in rear of the Roman left flank. Here the Numidian light horse had been fighting a very difficult action, refusing to close with their opponents but keeping them in check by constant skirmishing. Livy has an improbable story of how a detachment of five hundred of the Numidians pretended to desert to the Romans, were allowed to pass through their ranks, and then suddenly drew concealed swords and fell upon their rear; Polybius makes no mention of such an action and it would seem that the story can be safely disregarded as another of Livy's inventions to show the deceit and treachery of the enemy.

Under the impact of Hasdrubal's charge the Italian horse broke at once, and, having room to do so, fled in all directions. Once again—which makes it all the more creditable to all concerned—Hasdrubal got his men back under control. Only the Numidian light horse, not at their best at close quarters, were unleashed to follow the fugitives; the heavy horsemen were re-formed and led back to take position in rear of the Roman infantry centre.

Here too the battle had gone in perfect accordance with Hannibal's plan. Servilius and his Legions had pressed on after the retiring enemy, pushing them back until at first they formed a straight line with the flanking African infantry, and on until the line had become concave; at which point the Africans, until now very lightly engaged, wheeled inward to turn the Carthaginian front into a huge sack enclosing the Roman masses. Some of the outer Maniples of this mass turned outward to meet the new threat, but this seems to have been instinctive action by local commanders rather than a controlled movement; in any event the shock of the unexpected assault seems to have checked the Roman impetus, thus enabling the hard-pressed Gauls and Spaniards to gain their breath and reform before renewing the fight. It was at this stage that Hasdrubal's victorious horsemen thundered down on the Roman rear, delivering a succession of controlled charges which served to press the unfortunate mass of legionaries closer and closer together as their own weight of numbers became a disadvantage. All authorities agree that from this point the fighting degenerated into mere butchery as the Romans became packed so tightly that it was difficult even to lift their swords. Only those on the outer edges could do anything to defend themselves and, as one writer has said, those in the centre, though no cowards, must have died many deaths before they met their actual doom.

The Battle of Cannae lasted, in all, some eight hours and ended in the virtual annihilation of the Roman army. As usual, it is difficult to pin down the figures of losses on both sides. Polybius says that seventy thousand Romans were killed or captured, only three thousand escaping; Livy says that 45,500 infantry and 2,700 cavalry were killed, while two thousand escaped temporarily to Cannae, seven thousand into the smaller camp and ten thousand into the larger. These latter figures, however, ignore the fact that these camps were already garrisoned, and it can be assumed that the bulk of these troops never actually fought at Cannae. It seems much more likely that very few indeed of the main Roman infantry force broke out of the net: the two thousand who escaped to Cannae, where they were rounded up by the Numidian cavalry, may well have been either Velites or troops on the fringes of the Roman centre who never entered the main trap. After the battle Hannibal's army proceeded to assail both Roman camps, which either surrendered or were stormed, thus making the destruction of the Roman army complete.

A realistic appraisal of the Roman losses would seem to be in the region of fifty thousand dead and over twenty thousand prisoners as a modest estimate. This allows for Livy's claim that a body of ten thousand men escaped to Canusium; if this claim is incorrect then the figures of casualties must be increased still further. Bloodshed was heavy, too, among the senior officers of the defeated army. As we have already seen, the Consul Aemilius Paulus was killed: we have an affecting story of how he was found, sitting wounded on a rock, by a fleeing Tribune who offered him his horse, saying that as Paulus was the only man not to blame for the disaster he deserved to survive—but at that moment the Tribune was swept away by a party of pursuing Numidians who slew the Consul with javelins. It may or may not be true, but it smacks somewhat of post-battle justification of Paulus in order to make a scapegoat of the surviving Consul, Varro. He himself seems to have either fled or been driven from the field in the rout of the Italian cavalry, arriving at Venusia with only seventy horsemen. Also among the dead were the pro-Consul, Servilius Geminus and the ex-Master of Horse, Minucius Rufus, whom we assumed commanded the centre, two Quaestors, twenty-one Military Tribunes, eighty men of Senatorial rank and hundreds of knights.

In comparison, Hannibal's own losses were light: Livy assesses them at eight thousand while Polybius gives the figure of four thousand Gauls, fifteen hundred Spaniards and Africans and two hundred cavalry. Even if we take the higher figure this makes a loss of about twenty per cent, acceptable enough for such a complete victory, while once again it is noticeable that a good half of the casualites fell upon the replaceable element of his army. It must also be remembered that a percentage of the casualty figure would be wounded who were only temporarily lost to duty.

Cannae was thus a crushing defeat for Rome, a defeat which was made possible not by Roman stupidity, as has often been suggested, but by sheer brilliant planning and training on Hannibal's part. Many writers, even to this day, do not seem to have appreciated the implications of his planning in full—in many accounts one reads of the Carthaginian centre being 'unable to hold its ground' in face of the Roman attack, or of Hannibal having exposed his centre unduly by its positioning, whereas I hope I have made it clear that this was all part of the master-plan and that the centre was never intended to hold its original position but to draw the Romans ever deeper into the trap. There has been little appreciation either of Hannibal's brilliant insight into the tactics and characters of the Roman commanders; just as at Trebbia and Trasimene, he seems to have known exactly what his opponents would do in a given situation and fitted this neatly into his plans. As already mentioned, none of this would have been enough without the high standard of training and discipline displayed by all sections of the Carthaginian army; Hannibal depended upon this factor to bring his plans to fruition, and as we have seen all parts of the army carried out their assigned tasks perfectly.

Probably the biggest controversy over the whole of Hannibal's career hinges upon the events immediately following his greatest victory. We are told by several authorities that on the evening of the battle Hannibal was approached by his veteran lieutenant Maharbal, who exhorted to him to march at once on Rome.

'Let my cavalry go on ahead' he said, 'and in five days you will be dining in the capital'. Hannibal replied that this was easy to say but would need much thought, whereupon Maharbal burst out: 'Hannibal, the gods have taught you how to win a victory, but not how to exploit it!'.

Almost universally Hannibal has been condemned for his inexplicable error in not marching directly upon Rome after the victory. Most of his detractors have been civilian historians without much military knowledge or appreciation and their findings can therefore be dismissed fairly easily; but the criticism of Field-Marshal Montgomery, who wrote that Maharbal was right in saying that Hannibal did not know how to exploit success, is far more weighty. The opinions of so noted a General are not easily disregarded, but in this instance I must have the temerity to disagree with him.

Let us first consider the actual situation. Hannibal's army had just fought a long, hard action and must have been weary and battle-worn. It was, moreover, encumbered with almost half its own number of prisoners and mounds of booty. The distance from Cannae to Rome is about 250 miles so that it is difficult to imagine how Hannibal could have traversed it in five days. Possibly the cavalry could have done it in a forced march; the infantry, averaging probably fourteen miles per day, would have needed the best part of three weeks. Rome was not an open city: it was well fortified and garrisoned by two Legions—perhaps not fully trained field troops, but perfectly capable of manning walls—and had a huge reservoir of able-bodied citizens who could be armed and pressed into service in an emergency. It is true that on the news of Cannae the citizens were thrown into a panic, but the Senate certainly was not—on Varro's return, for instance, instead of berating him for his defeat they thanked him for not despairing of the Republic—and it is inconceivable that Rome would have surrendered upon the appearance of a handful of cavalry. It is barely possible that on the arrival of his full army Hannibal might have stormed the city: but even a successful storming would have been terribly costly, and it must be remembered—something Hannibal always had to bear in mind—that he had only one army to lose, and must always be careful with the lives of the core of this army. An unsuccessful storming would probably be his finish. Failing an assault, the alternative would be a regular siege, but against such the insignificant town of Saguntum, completely unsupported from without, had held out for eight months. What of the remaining Roman resources while Hannibal was besieging the city? There were two Legions in Cisalpine Gaul, two more in Sardinia, which could be concentrated fairly rapidly for relief operations, besides the thousands of fresh troops which could be raised to support them. In a very short length of time Hannibal would find himself in a most difficult position: besieging a great city, while at the same time having to detach large parts of his army to forage for supplies and being menaced by relief forces as strong numerically as his own army.

Too many people have assumed that, because Hannibal had enjoyed an unbroken run of victory until then, all he had to do was march up to a Roman army and defeat it. A study of his operations shows that he never did just that;

each fresh enemy was thoroughly studied and measured before it was encountered on Hannibal's own terms. In the situation we envisage, any fighting would be done by Roman choice, and Hannibal would know that he could not necessarily guarantee success. Under such circumstances the siege of Rome would be a horrible gamble, and Hannibal was not a gambler by nature. I venture to suggest that Field-Marshall Montgomery, a soldier with a reputation for caution and a fetish for always being 'balanced' before he undertook an operation, would have thought long and hard before he embarked on such a venture.

Even had the situation been more promising, however, we must look at it from the viewpoint of Hannibal's long term plan. His aim was not the capture of Rome, but the break-up of the Italian Confederacy; an attack upon its headquarters was not necessarily the best means of achieving this, since it might tend to rally support to Rome. What he desired was to persuade the Italian cities to revolt against Rome's supremacy. For this his best hopes lay in the South, and at last he was in a position to nourish any incipient revolt, since he was free to march where he pleased without a Roman army to dog his footsteps and overawe the disaffected. From this point of view alone it made sound common sense to turn away from Rome. It is unlikely that this was a snap decision on Hannibal's part; I think it very probable that his mind was already made up before the battle as to what he would do after he had won it, and the completeness of the victory probably reinforced rather than weakened his decision.

Chapter 11

Failure of a dream

The news of Cannae came as a shattering blow to Rome, and at first the city was panic-striken. At this time of crisis, however, the cast-aside Dictator, Fabius Maximus, once more took control and rallied the Senate. Under his direction riders were sent out to find the true facts of the situation, and orders were rushed off to Claudius Marcellus, then at Ostia about to leave with a fleet for Sicily, to disembark all available marines and hurry them to Rome. Eight thousand able-bodied slaves were purchased by the state and armed to aid in the defence of the city in addition to the urban Legions. Finally a new Dictator, Junius Pera, who had been consul in 245/4 BC, was appointed.

No sooner had this been done and the immediate panic calmed, than two items of good news were received. The first was that Hannibal was not, as had been expected, in full march for Rome, but was still encamped on the Aufidus; the second was from Varro, who had rallied the survivors of his army, some 14,500 in all, at Canusium. Accordingly Pera now ordered Marcellus to hand over command of the fleet to Furius Philus and proceed at once to Canusium and assume control of the troops there, thus releasing Varro to return to Rome. There were probably two reasons for his recall—in the first place it was probably felt that the troops would have little confidence in him after his defeat, and in the second it was constitutionally necessary, as we saw earlier, for an existing Consul to nominate the Dictator, and thus confirm Junius Pera in office. Arrangements were made to enlist a further six thousand young men in the city and arm them from any available source, while urgent requests for reinforcements were sent to the allied communities. In this way an army of some 25,000 men was eventually collected together, though its quality was obviously not of the best.

Meanwhile Hannibal had been occupied in reducing the Roman camps and dealing with his prisoners and booty. As before, the Italian prisoners were released and sent back to their homes. But this time, instead of selling the Roman captives into slavery, Hannibal offered to ransom them at a cost of five hundred *denarii* for a cavalryman and three hundred for a foot soldier. Ten delegates were selected from their number and these, together with the Carthaginian officer Carthalo, were sent to Rome to settle the ransom details. Carthalo also appears to have had Hannibal's authority to open negotiations with the Senate for peace, though we do not know what terms he was empowered to offer. Whatever they were, he was not given the oportunity to express them, for on entering Latin territory he was met by a *lictor* from the new

Dictator who refused him access to Rome. The ten delegates were allowed to proceed, but met a stormy reception in the Senate; after an angry speech by the ex-Consul Manlius Torquatus condemning the prisoners as cowards who should have died rather than surrender, the Senate voted not to ransom a single man and sent the ten delegates back to Hannibal's camp. There is a story that one delegate who attempted by trickery to avoid returning was actually sent back in chains.

It is difficult to decide on the correctness or otherwise of this Roman decision. There can be no doubt that it was handed out in the same spirit as the shooting of Admiral Byng after his failure at Minorca, as an example of *'pour encourager les autres'*—a sign that Rome's determination was unweakened, and an encouragement to any dispirited or wavering allies. On the other hand, though it may well have come as a blow to Hannibal, showing him that as yet there was no hope of a negotiated peace, it certainly did not deprive him of the ransom money, since he obtained this or more from the slave traders who promptly bought the unfortunate Romans from him; and it did deprive Rome of the services of approximately ten thousand trained soldiers at a critical time.

Most historians have recorded this as an example of Roman willpower and moral fibre; they tend to forget that it is comparatively easy to be tough when the decision does not affect you and your family—and few of the unfortunate prisoners would have come from Senatorial families! It would be interesting to know whether the decision would have been the same had the majority of them been relatives of the Senators. My own feeling is that the decision was typical of the unfeeling arrogance and disregard of human rights which was to characterise Rome throughout her history. Livy complains that the bulk of the sympathy for the Carthaginian cause in southern Italy during the ensuing period came from the common people while the aristocrats were largely pro-Roman. Can this be wondered at when the common people had before them the very differing examples of Hannibal's treatment of them and the unfeeling attitude of the Roman Senate?

If Rome herself stood firm, however, many of her allies did not. On receiving the news of Cannae, large parts of southern Italy declared for Carthage. Most of the Apulian towns at once opened their gates to the conqueror; as soon as Hannibal moved north-west into Samnium virtually all the Samnite tribes except the Pentri followed suit, and delegations came in from Lucania and Bruttium offering allegiance to the cause. It appeared that Hannibal's dream was becoming a reality, and that the Italian Confederacy was splitting apart at last. Hannibal had therefore to split up his forces; having occupied Compsa, a fairly central position which was yielded to him after its pro-Roman citizens had fled, he left all his booty and heavy baggage here and gave his brother Mago a strong force with which to accept the support of the other towns in the neighbourhood and in Lucania to the south. Mago was instructed to clean up the whole area, taking intransigent towns by force if necessary, and then himself to return by ship to Carthage to report on the position in Italy. Hannibal probably felt that at this point it needed a member of the Barcid family in Carthage to try and ensure full support for his plans; the more so since to date he appears to have received virtually nothing in the way of reinforcements, supplies or money from his home government. The brothers were never to meet again.

Meanwhile Hannibal himself moved west into Campania. It seems probable that at this point his hope was to gain control of some at least of the west coast seaports, which would make communication with both Carthage and Spain much easier. On the one hand it would rob the Roman fleet of both bases and sources of ships and men, while making these in turn open to the Carthaginian fleet. His first objective was therefore Naples; the defection of this city would have given a decisive lead to the others along the coast. Naples, however, was not prepared to secede; in fact, as Hannibal marched into her territory, the Neapolitan cavalry bravely, if somewhat foolishly, rode out to attack him. They met their inevitable fate, being ambushed and massacred by the Numidian light horse; but when he appeared before the walls of Naples Hannibal found the gates firmly shut and the city undoubtedly hostile. An assault was out of the question; quite apart from the cost in lives, it was hardly the way to endear himself to the inhabitants. The point which so many historians have missed in claiming that during the following years Hannibal seemed to have lost his edge because he did not attack and capture all the cities which resisted him, is that it was never his policy in Italy to take cities by force except in very exceptional circumstances. Captured cities were of little use to him; he could not spare the garrisons to hold down hostile populations. What he needed, and spent his time trying to inspire, was the free allegiance of tribes and towns which either saw him as a deliverer from Roman tyranny or, seeing him victorious, wished to join the winning side. He could not compel the Italians to join him against Rome; his hope for eventual victory lay in the free will of the local populace. Storming their cities and slaughtering their inhabitants was not exactly the best course indicated to bring this about.

Accordingly Hannibal turned aside from Naples; in any case at this moment a bigger prize was freely offered to him. Capua was the second city of Italy: in fact in some ways it exceeded Rome herself in wealth and culture. A feeling of jealousy for Rome had long been burning in Capua, and as early as the time of Trasimene there had been rumblings of discontent which had only been kept down by consideration of marriage relationships between Roman Senators and influential Capuan families and the presence in the Roman army of some three hundred Capuans of good birth, besides the Campanian levies. After Cannae these factors were no longer strong enough to hold the alliance together, and now the Capuan Senate sent envoys to Hannibal to offer him an alliance. The terms they offered were probably not those the Carthaginian General would himself have proposed, but he was not prepared to look a gift horse in the mouth; the accession of Capua to the cause of Carthage must in itself inspire many other towns to follow suit and shake the spirit of Rome, and was worth obtaining on almost any terms. Hannibal therefore agreed that Carthage should have no jurisdiction over Campania, that no Campanian citizen should be forced against his will to serve in the army, that Capua should retain its own government and that Hannibal should provide the city with three hundred Roman prisoners of good rank to be exchanged for the Capuan nobles then serving with the Roman army in Sicily. On the face of it, Hannibal therefore did not receive a great deal of military support, but he no doubt hoped and expected the co-operation of the thirty thousand men Capua could put in the field if she wished. He therefore marched north from Naples to Capua, where he met with a rapturous reception as he rode through the streets. The leading pro-Roman citizen, Decius Magius, was handed over to the Carthaginian commander, since he refused to renounce his allegiance to Rome. In direct contrast to Roman conduct in a similar situation, Hannibal merely shipped him off to Carthage instead of executing him; and in fact the ship, being caught in a storm, ended up in Cyrenaica where he received political asylum from the King of Egypt.

The defection of Capua was quickly followed by that of Atella and Calatia, but parts of Campania still remained loyal to Rome. With his army considerably reduced in numbers by the detachments operating in Bruttium and Lucania, Hannibal could not further disperse his troops. He therefore first moved back to try the spirit of Naples once more, and then, finding the seaport still hostile, turned toward the town of Nola, which lay in the open plain of central Campania and whose citizens seemed ready to join in the revolt against Rome. However, here he was forestalled: the nobles of Nola, still pro-Roman, had sent hurriedly to Marcellus, who was encamped at Casilinum, for assistance. Marcellus, arguably the best soldier Rome possessed at this time, acted swiftly, marching around behind the mountains and reaching Nola from the hills directly above the town. Arrived here, he bloodily repressed the pro-Carthaginian elements and, when Hannibal marched up, audaciously assailed his vanguard and, after some success, slipped away into the hills. Hannibal therefore withdrew and struck instead at Nuceria and Acerrae, both of which were still loyal to Rome. At both places he refrained from assault but compelled surrender by blockade; in each case he allowed all citizens still loyal to Rome to depart in peace, but then burned the city as a warning. The season was now approaching its end; but Hannibal attempted one last stroke before going into winter quarters. This was an attack on Marcellus' base at Casilinum, which was situated too close to Capua for comfort. The place, however, was held by a garrison of a thousand men who, having apparently slaughtered such of the populace as favoured Carthage, fought with the desperation of doomed men; and after some sharp fighting Hannibal abandoned the attack and went into winter quarters at Capua.

The year 216 BC had therefore been a fruitful one for Hannibal, even if the aftermath of Cannae had not reached his full expectations. The next year was to be something of an anti-climax. It began well enough with the capture of Casilinum, which eventually surrendered on terms when its garrison ran out of food; a Roman army in the neighbourhood under Sempronius Gracchus being unwilling to face Hannibal in the field, no relief was possible. A garrison of seven hundred Campanians took over the town, which then acted as an advanced post for Capua itself.

The Roman consular elections for 215 BC showed that the Fabian party was once more in control of the Senate. The two successful candidates were the Praetor, Posthumus Albinus and the Master of Horse, Sempronius Gracchus. Posthumus, however, was at the time campaigning against the Boii in Cisalpine Gaul, and before he could return to Rome to take up his new position he fell into an ambush. His army marched through a wood, in which the Boii had already sawn through all the trees bordering the road. At the right moment the trees came down, trapping and scattering the surprised Romans, who fell easy victims to the Gauls. The Consul-elect and 25,000 men died. Livy tells us that the Gauls cut off his head, hollowed out and gilded the skull and used it as a ceremonial vessel in their holiest temples—surely the strangest fate ever to befall a Roman Consul! This necessitated a bye-election, and the winning candidate was Marcellus: a worthy choice, one might feel. However, it would seem that Fabius did not think so—perhaps Marcellus was too much of a fighter for his liking—since he stage-managed an invalidation of the election on technical grounds and was then himself elevated to the vacant Consulship.

Rome was putting out every effort for the coming campaign season, fielding no fewer than fourteen Legions. The figure may even have been higher, since Livy's figures are somewhat confused; it is unfortunate that for this period of the war we cannot consult Polybius, since the latter parts of his History have largely disappeared, only fragments remaining. We are therefore forced to rely more heavily than usual on Livy and other Roman writers, who admittedly did have access to the work of the Greek historian. It seems fairly plain, at all event, that some seven Legions were fielded against Hannibal himself, though they were not concentrated under one command. Fabius himself took over the forces of the Dictator at Teanum, while Tiberius Gracchus with a second army was above Casilinum; Marcellus with a third was at Suessula on the right bank of the Volturnus; two veteran Legions from Sicily under the Praetor Laevinus were to the south watching Apulia, Lucania and Calabria; the garrison of Tarentum was greatly strengthened, and Varro was directed to raise new levies in Picenum.

Neither side seemed prepared to risk anything very much during this year. Following the policies of Fabius, the Romans were content to watch Hannibal and prevent him from gaining any further large-scale success, while Hannibal himself was waiting for the arrival of hoped-for reinforcements from either Spain or Carthage. Operations thus tended to be of a somewhat half-hearted nature. A Capuan attempt to seize the port of Sumae, south of Naples, was foiled by Gracchus, who according to Livy inflicted severe losses on the Capuans, and a subsequent attempt by Hannibal to take the place by a *coup de main* was also unsuccessful.

While this was going on Fabius moved from Teatum to Cales and captured three small towns in the area which had declared for Carthage. He then pushed on to join Marcellus at Suessula, which enabled Marcellus in his turn to move on to Nola, from which base he could harass the territory of Hannibal's Samnite allies. Hannibal's response to requests for help from his allies was to march against the focal point of their troubles—Nola itself. Here, however, he met another setback: Marcellus defended the town with great skill and he was eventually forced to withdraw. If we are to believe Livy, Marcellus even left the town and defeated Hannibal in the open field, though it seems more likely that what happened was a successful sortie against the Carthaginian foragers. Livy also claims that over two hundred Numidians and Spaniards deserted to Marcellus at this point; even if this is true, it is no clear indication of any large-scale failure of morale in the Carthaginian army. Desertion is a disease all armies suffer from, victorious ones as well as defeated ones, and by now Hannibal's men had been absent from their homes for four years; it is not surprising that some of them would be suffering from home-sickness.

If Hannibal himself had achieved little enough during the year, however, he had tied down the main bulk of the Roman armies, thus enabling his lieutenants and allies to prosper. Thus the last Roman stronghold in Bruttium, Petelia, fell to Himilco after a long siege, while the Bruttians, themselves. stormed Croton. Consentia and Locri both surrendered, and the far south of Italy, with the single exception of Rhegium, was now solidly Carthaginian. There is some evidence, also, that the Carthaginian Admiral Bomilcar did succeed in landing some few reinforcements, possibly including elephants, for Hannibal.

The year had also seen extensions of the war beyond Italy and Spain. The Carthaginian colonists in Sardinia had once again risen against their Roman masters and had appealed for help from Carthage. The mother city had despatched a fleet and army to their aid under one Hasdrubal the Bald; unfortunately bad weather had blown him off course to take refuge in the Balearics, and in the ensuing period the Romans had reinforced their own army in Sardinia. As a result, when Hasdrubal at last arrived and landed he was quickly defeated and captured, and the rising was bloodily suppressed. Better news, however, was that in Syracuse Rome's good friend Hiero had died and been replaced by his grandson Hieronymous, who promptly declared for Carthage—a great blow for Rome. Finally envoys from Philip of Macedon had reached Hannibal's camp and signed an alliance against Rome—though its implementation was somewhat delayed when the envoys unfortunately fell into Roman hands on their way home. The other bad news to reach Hannibal was that Mago had succeeded in obtaining reinforcements for him in Carthage, but had then been diverted instead to Spain as a result of a defeat suffered there by his brother Hasdrubal.

The consular elections for 214 BC were again a success for the Fabian party. Otacilius Crassus and Aemilius Regulus were originally elected, but on the insistence of Fabius both candidates were set aside on the grounds of unsuitability for military command, and he himself and Marcellus were finally elected for the coming year. It seems likely, in view of his repudiation of Marcellus the previous year, that he was not the colleague Fabius would have selected, but that in view of his successes during 215 BC it was difficult for Fabius to oppose him. The number of Legions in the field was again increased to a record total of twenty; of these, ten were actively engaged in the south against Hannibal while two more were assigned to Cisalpine Gaul and two to the defence of Rome, thus making a total of fourteen Legions directly or indirectly held down by the great Carthaginian.

Once again, however, the year's campaigning in Italy was to prove largely indecisive. Hannibal opened the season with an attempt upon Puteoli, but once again failed to secure the seaport he desired. After ravaging the territory of Naples he then made a feint at Nola to pin down Marcellus before hurrying off south to Tarentum, which he had good reason to believe would open its gates to him. This great prize, however, was denied him; the garrison had recently been strengthened and the gates were closed. Moreover, during his absence in the south things went badly for the Carthaginian cause in Campania. His lieutenant, Hanno, had been recruiting in Bruttium, and from there had marched north into Campania, heading for Beneventum. En route he was intercepted by Gracchus on the River Calor. Hanno had, according to Livy, seventeen thousand infantry, all freshly recruited, and about twelve hundred cavalry, mostly Numidians, while Gracchus' force consisted of the two slave Legions recruited after Cannae. Gracchus apparently promised his men their freedom in the event of victory, and as a result they fought so well that Hanno was decisively defeated, getting off with no more than two thousand survivors. Though he retrieved the situation somewhat by similarly annihilating a force of Lucanians loyal to Rome, Hanno's defeat must have come as an unpleasant shock to Hannibal. Further bad news was to follow: for Fabius and Marcellus now combined forces and stormed Casilinum, putting its Campanian garrison to the sword, and Fabius followed this up by ravaging Samnium and recapturing three towns. The year had thus gone steadily in favour of Rome, which was now beginning to regain the ground lost after Cannae.

The situation in Sicily at this time was extremely confused. It would seem that Hieronymus, while not engaged in active operations against the Romans, had certainly signed an alliance with Carthage, but was assassinated by anti-monarchist elements in the summer of 214 BC; a power struggle then developed in Syracuse, in which the decisive element turned out to be two agents despatched thither by Hannibal, named Hippocrates, and Epicydes. Syracusans by birth, they were dedicated to the Carthaginian cause, and by various trickeries and deceits succeeded finally in inducing the new Republic of Syracuse to formally declare war on Rome. Marcellus had meanwhile arrived in Sicily to take command of the Roman forces there, but it would seem that active hostilities did not commence until the spring of 213.

The consular elections for 213 brought to office Fabius' son Quintus and Sempronius Gracchus, but the planning for the campaign seems as before to have been mainly controlled by Fabius, who during these years was virtually Dictator of Rome in fact if not in law. The same main dispositions were made with the intent of keeping Hannibal under control rather than destroying him; those historians who accuse Hannibal and his army of sinking into sloth among the fleshpots of Capua during this period fail to note that the Romans still held him in far too much dread to face him in the open field or even to initiate a real offensive plan against him. Instead the overall strategy was much the same as that of the Allies against Napoleon in 1814, that of nibbling at the territory under his control but avoiding being brought to battle. Considering that Hannibal had still not received any considerable reinforcement other than the raw troops levied in Italy, this attitude amply refutes these uninformed criticisms.

In fact nothing of note seems to have happened in Italy during this year with the exception of the recapture of Arpi by Quintus Fabius. According to Livy this success was marked by the desertion of a further thousand of the garrison on the condition that they be allowed to return home. If true, this is possibly an indication that time was now on the side of Rome, and that the peripheral elements of Hannibal's army, with little prospect of loot now that they were defending rather than acquiring territory, may have been becoming less reliable.

The main attention that year was given to Sicily, where both sides were now putting forth considerable effort. The wisdom of the Carthaginian effort in Sicily has been questioned, and certainly at first sight it would appear that the troops and ships involved could have been better employed in Italy with Hannibal; but, as Lazenby has pointed out, a Carthaginian success in Sicily would have greatly improved Hannibal's position in Italy by making his seaborne communications with Carthage that much easier and giving him a securer base. It must also be remembered that Sicily had always had a fatal attraction for Carthaginian statesmen, and that the chance to re-open their cause in the island was probably more than they could resist. On balance, it would appear that Carthage's mistake was not to embroil her forces in Sicily but to conduct affairs there with such apparent ineptitude. It brings forcibly to us the fact that outside the Barcid family Carthage was desparately short of leaders of genius, either political or military.

Marcellus began operations in Sicily by laying siege to Syracuse itself and, as was to be expected of him, pressing it fiercely. While a land attack against the city was directed by Claudius Pulcher against the Epipolae plateau—which had proved the key to the city during its famous defence against the expedition from

Athens in the Peloponnesian War—Marcellus himself organised a seaborne attack on the harbour by lashing together a number of quinqueremes to form a floating assault platform. His attack, however, was thwarted by the efforts of the local genius, Archimedes, who turned his attention to military invention and produced a series of remarkably advanced machines, some of which dropped huge rocks on the Roman ships while others seized their prows in mechanical pincers and tipped them over. It has even been suggested that he succeeded in harnessing the sun's power by means of a huge lens and set the Roman ships on fire by this method. At all events, so successful was the defence that Marcellus was soon forced to give up the assault and convert the siege into a blockade.

He then turned his attention to reducing the other pro-Carthaginian towns of the island, but had no more than begun these operations when the Carthaginians landed an army of 25,000 foot, three thousand horse and twelve elephants under a General named Himilco and captured Heraclea and Agrigentum. Marcellus succeeded in defeating a Syracusan army and preventing the relief of the city, but in general affairs in Sicily went badly for Rome during the year, more especially after a typical piece of Roman brutality. The Roman commander at Henna, Lucius Pinarius, anticipating a revolt, coldbloodedly massacred the entire population. Marcellus, apparently feeling that this act would terrorise the Sicels into surrender, condoned it; but in fact it backfired, causing the greater part of Sicily to rise in revolt against Rome.

The consular elections for 212 BC marked the end of the road for the Fabian party which had been in power for so long. Rome had had time to recover from the gloom of Cannae, and was ready to turn once more to the forward policy of the Great Delayer's opponents. The new Consuls were Fulvius Faccus and Claudius Pulcher and the total of Legions was again increased to twenty-five. But before the new Consuls could take office, Hannibal had at last secured the seaport he had been seeking for so long. In 214 he had attempted unsuccessfully to secure Tarentum, the Greek city which had been Rome's last opponent in Southern Italy, but had found its gates shut against him. In the early months of 212, however, two Tarentine nobles, Niko and Philomenes, entered his camp with news of a conspiracy in the city to admit him. Hannibal was quite willing to offer Tarentum the same terms on which Capua had joined him; and arrangements were made for a night surprise. The two Tarentines made a habit of entering and leaving the city by night through a gate in the eastern wall, which was regularly opened at their signal. On the night concerned Hannibal, whose camp lay three days march from the city, suddenly approached Tarentum with a picked force of eight thousand foot and two thousand horse, and lighted a signal fire on a mound known as the Tomb of Hyakinthos. The conspirators within the city then assailed the Temenid Gate, to the north of the one used by Niko and Philomenes, slew the guards and succeeded in opening that gate. Hannibal, leaving his cavalry outside, at once marched in with seven thousand men and headed straight for the market-place; at the same time Philomenes, having led the remaining one thousand infantry up to the other gate, signalled for it to open. He and a companion were admitted through the postern; they quickly slew the guard and admitted several more soldiers, who overcame the rest of the gate guards and opened the doors to admit the rest of the Carthaginian infantry. In the general confusion most of the Roman garrison, turning out in small bodies, were easily disposed of, but the commander, Marcus Livius, succeeded in reaching the citadel, where he held out defiantly.

By daybreak, however, the town itself and its important harbour were securely in Hannibal's hands. The whole operation was a masterpiece of its kind and showed quite clearly that his hand had not lost its cunning. The capture of Tarentum was followed quickly by the defection to Carthage of Metapontum and Thurii, thus putting the whole strip of coastline under Carthaginian control. Rome, however, was now in a more aggressive mood, and the fall of Tarentum merely inspired the new Consuls to attempt the siege of Capua. They began by ravaging the Campanian countryside, thus preventing the Capuans from sowing and harvesting their crops, so that the city, short of food, cried out to Hannibal for aid. Hannibal, ever attentive to the needs of his allies, at once despatched Hanno from Bruttium with orders to make for Beneventum and there collect grain for the relief of the city. Hanno, having eluded the armies of Gracchus and Nero, set up a fortified camp some 2½ miles from Beneventum and began collecting food stuffs from the surrounding communities, at the same time sending messengers to Capua directing that wagons should be sent to his camp in order to bring in the supplies. It seems, however, that the Capuan authorities were slow to respond, and in the meantime, Flaccus was advised of what was happening. Marching at once, he arrived at the camp while Hanno and most of his men were out foraging, and attacked it vigorously. Despite a desperate resistance the camp was taken, together with all the supplies, and Hanno had to fall back into Bruttium in disgust.

Flaccus now called up his colleague Pulcher to join him at Beneventum, and the Capuans in terror again called on Hannibal for assistance. He at once despatched two thousand cavalry to the city; these horsemen caught the Roman vanguard by surprise and killed about fifteen hundred men, but the Consuls were not to be diverted, and proceeded to invest the city. Hannibal himself then came up at the head of the main army and took post at his old camp of Mount Tifata, overlooking Capua. It was plain to him that, rather than become involved in a siege, what was needed was a decisive victory in the field, and on the following day he accordingly drew his army out in order of battle. Somewhat to his surprise, perhaps, the challenge was accepted and battle was joined. Unfortunately we have no details of the fighting; even Livy seems to have had little idea of what happened. According to his account, the battle was in the balance when both sides sighted a fresh body of troops approaching; since neither side could tell whether they were friend or enemy, each decided to break off the action and withdraw, although it turned out that they were in fact the army originally commanded by Gracchus, who had somewhat earlier been ambushed and slain in Lucania.

Livy's account is decidedly suspect, since it would mean that both sides were extremely deficient in scouting and intelligence—a criticism which cannot normally be levelled against Hannibal. It is clear, however, that Hannibal was unable to gain a decisive victory; but his intervention was enough to drive the Romans away from the beleagured city, for Livy admits that on the following night they broke up their camps and marched away, Fulvius for Cumae and Pulcher for Lucania—though he suggests that this was merely a ruse to draw Hannibal's army away from Capua. Hannibal followed Pulcher; just what happened is difficult to decipher, but it is certain that about this time Hannibal scored a decisive victory over a Roman army in Lucania, killing sixteen thousand men, and it therefore seems more likely that it was Pulcher who met this defeat rather than that, as Livy suggests, he foxed Hannibal and doubled back to join his colleague. The whole sequence of events is typical of Hannibal's skill in separating his opponents and destroying an isolated portion of their forces, and once again refutes any stories of a diminution of his genius.

While Hannibal was thus absent, Fulvius resumed the siege of Capua. but Hannibal did not at once return to its succour. Instead he moved north-east into Apulia, where another Roman army under the Praetor Gnaeus Fulvius had been operating with some success. Livy would have us believe that easy successes had made this army soft and ill-disciplined, but this would appear to be another excuse for defeat. Hannibal caught the Praetor outside Herdonia and, having cut off his retreat, by judicous use of his cavalry, broke the Roman army at the first charge, so that of eighteen thousand men only a few hundred escaped.

Notwithstanding these defeats, the Roman Consuls continued to press the siege of Capua. Food supplies were gathered, so as to make foraging unnecessary, and reinforcements were summoned until three consular armies of six Legions and their allied contingents had drawn a ring round the doomed city. Work was at once begun on a wall of circumvallation, but before this was completed the Capuans sent off hasty appeals to their protector; Hannibal, however, was apparently not ready at this stage to force a general action, since he returned a vague answer that the Consuls would not resist his coming, and remained in the vicinity of Tarentum. The year therefore died away; it had certainly been more favourable for Hannibal than the previous one, since it had brought him the rich prize of Tarentum and two victories in the field. But as the siege of Capua began, the writing was on the wall, and he must have known that in 211 he had to either break the siege or see the beginning of the end of his dream.

However, if things had gone badly for Rome on the mainland, in Sicily Marcellus had triumphed. Toward the end of the campaigning season, by a brilliant night escalade he had seized possession of the heights of Epipolae, only to find himself then virtually besieged by the army of Himilco which had come up from behind him. Fortune, however, smiled on the Roman commander, for the Carthaginian army, encamped in the unhealthy lowland area, was soon struck by fever and melted away. A relieving Carthaginian fleet under Bomilcar, when faced by a somewhat inferior Roman squadron, hesitated to attack and finally sailed away; and the Sicilians accordingly lost hope and dispersed. Marcellus, taking his opportunity, stormed the city successfully; he had given orders that Archimedes' life was to be spared but, so the story goes, the old genius, deep in some problem, refused the order of a Roman soldier to go with him to the General, and was cut down without further ado. Following on this success, Marcellus turned swiftly against the remaining Carthaginian forces in the island and utterly routed them at the river Himera. Though some resistance lingered on, Carthaginian hopes in the island were now effectually quelled.

In the following year the Romans stuck grimly to the siege of Capua; though the besieged kept up an active defence and, in fact, had the better of a number of cavalry engagement between the lines, they could not break the wall of circumvallation, while the Romans were content to hold on and let famine do its grisly work. For a while Hannibal remained in the neighbourhood of Tarentum, where he was still trying to take the citadel held by Marcus Livius; but when it became clear to him that Capua's situation was becoming desperate, he marched rapidly and secretly to Mount Tifata, where he managed to concert operations with the Capuans, so that they attacked from within while he assailed the siege lines from without. In an operation of this nature there was not a great deal of room for the careful manoeuvres and deceptive planning which had won the great Carthaginian his best victories; in fact it called largely for hard fighting between the infantry, in which the Romans might have been expected to excel. Yet, so much had the Carthaginian infantry developed under Hannibal's care and training, that although the Capuan attack was easily repelled, Hannibal came within an ace of success. At one point his men actually broke through the wall with the help of some elephants, but the bridgehead could not be exploited, and Hannibal finally called off the attack and withdrew.

If Capua could not be saved by direct methods, then it was time to return to the tried and true ways of strategic manoeuvre—the indirect apporach, as it is termed by Liddell Hart. Rather than dash himself against the strong Roman position, Hannibal would draw them away by threatening a point they could not ignore—Rome itself. There can be little doubt that this was purely a strategic manoeuvre and that he had no thought of the actual capture of the city; the whole object was to draw the Roman field armies away from Capua and if possible manoeuvre them into a position from which he could force a decisive battle in his inimitable way. Having first communicated his intentions to Capua, so that that citizens would not think he had deserted them, four days after the unsuccessful relief attempt he slipped away by night into Samnium and, marching by way of Alba, Amiterum, Foruli and Eretum, he appeared suddenly before the walls of Rome.

Accounts of what followed differ. According to Livy, the Romans at Capua were warned of Hannibal's march and sent off Fulvius Flaccus with fifteen thousand men who, moving by the direct route of the Via Latinum, entered Rome at almost the same time as Hannibal was pitching camp three miles away from the city walls. This force, with the Legions already in the city, made a respectable army and, despite the initial panic in the city at Hannibal's approach, the Romans were soon able to put on a bold front and actually offer battle outside the walls. As it happens, however, the part of Polybius dealing with this period is available to us, and his account says that in addition to the regular two-Legion garrison the Consuls had enrolled a third Legion and were just completing the enrolment of a fourth; thus there was no need to summon troops from Capua, and not a man of the field force moved from the siege.

What is clear, however, is that Hannibal's move failed in its main purpose of raising the siege of Capua. He did not remain long in the vicinity of Rome, since, expecting the armies from Capua to be marching to the succour of the capital, he had no intention of being caught between them and the city garrison. Instead he soon broke up his camp and withdrew across the Anio river; he appears to have met with some difficulty here and had to fight a rearguard action against the city garrison which was following up his withdrawl, but gave them a bloody nose and slipped away without much loss. There being no point in returning to Campania—a second attempt on the Roman siege lines had no better prospect of success than the first—he instead marched hard for Bruttium in the hope of perhaps surprising the seaport of Rhegium, the one Roman strongpoint remaining in the area. In this he was doomed to further disappointment.

It is obvious that Hannibal had now written Capua off. As a staunch ally, he had done all he safely could to save the city; loyalty did not include throwing away his army in pointless attacks which were doomed to failure. Yet at this moment he must have been very close to despair. All that he had worked and hoped for was crumbling into ruin before his eyes. A lesser man would surely have given up, gambled perhaps on a last battle at Capua and lost his life rather than fight on. But Hannibal was not a lesser man, and the dream he was fighting for was not one of personal power and glory; he was the servant of Carthage, and while any hope remained for his city he would go on fighting and striving to the best of his ability. Capua might and probably would fall; but if his brother Hasdrubal succeeded in bringing him reinforcements from Spain next year, all the lost ground might still be regained. Perhaps he deluded himself that it was still possible to win; being Hannibal, it is more likely that he gritted his teeth and faced the facts but refused to give in. If true greatness only comes with adversity, then the next six years were to prove that Hannibal was no fair-weather soldier, and that his spirit could rank with the best.

Left to its own devices, Capua's will to resist crumbled rapidly. The disheartened citizen's clamoured for surrender; and after twenty-eight Senators had commited suicide rather than be taken alive, the gates were opened and the Romans marched in. The remaining Senators were all executed, as were the leading men of other Campanian cities which followed Capua's example; in the other cities the remaining populace was sold into slavery, but the commons of Capua seems to have escaped fairly lightly. Probably even Rome hesitated over making an example of a city second only to herself in Italy.

Chapter 12

Defeat on the Metaurus

In order to understand fully the background to Hannibal's operations in Italy, it is necessary at this stage to digress and look in some detail at what had been happening in Spain during his absence. It will be remembered that when the Consul Cornelius Scipio had failed to intercept Hannibal on the Rhône he had, while returning himself to Italy, despatched his army under his brother Gnaeus to continue on the way to Spain. Gnaeus disembarked safely at the Massiliot colony of Emporiae, which Hannibal had not had time to reduce; he then marched out and utterly defeated Hannibal's lieutenant Hanno, who had been left to hold the area north of the Ebro; Hanno himself was captured and his army virtually destroyed. The local Spanish tribes, which had been overawed but not subjugated by the Carthaginian presence, promptly declared for Rome; and thus at a blow Scipio had not only established himself in northern Spain but had cut overland communications between Hannibal and his base.

Hannibal had left his brother Hasdrubal as Viceroy in Spain with what seemed, no doubt, at the time an ample force. It would appear that Hasdrubal was taken by surprise by the arrival of the Roman army and the completeness of Hanno's defeat, for his effort in 218 BC was confined to a mere raid which achieved little except to inflict casualties on the crews of Scipio's ships. In early 217, however, he mounted a joint expedition, manning forty quadriremes to seize command of the sea while he himself marched up the coast with an army. The casualties of the previous year had apparently reduced the number of ships Scipio could man from sixty to thirty-five, but this was considerably offset by the support of twenty Massiliot vessels, and in an action off the mouth of the Ebro the Carthaginians were badly defeated, losing twenty-five ships. This seems to have discouraged Hasdrubal so much that he withdrew to the south, for when later that year Gnaeus was joined by his brother the two Scipios had no difficulty in crossing the Ebro and operating for some while south of the river. The campaign of 217 was hardly decisive but must be counted as a points win for Rome.

The operations of 216 and 215 give the distinct impression that Hasdrubal was not in the same class as his great brother either as a soldier or a leader of men. In 216 he was embarrassed by tribal uprisings which diverted him from his principal task, as instructed by the Carthaginian Government, of leading reinforcements to Italy. He seems to have protested that the very news of such a move would weaken the Carthaginian hold over the Spanish tribes, and it was not until a General named Himilco arrived with some five thousand reinforcements from Africa that he at last marched north in early 215. The Scipios met him on the south bank of the Ebro near a town called Ibera and, from all accounts, smashed his army completely. Hasdrubal seems to have used much the same tactics as Hannibal at Cannae, but to have had far less control over his troops, with the result that his centre failed to hold the Roman assault and his cavalry were never decisively engaged. The bulk of his infantry were lost but he seems to have got off most of his cavalry and elephants.

The main result of this disaster was that, far from Hannibal receiving reinforcements from Spain, those being prepared in Carthage under his brother Mago were diverted from Italy to Hasdrubal, as we have already seen. For the next few years operations continued indecisively, with both sides meeting with successes and defeats though, on balance, events would seemed to have favoured Rome. Livy has long involved accounts of decisive battles in impossible places, but the bulk of his story can be discounted as mere invention or wrong dating and placing of events. In 211, however, the Scipios felt strong enough to launch a large-scale offensive, just at the time when the Carthaginians had been reinforced and had three armies in the field under Hasdrubal himself, his brother Mago, and Hasdrubal Gisco. It is possible that the Scipios had become overconfident after several relatively easy victories, and it is certain that they reposed too much trust in the loyalty of their Spanish auxiliaries, for they made the mistake of dividing their forces and operating separately, Gnaeus against Hasdrubal Barca and his brother against the other two. The result was utter disaster. Publius Cornelius, attempting a night march to destroy an isolated Carthaginian force, fell into a trap and was killed with most of his army, while his brother, Gnaeus, deserted by his Spanish auxiliaries when they heard the news, tried to retreat but was brought to battle and similarly defeated and killed thirteen days later. With their deaths the whole balance of power in Spain swung decisively back to Carthage.

Once again, however, events seem to prove the uniqueness of Hannibal among the Carthaginian leaders, for little use was made of the victory. The Roman force left in Spain cannot have exceeded nine thousand men, yet this force under two very junior commanders seems to have had little difficulty in holding the line of the Ebro and even inflicting a repulse on Mago's army. Livy much exaggerated these successes but, even so, there seems to have been a kernel of truth in his claims. When the news of the disaster reached Rome, the Senate appointed Claudius Nero to the vacant command, giving him by all accounts a force of ten thousand infantry and a thousand cavalry with which to bring the army up to strength—little enough, in all conscience, with which to face the renascent Carthaginian forces, but to the Senate the main theatre of operations was still Italy, and would remain so as long as Hannibal was still at large.

Though Nero achieved nothing definite, he did succeed in keeping control of the coastal area north of the Ebro which served as the main base for Roman operations in Spain. At the end of the year, however, the Senate took a momentous decision—though at the time they doubtless had no idea of its crucial importance—when they appointed to the command in Spain the young Publius Cornelius Scipio, son and nephew of the dead Generals. It is interesting to examine this appointment in more detail, for it was a somewhat unusual one. Though the young man already had given good account of himself as a soldier, he had held no important office and as such would not normally be considered for such a command—why then did he receive it? The answer lies undoubtedly in the vagaries of Roman party politics. As already mentioned, to the Senate the most pressing theatre of operations was still Italy and the defeat of Hannibal; but Rome was now also engaged in military operations in Greece against the forces of Philip of Macedon, and there was a strong party in the Senate which favoured abandoning Spain—or at least giving it minimal attention—and making Greece the main secondary theatre. Young Scipio was now the head of the still very powerful Scipio gens, which undoubtedly favoured the Spanish theatre; moreover it was probably hoped that his relationship to the dead Generals would be of great use in following up their Spanish connections. If to this one adds the undoubted strength of his personality and strategic grasp, the appointment becomes a fairly logical one. It was to change the shape of the whole war.

Scipio reached Spain in the summer of 210 BC, bringing with him about the same number of troops which had accompanied Nero, so that the Roman strength in Spain would now be in the neighbourhood of thirty thousand plus any Spanish auxiliaries they had recruited. Very wisely, he embarked on no new operations during the remainder of the year, but spent it in exploring his new command, familiarising himself with his troops, the countryside and the Spanish tribes. Then in the winter he set about planning his masterstroke. This was no less than an attack on the headquarters of Carthaginian power in Spain, their capital, New Carthage. The idea was an audacious one but it was made practicable by the disposition of the Carthaginian armies, which were widely spread. Mago was in the vicinity of the Pillars of Hercules, Hasdrubal Gisco was in Lusitania, and Hasdrubal Barca was deep in the interior near the headquarters of the Tagus. All were far away from New Carthage, yet so confident were they of the city's invulnerability that it was only held by a garrison of a thousand men.

This decision shows that Scipio had already made the advance from being a good General to a great one. A good soldier, seeing the enemy so dispersed, would have planned to defeat them in detail; only a top-class commander would see the opportunity to cut right to the heart of the problem and have the audacity to put such a plan into operation. Scipio in fact kept his ideas entirely to himself, merely issuing orders for the fleet and army to assemble at the mouth of the Ebro as early as practicable in 209. Here he joined them with five thousand Spanish auxiliaries he had raised; he left three thousand foot and five hundred horse under Silanus to guard the Ebro, and marched rapidly south along the coast with about 25,000 infantry and 2,500 cavalry, while the fleet under Laelius coasted along abreast of him. Polybius avers that it took seven days for him to reach the objective, but this seems an impossibly short time for a march of three hundred miles: all we can be sure of is that Scipio marched fast and secretly and that he reached his destination before any word of his intentions could leak out.

New Carthage, or Cartagena as we know it today, lies on a jutting peninsula formed by the sea on the south and a large but fairly shallow lagoon on the north, the two being linked by a canal to the west. The peninsula thus formed is ringed by hills except to the south-west, and had been well fortified on all sides, though the obvious avenue of attack was of course the neck of the peninsula. It would appear that Scipio was well informed of the geographical features of the place, and particularly that the lagoon, which on the face of it was an insuperable obstacle, was in fact barely fordable, and that at times, when the wind was in the right quarter, it became even shallower and barely an obstacle at all. He thus made plans for his assault, having encamped on a hill overlooking the isthmus and thrown up a line of sketchy fortifications to cover his rear in case any Carthaginian relieving force should come up unexpectedly.

The Carthaginian commander had hurriedly armed some two thousand of the citizens to reinforce his garrison, and he initially placed these men to guard the isthmus wall, holding back his regulars to act as a reserve. Though these levies were foolish enough to sortie out and attack Scipio's men before the main assault began, with the natural result that they suffered unnecessary losses and were soon driven back inside the gates, they nevertheless put up a tough resistance when the Romans attempted to storm the isthmus walls, so that after some very hard and bloody fighting Scipio was forced to sound the recall. While this was going on the fleet had been similarly attacking the seaward walls, though it is not clear whether this was merely a bombardment with missiles or whether the ships actually tried an assault. All these activities had the effect of drawing the attention of the defenders away from the lagoon; and, when he saw signs that the waters were beginning to recede, Scipio renewed his attack on the isthmus and gave the signal for a special party of five hundred men to cross the lagoon. Passing though the shallow water, the Romans planted their scaling ladders and mounted the walls quite unopposed: sweeping round left-handed they then fell on the rear of the isthmus defence. The main Roman force poured in and began slaughtering everyone in sight, while Scipio himself headed direct for the citadel, where he received the surrender of the remains of the garrison.

Though there was considerable slaughter in the excitement of the assault, once the city was secured Scipio acted with a restraint which marked him apart from the general run of Roman commanders. Of the ten thousand prisoners taken, all the citizens were released to their homes, merely being instructed to be well disposed toward their new masters, and from among freed slaves he recruited the crews for eighteen ships he had captured in the harbour. Similarly, a number of Spanish hostages held in the town for the good behaviour of their tribes were sent home to their relatives to spread the good news of the Roman successes. This was not an isolated occurrence: throughout his career Scipio, like his great opponent, Hannibal, was to make war in as gentlemanly a fashion as possible.

The loss of New Carthage was a body blow to Carthaginian power in Spain. It had been their main base, and was consequently stocked with supplies and treasure; it was also the most convenient port for the delivery of reinforcements and other items from Carthage. Moreover, it was the centre of the silver mining area, and its loss cost the Carthaginians a large part of their annual revenue; while the release of the hostages meant a decided weakening of control over the tribes of the interior. Scipio did not push his luck by embarking on any further major enterprise that year; instead he devoted his time to rigorous training of his troops, turning his army into a fully-tempered weapon with a fine cutting edge.

The Roman General spent the winter back at Tarraco, where he received delegations from many Spanish tribes. In the spring of the following year he marched out to try conclusions with Hamilcar Barca. The latter had apparently made up his mind simultaneously to give battle; if he could defeat Scipio he could obviously regain much of the lost ground among the Spaniards, while he had resolved to fight in such circumstances that if things went wrong he could cut his losses and march for Italy even though with reduced forces. He therefore took up a defensive position at a place called Baecula, which has been tentatively identified with Bailen; he drew up his army on a flat-topped hill, which descended to a sloping terrace with a parapet-like rim. Here he awaited Scipio's attack. Scipio, who apparently misliked the strength of the Carthaginian position, encamped over against it, evidently hoping that Hasdrubal would oblige him by attacking. After waiting for two days in vain, however, he resolved to attack himself; very probably he feared that further delay might result in the separate armies of either Mago or Hasdrubal Gisco arriving to catch him between two fires. Once again, the resulting battle does not show Hasdrubal as a commander of the first order. Scipio sent in his light troops to begin with, attacking the lower plateau; this, as he intended, drew Hasdrubal's attention to this area and sucked forward his main infantry force, which manned the edge of the higher plateau. While their attention was thus diverted, he launched an attack round both flanks and succeeded in seizing commanding positions before Hasdrubal's wings could occupy them. Seeing that things were going badly, Hasdrubal, as he had already determined, cut his losses by abandoning the troops on the lower plateau; he made a skilful withdrawal and got away a good two-thirds of his army, including his elephants, cavalry and all his treasure.

Scipio's political opponents in Rome were later to castigate him for allowing Hasdrubal to escape with the greater part of his force and make for Italy, but it is difficult to see how this could have been prevented without throwing away all Scipio had so far achieved in Spain. If he had launched his army in an all-out pursuit of Hasdrubal he might still have failed to destroy him before he could reach Italy, while he would have abandoned Spain to the armies of Mago and Hasdrubal Gisco which were still very much in the field. In fact, Scipio probably calculated that by now the Roman armies in Italy were strong enough to take care of themselves, and that his task in Spain would be made a lot easier by Hasdrubal's withdrawal.

Scipio seems to have assumed that Hasdrubal would follow his brother's route across the eastern end of the Pyrenees, for he made the token gesture of sending small forces to hold the passes controlling this route. Hasdrubal, however, did nothing of the sort: instead he moved west to the Atlantic coast and marched round the western extremity of the mountains, entering Gaul by way of the Bidassoa and the Adour. Still keeping to the west, he completely avoided the Mediterranean area, moving instead into the country of the Averni and crossing the Rhône in the neighbourhood of the modern Lyons. Then he went into winter quarters and recruited what Gauls he could to replace the losses at Baccula.

Early in 207 Hasdrubal set out on the final leg of his march for Italy. Though we cannot be entirely sure of his route, all the evidence points to his following Hannibal's route for most of the way, thus taking advantage of the various engineering works which had been carried out during the original march, but that where Hannibal had been led astray by his guides into a minor pass at the end of the crossing, Hasdrubal carried on down the main route, most probably the pass of Mont Cenis. It would appear that he met with no opposition from the mountain tribes and that his army suffered little from the elements; the latter would doubtless be explained because he was crossing at a different season of the year; as for the former, Creasey suggests that the mountaineers had opposed Hannibal because they thought he meant to take away their lands, but in the meantime they had learnt of the war in Italy and, realising that Hasdrubal's army was merely passing through, refrained from opposing him and indeed sent many of their young men to join him. I find this reasoning rather specious; the attacks on Hannibal seem to have been occasioned by the wish for loot rather than anything else, and the same temptations would have been open during Hasdrubal's passage. A better explanation may be that for one thing Hasdrubal's army was in better condition to defend itself than Hannibal's, since it was fresh and rested after the winter, and for the second that Hasdrubal, being well supplied with money, successfully bribed the tribes to give him free passage. Undoubtedly also he had been furnished with full details of Hannibal's march and thus was not breaking new ground as had his brother.

Be this as it may, the news that Hasdrubal was in Italy with a powerful army came as a shock to the Senate, many of whom gave him an inflated military reputation both from reports of his out manoeuvring of Scipio in Spain and his easy passage of the Alps. Though they had known in advance that he had wintered in Gaul, it would seem that they were taken by surprise at the ease and rapidity of his advance and had not completed their preparations when he debouched into Cisalpine Gaul. Fortunately for Rome, the time they needed was given back to them when Hasdrubal, instead of pressing on to the south, halted in Cisalpine Gaul and laid siege to the Roman colony of Placentia. For this he has been castigated by Livy, but it may well be that he had good reasons for his actions. It would be necessary for him to reassure the local Gallic tribes and persuade their warriors to join him, and the capture of Placentia would be an ideal way in which to do this; moreover, he probably wished to wait for the season to draw on a little so that he could be sure of forage for his animals. Armies which, to a large degree, live off the country are very much tied to the local agricultural conditions, which is a point many historians tend to miss.

It is now necessary to go back several years and see what had been happening in Italy since the fall of Capua. In 210 BC Marcellus had been elected to the consulate and given the chief command against Hannibal; he had signalised his return to the Italian theatre by recapturing the town of Salapia, which was betrayed to him despite a ferocious defence by its garrison of five hundred Numidians, and storming Marmorea and Meles in Samnium, which province Hannibal had virtually abandoned. But while Marcellus was thus engaged, his colleague the Proconsul Fulvius Centumalus attempted a similar capture of Herdonea in Apulia, where certain of the leading citizens had intimated that they were ready to change sides. Hannibal was then in Bruttium; but, apprised by his spies of the move, made one of his rapid surprise marches and fell upon the Roman camp before Fulvius had any inkling he was even in the neighbourhood.

Fulvius himself and eleven out of twelve military Tribunes were killed, and the Roman force was utterly destroyed; the dead certainly numbered seven thousand and may have reached the higher figure of thirteen thousand. Marcellus at once marched to restore the situation, and there seems to have been a three-day battle at Numistro in Lucania. Livy says the battle was drawn but that Hannibal conceded defeat by withdrawing, while Frontinus avers that the battle was a Carthaginian victory. It seems likely that Hannibal was primarily concerned with giving Marcellus a bloody nose but refused to be drawn into a major engagement, slipping away successfully when he had achieved his object. The rest of the year was spent in mere skirmishing, with Hannibal being content to protect his control of Calabria, Lucania, Bruttium and much of Apulia. There was also a Carthaginian success at sea when the Tarentine fleet intercepted and defeated a Roman squadron endeavouring to throw supplies and reinforcements into the beleaguered citadel of Tarentum.

For the following year Fulvius Flaccus and Fabius Maximus were elected Consuls, but Marcellus retained command of his army watching Hannibal; Flaccus was to conduct operations in Lucania and Bruttium, while Fabius with two Legions and a fleet would attempt the reduction of Tarentum. For the first time, however, the Latin colonies appear to have shown their war-weariness; twelve out of the thirty refused point blank to supply their quotas of men, and the Senate, fearing to push the issue, were forced to acquiesce. It is interesting to note, as Lazenby points out, that the recalcitrant twelve were the inner ring of colonies, whose troops would be largely used for the remoter campaigns, while the outer colonies, whose soldiers would be fighting in defence of their own homes, continued to levy men without protest.

The campaign opened by the garrison of Rhegium breaking out and committing widespread depredations in Bruttium. This was intended to draw Hannibal off in this direction, and it achieved its aim. although we again have too little detail, it seems clear that he engaged Marcellus twice, beating him on both occasions and so crippling his army that it was unable to interfere with Hannibal's march. The Carthaginian commander then hastened off to restore the situation in Bruttium, but during his absence Fabius was successful in recovering Tarentum; he had planned a combined sea and land attack, but at the last moment was aided by treachery from within, the walls being betrayed by a Bruttian officer. The Romans burst in and, after some fierce fighting in the market-place, the town was successfully taken. Carthalo, the Carthaginian officer whom we have met on several occasions before, was killed here in command of the garrison. Hannibal, who had routed the Rhegium troops outside Caulonia, hurried back to try and save the city, but was too late. After trying to tempt Fabius out to engage him, he then made another of his rapid withdrawals, laying an elaborate trap at Metapontum, which Fabius was led to believe would follow Tarentum's lead and go over to him. From all accounts Fabius was only saved from falling into the trap because the religious omens were bad and he refused to march.

It is clear that the year was a bad one for Hannibal, despite his successes in the field. While he was still more than a match for any of the Roman armies—as is clear from his defeats of Marcellus—and his movements were as rapid and incisive as ever, there were too many Roman forces in the field for him to be able to frustrate them all; while he was engaged with one, the others could profit from his absence, and the result was a general fall in the morale of his allies, who saw a steady erosion of the area under his control. To combat this he needed more troops desperately and only a successful junction with Hasdrubal could swing the balance back toward Carthage.

In the following year, 208 BC, Marcellus was again elected Consul, his colleague being Quinctius Crispinus. The latter was the first to take the field, making an attempt on Locri which was foiled by Hannibal. He then marched to join Marcellus at Venusia, and it appears that the two Consuls had every intention of engaging Hannibal in a decisive battle to the death. Unfortunately when the two Consuls rode out with a cavalry escort to reconnoitre the ground between the armies, they were ambushed by Hannibal's Numidians: Marcellus was killed, with the bulk of the escort, and Crispinus was wounded. The death of Marcellus was a bitter blow to Rome. Though obviously not in Hannibal's class as a commander, he was a veteran fighting soldier who was never cast down by defeat and had served Rome well. Hannibal, as was his wont, had Marcellus buried with full military honours; but, also typically, made use of the dead Consul's signet ring to try and secure the possession of Salapia. The plan unfortunately misfired and cost him six hundred men who were trapped within the city. Fortunately this mishap was promptly offset, for Hannibal turned at once in the direction of Locri, which was once more being attacked by a Roman force under Cincius Alimentus. Part of the Roman force was ambushed, with a loss of two thousand slain and fifteen hundred captured, and the Locri garrison having sallied out and engaged the attention of the main besieging force, Hannibal's cavalry fell furiously upon their rear and utterly routed them.

For the decisive year of 207, Rome elected as Consuls Claudius Nero, a soldier of proven worth, and Livius Salinator, a Senator who had for some time been in self-imposed retirement following a disgrace in 218. Salinator with a regular consular army was to cover the north against Hasdrubal, while Nero with a second faced Hannibal in the south. Terentius Varro and Porcius Licinus had similar strength armies in Etruria and Umbria respectively in support of Livius, while Fulvius Flaccus and Claudius Flamen had a further two in Bruttium and Calabria to support Nero. When we add a single Legion at Capua and the two urban Legions at Rome, this makes a total of fifteen Legions deployed in Italy against the two Barca brothers.

The Romans had the advantage of the central position, which would make it much easier for them to concentrate against either of the Carthaginian armies. Hannibal and Hasdrubal had the grave disadvantage that neither knew the other's plans, and it was vital that they get into communication and concert operations. For Hasdrubal the situation was relatively simple: he merely had to decide on which route to take on his southward march. As with Hannibal earlier on, he could decide to move by the east coast or the west, and the Romans had had to guard against both by locating an army in each area—the intention being, presumably, that as soon as his direction was determined, Livius Salinator would move up to join either Varro or Licinus as the case might be. For Hannibal the problem was far more acute: in order to meet his brother he must march far to the north with the great bulk of his forces, leaving his territories of Bruttium and Lucania defenceless against the large Roman forces which would still remain in these areas. It was therefore essential that he know well in advance the direction and date of Hasdrubal's march, so that he could delay his own move for as long as possible.

Having given up the siege of Placentia, Hasdrubal at last began to move south, by the eastern route, sending off at the same time a patrol of four Gauls and two Numidians with a letter to Hannibal. Unfortunately we do not possess the full text of this letter, so we are still somewhat in the dark as to his intentions. The messengers, having safely traversed the length of Italy, made for Tarentum rather than for Hannibal's current camp at Metapontum, and there they fell into Roman hands. In the past, historians have always assumed that this was a disaster which doomed the whole Carthaginian campaign, since from this point on the Romans knew what Hasdrubal proposed to do while Hannibal

remained in ignorance. Lazenby, however, puts forward an entirely new
theory—that, in fact, the whole letter was a trick designed to divert Roman
attention and was intended to be captured. On the face of it this may seem fairly
preposterous, but Lazenby is able to make out a rather good case; what it needs
for real proof is the full text of Hasdrubal's letter. Livy only says that it told
Hannibal he hoped to meet him in Umbria—a vague statement indeed.
However, from the responses of Claudius Nero it seems likely that Hasdrubal
actually mentioned that he would move originally by the eastern route but
intended to cross the Appenines somewhere south of the via Flaminia, whereas
we know that in fact he did not turn west but kept on down the east coast. On
this basis Lazenby bases his suggestion that Hasdrubal, fearing a Roman
concentration on the east coast, hoped by planting this letter on them to induce
them to make their concentration further west and allow him to slip past. He
makes two other good points: that Hasdrubal was probably not naive enough to
think that his messengers could, despite being obvious foreigners, slip
undetected through the length of Italy to reach Hannibal, and that Hasdrubal
could hardly expect Hannibal to march so far north to meet him. The first point
is somewhat invalidated by the fact that the messengers did just that, and that if
they had gone to Metapontum rather than Tarentum they would have reached
Hannibal safely—though here again, were they deliberately sent to the wrong
place by Hasdrubal? This hinges on whether he knew of the fall of Tarentum,
and we lack knowledge on this point. The second reason, that Hannibal could
not be expected to march so far north, is considerably stronger; the half-way
mark between the two brothers would be nearer Samnium than Umbria, and
since Hasdrubal would not necessarily expect his brother to have started north
until he received a message, it seems logical to have expected the junction point
to be fixed further south than north. The argument is an interesting one which it
is impossible to solve; all we can say definitely is that if it was intended to
mislead the Romans it failed in its intentions, and in the end did more harm than
good. What does seem almost unbelievable is that Hasdrubal apparently made
no other attempt to communicate his intentions to his brother; despite the
difficulties involved, one would have thought that the importance of the matter
would have outweighed them.

At all events, Hasdrubal moved south-east, pushing the army of Licinus
before him. At some point—where, we are not told—Licinus was joined by the
Consul Livius Salinator, but we cannot be sure whether it was at this point that
the combined armies decided to attempt halting Hasdrubal's advance, or
whether they continued to fall back after the junction. Livy's account of
Hannibal's movements at this time is also, unfortunately, completely
unreliable, since it makes no sense at all and, in the usual way, makes out every
encounter between him and the Romans to have been a Carthaginian defeat. It
seems plain, however, that at the beginning of the campaign Hannibal was in
Bruttium, and that having concentrated most of his army he then advanced into
Lucania, probably with the dual intention of bolstering up his shaky allies and
as the start of a general northward movement. Livy tells us that at Grumentum
he fought Nero and was severely mauled, losing eight thousand men and a
number of elephants. While there is little doubt that the armies were engaged
here, since Hannibal then continued his march unchecked into Apulia, there can
be little doubt that, in fact, Hannibal merely handed Nero off in passing and
continued on his way. Nero, it seems, made a fairly rapid recovery and followed

hot on Hannibal's tracks, so the wily Carthaginian doubled back to
Megapontum, where he picked up further troops, and then, having misled Nero
by a lunge at Venusia, slipped off north-east to Canusium.

It was apparently at this point that the intercepted letter reached Nero, and
that he made the decision which was to give him his place in history. Sending off
a despatch to warn the Senate of what he was doing, and speedy horsemen to
make arrangements for food and drink to be waiting en route, he selected a
picked force of six thousand infantry and a thousand cavalry from his army,
slipped secretly out of camp and headed north at top speed to join Livius
Salinator.

The march seems to have taken six to seven days, which for a distance of
approximately 250 miles is extremely good going—though undoubtedly the way
was eased considerably by the arrangement Nero had caused to to be made, and
it seems unlikely that the infantry actually marched every step of the way,
transport being provided wherever practicable. Even so, it was a remarkable
march, and at the end of it Nero's force slipped secretly into Livius Salinator's
camp on the river Sena. The two Consuls held a hasty meeting: Livius suggested
that Nero's men needed time to recover from their march, but Nero insisted
that, in order not to lose the advantage of surprise, battle must be given on the
morrow. Accordingly in the morning the Roman army deployed for battle.

On his side, Hasdrubal was apparently ready enough to fight, and in his turn
deployed for action. However, we are told that on riding forward to reconnoitre
the enemy lines, he thought that there seemed to be more of them than he had
expected, and that the equipment of some of them looked dusty and unkept,
while the horses of some of the cavalry looked jaded, as though they had made a
long march. Being suspicious, he drew back his troops and ordered instead that
horsemen should be sent out to scout the Roman camps, while attempts should
be made to pick up prisoners for interrogation. The scouts returned to tell him
that in the Consul's camp the trumpets had sounded not once but twice,
indicating that both Consuls were, in fact, present. It may seem illogical that
such a well-kept secret should be disclosed by such a piece of stupidity, but it is
completely in accordance with army routine that things are done by the book,
and no one told the unfortunate trumpeter that the usual drill was not to be
followed. As it happened, the disclosure was to have little effect on the result.

Some historians have wondered why, when he was apparently ready enough
to give battle against forty thousand men, Hasdrubal hesitated to face a further
seven thousand. There are several good reasons for this. We are not sure of
Hasdrubal's strength, but it seems certain that he was little if anything superior
in numbers to the original Roman army; an addition of seven thousand men
thus gave the Romans a very big advantage. But, in fact, Hasdrubal had no
means of knowing how many reinforcements Nero had brought, and may well
have expected that the number was greater than it actually was. More important
still, however, would be his reaction to the fact that Nero was there at all, and,
by implication, what had happened to Hannibal—had he suffered a decisive
defeat so that Nero could safely march north? In the circumstances it would be
far better to avoid battle until the situation was clearer, and we cannot fault
Hasdrubal on this.

Accordingly, that night he left his campfires burning and slipped away; but
unfortunately, as both Livy and Polybius agree, he was deserted by his guides,
and, in the confusion of a night march, the army lost its way and by dawn had

failed to find a suitable ford across the Metaurus. Since he would obviously have known his way back by the seacoast route which he had recently traversed, this indicates that he was heading west, probably with the intention of striking across the Appenines and marching round the Roman armies to try once more to make contact with Hannibal if the latter was still in the field. The night march took its toll of the army, which must have made about thirteen miles before reaching the Metaurus, and there was considerable straggling. Shortly after dawn the rearguard found itself under attack from the Roman cavalry, and Hasdrubal, seeing that he could not give his opponents the slip, made an attempt instead to throw up a fortified camp. In this he was frustrated, partly by the exhaustion of his men and partly by the promptness of the Roman pursuit, and accordingly he deployed for battle on the best position he could find.

The Metaurus in this area flows through a fairly wide valley bounded by hills, the river itself running between very steep, high banks, and the whole area being rather heavily wooded. Hasdrubal drew up his army with its left resting on the river and covered by a steep, difficult ravine. During the retreat his Gallic troops seem to have got completely out of control—another indication that Hasdrubal, unlike his great brother, had been unable to knit together his heterogeneous army—and a good proportion of them were now drunk and incapable of action. Such as were still fit to fight were therefore posted on the left, which was behind the protection of the ravine. In the centre, apparently some way from the Gauls and beyond the ravine, stood his Ligurian infantry, with the elephants covering their front, and his right flank was covered by his most reliable troops, the Spanish veterans. Neither Polybius nor Livy make any detailed mention of the Carthaginian cavalry, and the implication is that Hasdrubal was deficient in this arm.

Seeing the Carthaginians drawn up for battle, the Consuls similarly deployed and advanced to the attack. Nero was posted on the right flank, nearest the river, with his own troops, Licinus' two Legions held the centre, and the two of Livius were on the left. The action was opened by Hasdrubal, whose hope was obviously to beat the Roman left and centre before their right could intervene. He accordingly sent forward his elephants, who seem to have been fairly effective, doing considerable damage to the Roman lines, and followed up with his infantry, so that a ding-dong struggle was soon raging, in which the Carthaginians seemed to be slowly gaining the upper hand. Nero, meanwhile, had found that the ground to his front made it virtually impossible for him to come to grips with the Gauls. Showing a dash and initiative unusual in a Roman General of this period, he detached two thousand men from his wing, marched them across the back of the Roman centre and left, and then swung them forward to crash into the open flank of Hasdrubal's Spaniards.

The impact of this fresh force was too much for Hasdrubal's weary veterans. After a short struggle they gave way, and from that point on the battle degenerated into a mere slaughter as Nero rolled up the Carthaginian line. Hasdrubal himself, when he saw all was lost, apparently charged into the thick of the battle and fell sword in hand. Polybius says that he had done all that a good General could and, indeed, it does seem that but for the inspired intervention of Nero he would, at the worst, have escaped with a drawn battle. On the other hand, however, his initial deployment exposed him to just such a stroke—as did that of the Romans—and it is difficult to believe that Hannibal in similar circumstances would have been caught in such a way, or would have failed to carry out some such move against the Romans themselves. The plain fact, however, is that other Carthaginian armies were never as well trained or integrated as Hannibal's had become, while their leaders rarely showed any superiority over their Roman opponents.

Nero wasted no time resting on his laurels, being extremely concerned with what might be happening in southern Italy in his absence. Accordingly, after giving his men no more than a few hours rest, he hastened back to the south, making the trip, if we are to believe Livy, as fast as he had done on his initial march north. Hannibal in the meanwhile had progressed no further north than Larinum, and seems for once to have been completely hoodwinked, having no suspicion of Nero's absence. The first news he had of disaster was when his brother's severed head was hurled at the feet of his outposts and captured Carthaginian officers were paraded before them. This savage action, so typical of the callous brutality never far from the surface in the Roman character, was in complete contrast with Hannibal's own treatment of fallen Roman Generals; in his brother's glazed eyes Hannibal must have seen the end of all his dreams. The last hope of reinforcements had gone; from now on he was condemned to the defensive in what was virtually a secondary theatre. His thoughts must have been bitter indeed.

In Rome, naturally, jubilation reigned. At the beginning of the year the situation had looked grimmer than it had been at any time since Cannae, with the undefeated Hannibal still loose in the south and the menacing figure of Hasdrubal coming down from the north with fresh forces. Now the biggest menace, or so it seemed, had been swept away and for the first time in ten years a Roman army had won a decisive victory on Roman soil. There can be little wonder that the victorious Consuls were accorded a triumph, or that the main plaudits were received by Claudius Nero: little as one may like him as a man, as a soldier one must admire his obvious talents, for the victory on the Metaurus belonged to him and him alone.

Chapter 13

Scipio Africanus

After the victory of Baecula, Scipio seems to have spent the following year quietly in Spain; the only activity recorded by either Polybius or Livy is the defeat of a new Carthaginian commander, Hanno, who was caught while on a recruiting mission and routed by part of Scipio's force. Scipio himself invaded the Baeticia in an attempt to bring Hasdrubal Gisco to battle, but the latter seems to have dispersed his army in garrisons among the various towns; and Scipio did not attempt any large-scale sieges.

By the following year, however, news of the Metaurus had no doubt reached Spain; at all events, Hasdrubal Gisco now decided that a waiting game was no longer the correct policy. He and Mago together had succeeded in recruiting their army to a total of some seventy thousand foot and four thousand horse, and early in the spring he advanced to Ilipa, which has been identified as Alcala del Rio, on the right bank of the Guadalquivir some nine miles from Seville. Scipio, who had similarly assembled his troops at Castulo, advanced down the Guadalquivir to meet him with an army numbering 45,000 foot and three thousand horse. The Carthaginian cavalry tried a surprise attack as the Romans were pitching camp, but were beaten off; and for several days the armies remained motionless while the cavalry and light troops bickered between them.

Each day, however, the Carthaginians deployed and offered battle, and Scipio, studying their deployment with care, saw that it was always the same—their Africans holding the centre and the Spaniards on the wings, with their thirty-two elephants posted in front of the Spaniards. Scipio had two problems to solve—he was heavily outnumbered, and he did not altogether trust his Spanish auxiliaries. His solution was worthy of Hannibal himself. Each day he similarly deployed but refused action, in the same mode as Hasdrubal Gisco with his Romans in the centre and the Spaniards on the wings—but on the day he finally chose to fight, he not only deployed early but reversed his order of battle, so that the Spaniards now held the centre and the Romans the wings. Hasdrubal Gisco seeing the enemy advancing against him, had to draw up his army in haste and had no time to alter his own dispositions, so that the two armies engaged with, in each case, the weaker auxiliaries faced by the enemy veterans.

As usual, the action was begun by the light troops and cavalry on either side, and for some time the main infantry lines remained stationary. As the day drew on, however, Scipio recalled his skirmishers, directing them to fall back through the intervals of his main line and reform in its rear. His main line now advanced, but not, as Hasdrubal Gisco had assumed, for a direct frontal confrontation. Instead, the Spanish centre moved forward in line at a slow pace, but the Romans on either flank turned outwards into column and moved to their flanks until the heads of their columns were opposite the extreme flanks of the Carthaginian line, which had originally extended some distance beyond that of Scipio. Arrived here, the columns then wheeled round and advanced toward the enemy, until within charging distance, when they deployed back into line and the cavalry and Velites, who had been following in their rear, came up on the outer flanks, thus completely outflanking the Carthaginian army.

This was a daring and skilful movement, proving not only Scipio's tactical skill but the advanced state of training of his troops, who must have moved like a well-drilled machine. By this superb battlefield manoeuvre he had, in effect, re-created the Cannae situation in reverse by entirely different means, and without at any time jeopardising his position; for, had the African centre of the enemy advanced to the attack while he was in the process of making the move, his flanking columns could at once have deployed into line and assailed its flanks with devastating effect.

The Roman light infantry on the flanks of Scipio's line now came into action against Hasdrubal Gisco's elephants, which apparently had moved to the flanks to attempt a counter against the envelopment. The Roman missiles had a deadly effect, with the result that the great bulk of the elephants stampeded back into their own cavalry and outer infantry, throwing them into confusion. The Roman infantry then fell upon the Spaniards on either wing: these seem to have put up a spirited resistance but were gradually overborne and pressed steadily back until eventually they broke and took refuge in the Carthaginian camp. Meanwhile the African centre had remained halted, unable either to charge forward or to turn to its flanks for fear of being itself outflanked; and presumably Scipio would now have turned inward to finish it off in true Hannibalic style. At this precise moment, however, there began a violent thunderstorm which prevented further fighting, and both armies withdrew to their camps.

It was Hasdrubal Gisco's intention on the following day to hold firm in his fortified camp, but the bulk of his Spaniards, feeling no doubt that they had been left to bear the brunt of the fighting without assistance, now began to desert in large numbers; and accordingly the following night he ordered a retreat, with the intention of making for Gades. Scipio, however, was alert, and his troops, marching hard, secured the fords over the Guadalquivir (Baetis) before the Carthaginians could reach them. Hasdrubal Gisco was forced to push on along the right bank, but was so hard pressed that eventually he had to turn at bay. In the ensuing action he was utterly defeated, only six thousand men escaping from the field, and even these were rounded up and forced to surrender next day. Hasdrubal Gisco, Mago and the Numidian prince Masinissa managed to escape to Gades, but the Battle of Ilipa and its aftermath sealed the doom of the Carthaginian empire in Spain.

Scipio had already formed the intention of carrying the war into Africa, but realised full well the importance of gaining allies in Numidia before he did so. Shortly after the Ilipa operations, therefore, at the suggestion of the Numidian king, Syphax, with whom he had already been in touch, he personally embarked on a warship and sailed across to Africa, where he had meetings with the king which seem to have resulted in some sort of formal treaty. Just what promises

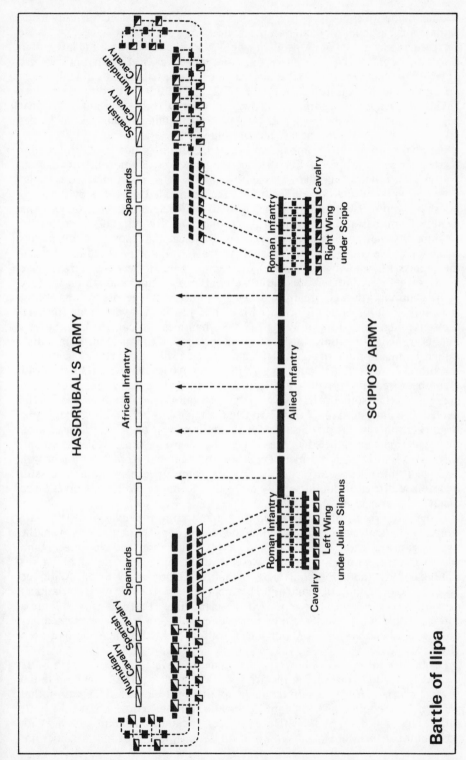

Battle of Ilipa

Syphax made we cannot be sure, but it is very probable that he was only using Scipio as a bargaining counter to pry concessions out of Carthage, for, as we shall see, it was not he but Masinissa who was eventually to drive the last nail in Carthage's coffin. Scipio returned to Spain, moreover, to find that all was not as well as he had expected. In his absence the interior tribes had suddenly taken up arms, and he was forced into a number of punitive expeditions, besides having to quell a mutiny among his own troops. It was thus the end of the year before Spain was fully quiet and the last Carthaginian stronghold at Gades taken, when Scipio could at last return home to Italy.

On Scipio's return to Rome he was elected Consul for 205 BC, with Licinius Crassus as his colleague. After the election, however, Scipio put forward his master-plan for finishing the war—an invasion of Africa mounted from Sicily. This met with considerable opposition in the Senate, led as always by the arch-priest of caution, Fabius Maximus, who wished Scipio instead to command against Hannibal and finish his menace once and for all. There are several versions of what actually took place, but it is clear that most of the Senate's objections were constitutional rather than strategical, and it would appear that the reports of grudging allowances of troops and half-hearted support have been exaggerated. Fabius' objections were, after all, sound enough on the face of it, Hannibal, though greatly reduced in numbers and territory, was still at large in Bruttium, while his brother Mago had just landed with some fourteen thousand men in Liguria, drawing off a Roman army to contain him. Surely, Fabius argued, it was only sensible to send their best General against Hannibal, rather than let him sail off on what might well be a wild goose chase? Scipio, on the other hand, pointed out that by invading Africa he would surely draw Hannibal after him, for the Carthaginian position there was weak, and he had every hope that some at least of their allies would desert them as soon as he landed. It would seem that Scipio had two main reasons behind his strategy: one would certainly be his predilection for the indirect approach and the attack on the weaker partner rather than the stronger, as shown at Ilipa; while the second was possibly that he felt a mere expulsion of Hannibal from Italy might well lead, in Rome's war-weary state, to a compromise peace, while a successful invasion of Africa would inevitably mean that Rome would be in a position to dictate whatever terms she pleased.

It therefore seems unlikely that, once committed to the invasion, the Senate would deliberately have refused Scipio adequate troops. In fact he was given the two Legions already in Sicily, a force of seven thousand volunteers and whatever other additional troops were available in the island—making, as Lazenby says, about the equivalent of a four-Legion army in all. With the necessity to contain both Mago and Hannibal in Italy, provide garrisons and an expeditionary force in Greece as well, it seems likely that this was as large a force as could be spared. Scipio certainly does not seem to have expressed any doubts of his ability to carry out the operations with the forces he had been given.

On his arrival in Sicily, however, he seems to have found that much more needed to be done in training his army than he had expected, for despite the relative urgency of his mission he made no attempt to launch the invasion that year, merely sending his lieutenant Laelius to raid the African coast with some thirty ships. This Laelius did with great success, in addition making contact with the Numidian prince Masinissa, who had recently been leading a somewhat chequered career. Numidia was in fact divided into two main areas, one of which was ruled by Syphax and the other, albeit as a feudatory of Syphax, by Masinissa's father Gala. When Masinissa returned home from Gades, however, he found that his father had died and that, due to the somewhat complicated inheritance procedures of the country, his claims had been ignored. He promptly raised an army and took possession of the country, only to be driven out by Syphax, who was egged on by Hasdrubal Gisco, the latter rightly suspecting that Masinissa had thrown in his lot with Rome. Masinissa had subsequently made two further attempts at securing his principality, each one failing in face of superior force, but he was still in the field with a sizeable force and eagerly awaiting Scipio's arrival. The very fact that the young prince had been able to raise more followers after two defeats shows that he was a charismatic character who would be a great asset to the Roman cause.

Scipio's timetable may possibly have been thrown out also by events at sea, where the Carthaginian fleet had been unusually active in support of Mago and had absorbed the attention of the ships which had been earmarked for the African invasion; and an enterprise in Italy which had needed his personal attention. This was the capture of Locri, which had been betrayed by its citizens to a force sent by Scipio on their request. Unfortunately for them the Carthaginian garrison had escaped into the citadel and, on the news that Hannibal was marching to their aid, Scipio himself felt impelled to hurry to the town. Livy makes much of this first encounter between the opposing Generals, since Hannibal on arrival avoided an action and merely extricated his garrison and withdrew; but it is very likely that this is all he ever intended, since the troops would be of more importance to him than trying to hold down a hostile town. In which case, of course, the credit which Livy awards to Scipio is rightly due to Hannibal for securing his limited objectives. As it happened, the capture of Locri turned out to be more of an embarrassment than an asset to Scipio, for the officer he left in command behaved extremely badly and embroiled Scipio in some awkward disciplinary proceedings. All these matters probably helped to delay his preparations until the season was over.

Scipio's consulship ended in March 204 BC, but he was confirmed in his command of the African expedition. Nevertheless it was probably June before he actually sailed. Estimates of his strength vary—Livy, for instance, gives three figures, ranging from ten thousand infantry and 2,200 cavalry to a combined total of 35,000 men. The lower total is ridiculously small, and it seems likely that while the cavalry figure was right, the infantry figure covers only the Roman contingent, ie, two reinforced Legions. If, then, we assume that the cavalry would be the usual proportions, we would have six hundred Roman horse and sixteen hundred allies, which would indicate an allied infantry force in the neighbourhood of sixteen thousand giving a final total of 28,200. This is the figure used by Lazenby, and is probably as near the truth as we are going to get.

When it comes to the invasion fleet, we have sound enough figures: the troops were embarked in four hundred transports with an escort of forty warships. The escort figure seems astonishingly low, even given the unenterprising use of the Carthaginian navy to date, and its record of constant defeat by inferior Roman squadrons, but it seems probable that although Scipio had more ships available—we know there were thirty in Sicily originally and that he brought thirty more when he first landed there—he had not the men available to man them. Even so it was taking a grave risk; at the most conservative estimate one would expect the Carthaginians to be able to launch fifty ships at this time, and there was no guarantee that their supine behaviour would continue. A Roman squadron of forty ships encumbered with four hundred transports might have been hard pressed if intercepted by even fifty Carthaginian galleys. As it happened, however, Scipio had estimated the risk correctly; had he in fact met with disaster he would probably have been castigated for rashness, but since the expedition succeeded we can merely applaud his daring. The passage from Lilybaeum to Cape Farina, where the army disembarked, was uneventful, not a Carthaginian ship being sighted, the weather foggy at night but with a favourable wind. Having disembarked, the troops moved inland a short distance and took up a position on a low range of hills, while the fleet moved off to reconnoitre the town of Utica, which was some thirteen miles to the south and was to be Scipio's first objective. The first encounter occurred when the Roman outposts were attacked by a force of five hundred Carthaginian cavalry under an officer named Hanno; but this force was soon defeated and dispersed, Hanno himself being killed. Scipio then proceeded to ravage the neighbourhood and capture an unwalled town, the booty from which was loaded on to the transports and sent back to Sicily as evidence of a success. At this point Masinissa joined up; he brought with him a force which has been variously estimated at from two hundred to two thousand horsemen.

According to Livy there now occurred a second cavalry action, against some two thousand men under yet another Hanno, who were lured into a trap by Masinissa, who used the standard Numidian tactic of a feigned retreat until Scipio's cavalry hit the enemy in flank. It is, of course, possible that there were two cavalry actions, but it seems stretching probability a little too far that in both actions the Carthaginian commander should be called Hanno—though this was a favourite Carthaginian name—and that he should be killed. The matter is not of great importance: all we can be sure of is that Scipio did manage to dispose of all the available Carthaginian mounted troops in the vicinity, thus giving himself freedom of manoeuvre. He therefore made a week-long raid into the interior, returning laden with further booty, which he again shipped off to Sicily—the transports having meanwhile returned laden with provisions—and then marched off to lay siege to Utica. But after forty days, with no signs of the city's resistance weakening, scouts reported the approach of two armies, one of Carthaginians under Hasdrubal Gisco and the other of Numidians under Syphax, and Scipio prudently abandoned the siege and withdrew his army into fortified winter quarters two miles east of the town, where there was a suitable peninsula.

Thus far he had achieved little enough, and though his small successes were doubtless enlarged in reports to Rome, the Senate cannot have been overjoyed with the results of what had been billed as the knock-out blow in Africa. However, his credit was good enough for his *imperium* to be confirmed for the following year, and in the meanwhile he occupied the winter with negotiations with Syphax. Ostensibly he was attempting to induce the latter to change sides, but it is fairly clear that his main intentions were to gain full information of the size and disposition of the enemy forces, ready for the resuming of operations in the spring. In this he was assisted by the fact that, although Hasdrubal Gisco and Syphax were allies—in fact the king had married the Carthaginian General's daughter—the two armies were encamped separately some two miles apart and about six miles from the Roman camp.

Although Livy does his best to whitewash the actions of the Roman commander, it would seem that Scipio on this occasion was not above acting in a manner which was at the least underhand and indeed smacks of treachery; had it been committed by a Carthaginian, Livy would doubtless have been full of indignation against Phoenician deceit. He allowed Syphax and Hasdrubal Gisco to believe that he was virtually ready to accept peace on the basis of a Roman evacuation of Africa in return for a Carthaginian evacuation of Italy, and while they were thus lulled, launched a sudden night assault on both camps. In fact, I personally would consider him to have been justified in his actions by circumstances, but it is apparent from a close study of the various authorities that even the Roman sources felt a certain guilt over the affair. At all events, the plan worked: Scipio's men fired the Numidian camp, and the unfortunate inmates, thinking the fire to be accidental, tumbled out half-dressed to fight the flames and were slaughtered while helpless or burned to death in their flaming huts. In the Carthaginian camp, Hasdrubal Gisco's men, similarly thinking the blaze an accident, turned out to assist their allies and were ambushed by the Romans as they did so. Casualties in this well-handled affair have been considerably exaggerated, since Hasdrubal Gisco and Syphax were able to field substantial forces not a great deal later in the year, but for the moment their armies were taken out of the play, and Scipio was left free to resume the siege of Utica.

As it happened, Syphax was joined at this time by a force of four thousand Celtiberian mercenaries, so that by the end of April he and Hasdrubal Gisco were able to concentrate an army of probably thirty thousand men at a place called the Great Plains: this has been tentatively identified as the plain of Souk el Kremis beside the River Bagradas, about seventy miles from Utica. On hearing of their presence here, Scipio left about half of his infantry to continue the siege of Utica, and marched south with the rest of the infantry and all his cavalry. It seems likely that Masinissa's contingent had by now swollen in size following the misfortunes suffered by Syphax, and that Scipio's mounted arm was thereby much enlarged. Probably in all he had some twenty thousand men, leaving him heavily outnumbered but almost certainly superior in quality.

After a five day march Scipio reached the vicinity of the enemy, but there were three days of minor skirmishing before, on the fourth, battle was joined in earnest. Syphax and Hasdrubal Gisco deployed their combined forces with the Carthaginian cavalry on the right, then the Carthaginian infantry, next the Celtiberians, followed by the Numidian infantry, with the Numidian cavalry on the left. Scipio placed Masinissa's horsemen on his left and the Italian cavalry under Laelius on the right, and seems to have had his Roman infantry in the centre with allied contingents on either flank. Scipio's tactics were somewhat reminiscent of Ilipa, in that he held back his centre initially while attacking with his flanking cavalry and infantry. On both wings the cavalry charged first, quickly routing their mounted opponents, and then swung inward just as the allied contingents engaged the enemy infantry. These also gave way very rapidly at about the same moment as Scipio's slower moving Roman centre engaged the Celtiberians. Since the flanks of these latter were now exposed, while the Roman Hastati engaged them frontally the Principes and Triarii from the second and third lines swept round to hit them in flank, and the four thousand mercenaries, though fighting desperately and courageously, were slaughtered to

the last man. A good part of the rest of the army escaped, since it had not stayed long enough to do much fighting; but Scipio's swift victory had the effect of destroying all confidence among the Carthaginians and their allies and leaving him in complete control of the hinterland.

Carthage itself was now in considerable panic, and it was decided, much too late, to launch the fleet against Scipio, in an attempt to raise the siege of Utica. Scipio, who after the Great Plains had marched boldly up to the vicinity of Carthage, capturing Runis, had to rush back to Utica to organise the meeting of this threat, for his ships were in no case to fight a normal naval action, being greatly encumbered with siege equipment. He accordingly drew them all up in a mass, warships in the centre and transports on the outside, and manned them with picked troops. The Carthaginian fleet at first waited expectantly outside Utica for the Romans to come out and fight, but at last had to attack Scipio in position. The result was tactically indecisive, though the Carthaginians claimed a victory since they were able to capture sixty transports which they managed to detach from the Roman battle-line; but since they then returned to Carthage leaving the siege still secure, strategically it must count as a Roman success.

Meanwhile a more important success had been gained elsewhere. While Scipio himself and the main infantry force had returned to the coast after the Great Plains battle, Masinissa, Laelius and all the cavalry had pursued the fleeing Syphax into Numidia. Masinissa's own tribesmen at once rallied to him, but Syphax was able to raise fresh troops and turn at bay. In the ensuing action, however, his raw army was again utterly routed and he himself captured. Masinissa was now installed as King of Numidia, and by this result the excellent Numidian cavalry now became the allies of Rome instead of Carthage. From that day on Scipio could be sure of cavalry superiority in an area where such an advantage counted doubly.

The news of the defeat of Syphax was the last blow for Carthage. Orders were at once sent to Italy for both Hannibal and Mago to return home as rapidly as possible, and at the same time a deputation of thirty nobles was sent to Scipio's camp to ask for peace terms. Scipio was perfectly ready to treat, but his terms were harsh: Carthage was to withdraw her troops from Italy, Spain and the Mediterranean islands, hand over all prisoners and deserters, surrender all except twenty warships, deliver a vast quantity of supplies to him, and pay a large war indemnity. Nevertheless, after some debate, the Carthaginians agreed to these terms, and envoys were accordingly sent to Rome to ratify the treaty. It would seem that by the time the envoys reached Rome both Carthaginian armies had already embarked for Africa; and there is considerable dispute as to whether, in fact, the Senate did ratify the treaty. Livy says not: according to him the envoys were sent away empty-handed, since the Senate agreed that Carthage was only awaiting the return of Hannibal before recommencing hostilities. Polybius on the other hand states definitely that the treaty was ratified.

What had been happening in Italy during Scipio's expedition? To deal briefly with Mago, that worthy had, as we noted, landed in Liguria with an army, and after some local recruiting, had advanced inland. Here, however, he was defeated and he himself wounded, but managed to extricate a good part of his army and bring it back to the coast. On receiving the orders from Carthage he duly embarked his troops for Africa but, according to Livy, he died of his wounds en route. Hannibal meanwhile had been restricted to the area of Bruttium, but in 204 had won a victory over the Consul Sempronius Tuditanus near Croton. Livy as usual claims that Roman reinforcements then arrived and Tuditanus in turn defeated Hannibal, which almost certainly means that Hannibal made one of his skilful disengagements when outnumbered. In the autumn he too at last abandoned Italy, taking with him those troops who wished to leave; we have no record of their number, but it does not seem to have been a very considerable force. His numbers must have been steadily decreasing over the last few years, and part at least of his Italians would no doubt have preferred remaining behind.

It is difficult to understand the events which followed. A convoy of two hundred Roman transports, laden with supplies for Scipio, and escorted by thirty warships, was en route to Africa when it was scattered by strong winds. The warships safely made Cape Farina, but the transports, not having oars, were driven across to the west coast of Cape Bon, in full view of the citizens of Carthage. Possibly short of food after diverting such huge supplies to Scipio, the Carthaginian magistrates allowed themselves to be persuaded to send out Hasdrubal Gisco with fifty warships to collect the helpless transports. This in itself was foolish enough: what followed seems little short of madness. Scipio's reaction was mild enough: he despatched envoys to Carthage to tell the government that the Senate had ratified the peace treaty, and to express astonishment at Hasdrubal Gisco's warlike act. It was therefore open to Carthage to apologise and make amends and preserve the peace. Instead, the envoys were cavalierly dismissed, and as they returned home by sea their ship was attacked by Carthaginian warships and heavy losses inflicted. It has been suggested that this was the result of Hannibal trying to prolong the war, but I find this difficult to believe. Hannibal was too intelligent not to know by now that the war was irretrievably lost, and since his motives had never been personal gain or glory such attitudes would be foreign to him. It seems much more likely that the war party in Carthage which had originally backed him, but had failed signally to support his enterprise with troops and supplies, now assumed that because he was back in Africa he could automatically reverse the situation. They were not themselves soldiers and had little grasp of the true military situation. It may well be that the whole business of the peace negotiations was merely to gain time enough for Hannibal's return, or it may be that the fact of his return was enough to spur on these irresponsible magnates to the action they took. Whatever the cause, it sealed the final doom of Carthage.

Scipio began operations by marching up the Bagradas valley, ravaging the countryside with fire and sword and thus effectively destroying the food supplies on which Carthage relied. He also had a secondary purpose, in that his march carried him toward Numidia and a junction with the forces of Masinissa, without whom his prospects of a successful general action were decidedly poor. Hannibal at this time was at Hadrametum on the coast, trying desperately to lick his army into shape and to raise cavalry of his own. In this he was not particularly successful, though remnants of Syphax's supporters did come in with a certain number of men. Time, however, was against him: on the one hand, representatives from the city and from the townships along the Bagradas were beseeching him to give battle to Scipio before he did more damage, while on the other, he knew the necessity of fighting before the Romans effected their junction with Masinissa. Accordingly he broke up from Hadrametum and marched west to a place called Zama, probably hoping to interpose between the two allies and force Scipio back toward the coast.

On his arrival at Zama, Hannibal sent envoys to Scipio's camp suggesting that they meet personally. It has been suggested that this was simply a ruse to hold Scipio in place so that he could be brought to battle before Masinissa arrived, but I think it unlikely, for Hannibal did not follow it up by moving toward the Roman camp until some days later when Scipio—having effected his junction with Masinissa—sent word that he was ready for a meeting. Hannibal then broke up his camp at Zama and advanced to the vicinity of that of Scipio. No-one has been able to offer a satisfactory identification of the area, but this is unimportant as terrain was not to play a significant part in the events which followed; any open stretch of ground might therefore be the battlefield of Zama.

Hannibal and Scipio then held their meeting somewhere between the two armies, accompanied only by an interpreter—though both men were fluent in Greek and it is probable that Hannibal was familiar with Latin. There is no reason to doubt the accounts we have of their conversation. Both knew full well that if they fought, it would not be to decide the outcome of the war—that was already irretrievably lost to Carthage—but the peace. If Scipio won, Carthage must accept any terms he liked to offer: if Hannibal was victorious, the most Carthage could hope for was a negotiated peace, perhaps marginally better than the terms which had already been agreed and then rejected. It seems likely, therefore, that quite apart from any personal curiosity about each other, both Generals sincerely wished to avoid unnecessary bloodshed, though they must have known that agreement was unlikely.

Hannibal began the discussion by praising Scipio's achievements but warning him that he had been fortunate and that fortune was notoriously fickle—why fight if it was not necessary? He offered essentially the same terms as those already agreed but with one very important omission—that of the surrender of all deserters. If this had been enforced, technically it would have included every Italian in his ranks, meaning probably fifty per cent of the veterans he had brought back with him, and would have doomed them to certain and cruel death. He was not the man to save his city by such a betrayal. Scipio, predictably, answered that it was the Carthaginians who had broken the truce, and why should they now expect to get better terms than those previously agreed? The meeting therefore ended in deadlock, and the two Generals parted in the knowledge that tomorrow would bring battle.

Unfortunately neither of our prime sources, Polybius and Livy, states numbers for either army, and we are forced to rely to a certain extent on extrapolation and inspired guesswork. Polybius does say that Hannibal's casualties amounted to twenty thousand dead and about the same in prisoners, and that his army was virtually annihilated: thus we can assume that his strength was in the neighbourhood of forty thousand. This is borne out to some extent by the fact that several writers have stated that his first line numbered twelve thousand; if we assume that the second and third were roughly similar, this gives us 36,000 infantry. Since we know he was heavily outnumbered in cavalry and that Masinissa had four thousand Numidian horse plus the Roman cavalry contingents, a reasonable figure for Hannibal's mounted arm would be four thousand, which coincides quite happily with our total of forty thousand. It seems likely therefore that this figure is correct to within a thousand or two either side. He had in addition eighty elephants, a fact which is stated by all our sources. On the Roman side, we know that Masinissa brought in four thousand horse and six thousand foot, and there is a strong possibility that six hundred more Numidians were contributed by a chieftain called Dacamas. For Scipio's own troops, if we start from our original figure of 28,000 men and allow for losses in battle and detachment in garrison, a reasonable assumption seems possibly 25,000, of whom about 2,000 would be mounted. This is as close as we are likely to get, and shows us that Hannibal was outnumbered in cavalry but had a substantial superiority in infantry, plus his elephants.

What figures do not show, of course, is the quality of the opposing armies. We know that by now Scipio's was extremely highly trained and full of confidence—probably at about the same level, and for the same reasons, as Hannibal's had been at the time of Cannae. Masinissa's cavalry would have been of the usual high quality, but we cannot make any guess at the worth of his infantry save that they would undoubtedly be skirmishers rather than infantry of the line. Hannibal's army, on the other hand, was a mish-mash of hastily thrown together elements. Its core, of course, was made up by his own veterans, who would be every bit as good as Scipio's men; he also had about twelve thousand mercenaries from Mago's army who were at any rate professional soldiers and therefore of reasonable worth. For the rest, Carthage had provided him with possibly the same number of citizen troops and hastily raised Africans: even if their courage was not in question their training certainly was and they could hardly be relied upon against veteran legionaries. Of Hannibal's horsemen we have no information, but we have no real reason to suppose that his Numidian cavalry were any better or worse than those following Masinissa. Finally his eighty elephants, while formidable on paper, were young and only partly trained, quite unused to battle conditions.

Scipio drew up his army in fairly conventional order, with the exception that instead of his three lines of Hastati, Principes and Triarii being drawn up in the *quincunx* or checkerboard pattern, he ranged them directly behind each other in order to make lanes down which it was hoped to shepherd the Carthaginian elephants. This was in fact the formation adopted so disastrously by Regulus many years earlier, but Scipio improved it by adopting a loose formation instead of herding his men closely together as Regulus had done, and stationing all his Velites in the lanes with orders to fall back in front of the elephants or, if this proved difficult, to right and left between the lines. He placed his Roman/Italian horsemen under Laelius—possibly plus Dacamas' Numidians—on his left and Masinissa with his whole force, infantry as well as cavalry, on his right.

Hannibal's deployment was somewhat similar to Scipio's. He in fact divided his infantry into their three component forces and used them as separate lines. In the first line stood Mago's men, Ligurians, Gauls, Moors and Balaires, a mixture therefore of skirmishers and line infantry. Fairly close behind this front line stood the new Carthaginian and African levies; and at a distance of perhaps two hundred yards to the rear were placed his veterans as a reserve. His Numidian horsemen were on the left and his Carthaginians on the right, and finally his eighty elephants were distributed in one long line along the whole of his front. For the first time in his career, Hannibal was fighting on ground not of his choosing and with an inferiority in the mounted arm: like Varro at Cannae, therefore, he had to rely on winning in the centre before his vulnerable wings could bring disaster upon him.

After some brief skirmishing, Hannibal ordered his elephants to charge all along the front. Scipio, however, had given orders that when they did so every trumpet and horn in his army should be sounded simultaneously; and a large proportion of the elephants, being young and untrained, were terrified by the sudden sound and stampeded back. They seem to have been more affected on the wings, where their sudden retreat apparently disordered both Carthaginian cavalry wings. Seeing this, both Masinissa and Laelius ordered their horsemen to charge home, and in a few brief moments Hannibal's horsemen were broken and driven from the field in rout. It has been suggested that, knowing his inferiority in cavalry, Hannibal had directed his wings to give way and draw off the Roman horsemen; this is possible but seems unlikely since, if his men had withdrawn under orders, surely they would have resumed the action later, whereas in fact they took no further part in the battle.

Masinissa and Laelius having followed in pursuit, for the moment the cavalry of both sides had vanished. Those elephants in the centre which had not stampeded backwards had in the meanwhile been successfully herded down the lanes betwen the Roman Maniples, though they seem to have inflicted considerable casualties on the Velites in doing so. It was now time for the main business to commence, and the Roman and Carthaginian first lines met with a crash. The fighting between them was severe, both sides struggling desperately, but gradually the Romans got the upper hand as the Principes came up to the support of the Hastati, until at last the mercenaries gave way and broke for the rear. Hannibal had apparently given orders for his second line not to allow the broken first to pass through it, for Polybius tells us that the routed mercenaries tried to cut their way through in their panic and caused some disorder in Hannibal's array.

With the mercenaries cleared away, the Roman first line, supported by the second—though some writers claim that the Principes had not yet been involved—attacked the Carthaginian and African second line. Despite what some sources claim, this line seems to have put up almost as good a display as the first; and when they finally broke and gave way, only to find that Hannibal's third line was similarly solidly between them and escape, a good few

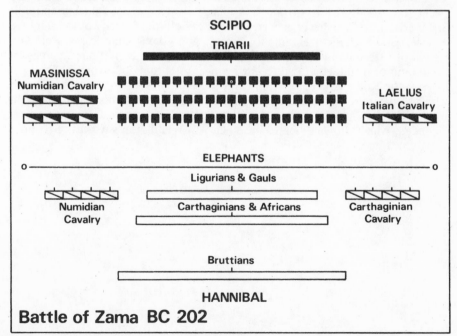

Battle of Zama BC 202

of them seem to have rallied upon its flanks. But though the two first lines had given a good account of themselves, they had not achieved in full what Hannibal had hoped, which was to draw Scipio into committing his reserve line of Triarii. With these still untouched, it would have been foolhardy for the Carthaginian reserve to have charged the Roman first and second lines and thus given Scipio a chance to use his favourite enveloping tactics. Scipio similarly wished to re-order his forces before the final decisive fight, and accordingly his trumpets sounded the recall and his weary Hastati and Principes fell back through the litter of dead and wounded.

These preliminary engagements had left the hard core contestants very evenly balanced in numbers and quality, and after a short lull Scipio gave the order for his re-formed line to advance. Since Hannibal's men were largely armed and equipped in the Roman style the ensuing combat could easily have been mistaken for a civil war, and was contested with as much bitterness. Both sides were fighting, not just for victory, but for their own pride in themselves and their commanders, and neither was prepared to yield an inch. It would seem, however, from most accounts, that any small advantage there was, was moving in favour of Hannibal when suddenly the victorious horsemen of Laelius and Masinissa re-appeared upon the field. Their arrival settled the issue: Hannibal's veterans, refusing to run, died where they stood, fighting on in grim despair.

Unlike his brother Hasdrubal, who in similar circumstances had thought only of himself and died sword in hand, Hannibal took the larger view and, when all was inextricably lost, escaped with a few horsemen. Very probably he would have preferred to die with his men, but as always, he thought of Carthage first: alive, he could still hope to have some influence on events and continue to serve his country in peace as he had in war. His army virtually ceased to exist: as already noted, Polybius assesses the casualties as twenty thousand dead and twenty thousand prisoners, though Appian's figures are 25,000 dead and only 8,500 prisoners. Whichever is correct it shows both the ferocity of the fighting, and the completeness of Hannibal's defeat. As to the Roman losses, Polybius' figures of fifteen hundred killed seems ridiculously low, even if one assumes the usual ratio of wounded at two to one giving a total of 4,500. Appian, however, assesses the Romans killed at 2,500 and those of Masinissa at a higher figure, which seems more appropriate; by using the same formula this would make the total of Scipio's losses probably five thousand dead and at least as many more wounded, which shows Zama to have been, in Wellington's words, 'a damned close run thing'.

Chapter 14

No peace for Hannibal

After his defeat at Zama, Hannibal retired to his original camp at Hadrametum, but from here he was quickly summoned to Carthage. Scipio in the meanwhile, having rested his army and dispersed a force of Numidian cavalry which had apparently been raised by the supporters of the dethroned Syphax, began his march back to the coast, and was met on his way by Carthaginian envoys asking for peace. Though these were told roughly to go away and return when he had encamped at Tunis, the terms they then received were, in the circumstances, lenient enough: Carthage was to retain her African possessions—though there is some dispute as to what boundary was set on these—but must cede everything else to Rome, surrender all warships except ten triremes, make reparations for breaking the truce, hand over all prisoners, deserters and runaway slaves, and pay a war indemnity of ten thousand talents of silver spread over fifty years. In addition, she must feed and pay Scipio's troops until they withdrew, promise not to train elephants or hire mercenaries, and was denied the right to make war on any nation outside Africa, or within Africa without Rome's approval. Finally, she was required to be the friend and ally of Rome by land and sea (in other words, her vassal) and to give up one hundred hostages from among her nobility.

These terms were read out to the Carthaginian Assembly, at which Hannibal was, probably for the first time ever, present. One rash member, apparently named Gisco, rose to speak against them and for a continuation of the war: Hannibal, appalled at such stupidity, forcibly dragged him from the rostrum and then, apologising gracefully for his ignorance of civilian customs, pointed out that the Assembly should be grateful that Rome left them anything at all, since they were powerless to oppose her. His pithy remarks convinced the Assembly, and the terms were forthwith accepted. Carthaginian ambassadors were then sent to Rome to ratify the terms; there was some debate in the Senate, not necessarily over the terms themselves but more, it seems, as to whether Scipio should be allowed to reap the full glory of ending the war or whether the current Consul should be sent out to do so. Eventually, however, this political bickering was decided in Scipio's favour and the peace was duly ratified.

It is possible that Scipio's leniency was coloured to some small degree by the personal regard he had formed for Hannibal; there was, for instance, no demand for the great General's extradition or for any reprisals against him or his family. There is, in fact, a tradition that years later the two Generals met again at Ephesus, and talked as old friends, showing once again that it is usually the politicians rather than the soldiers who harbour animosity and desires for revenge. Scipio is said to have asked Hannibal who he considered to have been the world's three greatest soldiers, and to have been told Alexander, Pyrrhus of Epirus, and himself. 'And supposing you had won at Zama?' asked Scipio. 'Then I would have ranked myself first of all', replied Hannibal. A graceful compliment enough—but in fact, had Hannibal won at Zama, who would ever have ranked Scipio among the world's great Generals?

After the departure of Scipio's army, Hannibal resigned his commission and retired into private life. For a man of his restless ability, however, it was impossible to stand by and watch his country founder in a sea of greed and inefficiency, and it would seem that he soon began to use his influence on behalf of the people of Carthage as opposed to the aristocracy. It will be remembered that the Barcid family did not count itself among the great aristocratic families but rather among the middle class: and Hannibal can have had little sympathy for the idle rich who had made themselves life tenants of the Carthaginian Government and in doing so were either lining their own pockets or turning a blind eye while others did so. Finally, when the hereditary Council of Judges declared that the country could not meet the annual war indemnity and that consequently a tax would be levied upon the populace—but not the aristocracy—Hannibal was elected Shofet in 196 BC. He at once set in hand an effective procedure of financial reform that within only a few years Carthage's internal economy was in better case than it had been before the war, while he also succeeded in abolishing the aristocracy's hereditary privileges, and making the government truly elective, thus establishing what was probably a truer democracy than that of Rome.

It was probably unfortunate for Hannibal that his rise to power in Carthage coincided with a fresh Roman involvement in the East. After the peace with Carthage, Rome's attention had turned once more to Greece, where hostilities were soon resumed with Philip of Macedon. Peace had been made in 205 largely because Rome's main concern then was with the war against Carthage: with that safely out of way, war was declared again in early 200 BC. After some fairly indecisive campaigning, the victory of Flaminius at Cynocephalae in 197 brought that war to a successful conclusion, but this had the effect of establishing a firm Roman presence in Greece; and this in turn brought Rome into contact for the first time with Alexander's successors in the old Persian Empire.

The series of wars in Asia Minor after the death of Alexander had failed to re-establish his empire, but as the years passed there had emerged what appeared to be a strong kingdom in Syria which controlled much of Alexander's eastern dominions. Its current ruler, Antiochus, regarded himself, however, as a Greek rather than an Asiatic, and as such laid claims to vague authority in Greece which sooner or later was bound to bring him into conflict with Rome. Hannibal's enemies in Carthage, finding themselves impotent to oppose him at home in face of his popular support, decided therefore to use against him the fear which his name still inspired in Roman breasts, and sent an embassy to Rome to accuse him of secretly conspiring with Antiochus to renew the war with Rome. Hannibal, they said, was using the reformed finances of Carthage to re-arm and prepare for war, and they begged Rome to remove him before he involved their country in a new disaster.

Whether there was, in fact, any truth in these stories we cannot be completely sure. Hannibal may indeed have had communications with Antiochus, but there is no evidence that if he had he was party to any plot for a renewal of the war. It seems most unlikely that a soldier and statesman of his stature could have believed that such a war could now succeed, and there is certainly nothing to show that he was making any warlike preparations. But, as the conspirators had anticipated, the very thought of Hannibal once more in arms against them was too much for the judgement of the Roman Senate. To do him justice, Scipio Africanus spoke up in Hannibal's favour, but to no avail: and in 195 an embassy sailed from Rome for Carthage. Ostensibly its purpose was to mediate between Carthage and Masinissa over a boundary dispute; but friends of Hannibal (it may be inspired by Scipio himself) sent him prior warning that they would demand that Carthage hand over Hannibal to Rome.

Rather than make his safety an issue which might destroy Carthage, Hannibal at once made arrangements for flight. On the day that the Roman envoys landed he rode out of the city to his villa at Hadrametum, where he boarded a small ship and sailed eastward to Tyre. Here he was received rapturously by his Phoenician countrymen, but he made only a short stop before journeying on to Ephesus and the court of Antiochus III. The Syrian king was just back from a successful campaign in the East: Hannibal now laid before him a well-constructed plan for the inevitable war with Rome.

Strike now, he urged, while Roman armies were tied up in Spain, where there had been a massive uprising of the tribes. Let Antiochus himself lead an army into Greece, while his large fleet landed Hannibal and a second army in Italy; with massive naval and financial support the early successes of the Second Punic War could be re-created and Rome's eastern expansion blocked. But the Syrian kingdom, for all its outward power and military might, was decadent and rotten; Antiochus himself was a typical Eastern tyrant, afraid to entrust anyone with overmuch power lest it was turned against him, and accustomed to wars in which there was much political manoeuvring and little real fighting. He expected a conflict with Rome to follow the same pattern and saw no advantage in hurrying things. He kept Hannibal at court, the object of much ostensible admiration and secret denigration by court officials, but rejected his advice.

There can be little doubt that the spartan Hannibal was ill at ease in the gilded luxury and decadence of the Syrian court. Though he spoke Greek fluently, he was not by nature a philosopher or a master of debate, and his years of authority had not prepared him for the role of supplicant and advisor. Abstemious in his habits, the gay Syrian courtiers must have regarded him as the skeleton at the feast. Moreover, he was too outspoken in his opinions of the Syrian army, whose military virtues—if any—were hidden beneath showy exteriors and a general air of ostentation. He publicly doubted their ability to face the Roman Legions, a statement which did not exactly increase his popularity.

In 192 BC, however, Antiochus at last moved, sending an army of some ten thousand men into Greece; a move of monumental stupidity, for it was not strong enough to do anything particular, but enough to provoke Rome into hostilities. The Aetolian League sent four thousand men to join him, while the rest of Greece remained aloof. Antiochus, who had brought Hannibal with him on the expedition, therefore fortified the Pass of Thermopylae, holding it with his own men while Aetolians held the hill trails above. The Romans, without calling up any reinforcements from Italy, at once drove the Aetolians from their positions and drove down to destroy the Syrians: Antiochus fled to his ships and sailed back to Ephesus. One can imagine Hannibal's chagrin and his contempt at the fighting qualities of the Syrians.

In Rome, however, the news that Hannibal was in the field again—for they had no knowledge of his powerlessness—prompted the despatch of Scipio Africanus to Greece, though his brother Lucius was nominally in command. Antiochus was at first undisturbed by his defeat, thinking that a peace with Rome could easily be patched up. Disillusioned, he began too late to prepare seriously for war, only to find Scipio's army marching through Greece for the Dardanelles and a combined Roman-Rhodian warfleet blockading Ephesus itself. Giving in at last to Hannibal's pleas for action, he sent him to Tyre to raise a Phoenician fleet. It may seem strange that the greatest soldier of the age should have been employed as an Admiral; but in those days a General was expected to be able to double as an Admiral as well, and in many respects the tactics of seafighting differed little from those of land.

Hannibal acted promptly: if he could bring his small fleet back from Tyre quickly enough he might break the Roman blockade and enable the Syrian army to beat Scipio to the Dardanelles and prevent his crossing into Asia. Off Side, however, he was intercepted by the Rhodian fleet, then the best in the world. The Tyrian ships were mainly large craft, designed to fight the Roman quadriremes: those of Rhodes were triremes, fast and graceful and handled with deadly skill. Though Hannibal's squadron on the left of the line did well, more than holding its own, the inshore squadron under Appollonius was quickly defeated, and Hannibal was forced to turn back to Tyre. It was his first and last experience of command under Antiochus.

With his navy checkmated, Antiochus abandoned the defences of the Dardanelles and withdrew into Asia to raise more men. In 190 BC he stood at Magnesia to fight, at the head of some seventy thousand men. Looking at their ranks gleaming with gold and silver, their commanders resplendent in jewels and silks, he turned to Hannibal, who still accompanied him as an advisor though his advice was regularly ignored, and said, 'Will not this be enough for the Romans?' 'Yes', replied Hannibal in grim jest, 'enough even for them, though they are the greediest nation on earth!' In the battle which followed the Roman veterans swept the field with ease, and two years later Antiochus was forced into humiliating peace. One of the terms was that he hand over Rome's arch-enemy; but to give him his due, he arranged that when the time came, Hannibal had disappeared.

From Syria Hannibal made his way to Crete, to a place called Gortyna. It seemed a good enough refuge. Crete was then off the beaten track, a haunt of pirates and sea-raiders; perhaps Rome would not seek him there. There is a story that, distrusting the honesty of the local sea-rovers, he deposited in the temple treasury a number of heavy jars which ostensibly contained his wealth, while actually keeping his money hidden in some bronze statues of the Phoenician gods which he openly placed along the path outside his villa. How long he stayed hidden in Crete we do not know; but, as he was to discover, Rome had a long arm. One day a Roman naval squadron under Fabius Labeo anchored in the Cretan harbour and demanded a cessation of pirate raids on Roman shipping. Fearing that his hosts, in their anxiety to propitiate Rome, would betray him, Hannibal slipped away again.

From Crete he sailed east, through the Straits and on into the Black Sea. He is supposed to have spent some time in Armenia, but we know that eventually he ended up in the petty kingdom of Bithynia. There is a story that Scipio Africanus knew of his presence there, but kept his own counsel: it may not be true but, it would have been in character for Scipio. For two or three years Hannibal lived quietly at Libyssa, a fishing village near Nicomedia, paying occasional visits to the court of King Prusias. In 183 BC, however, Bithynian envoys were summoned to Rome to settle differences between their country and the neighbouring one of Pergamum; and while there one of them mentioned Hannibal's name. The very name itself was still enought to make the Senate uneasy: Flaminius was sent to Bithynia to demand that the great Carthaginian be handed over to him.

King Prusias was in no condition to resist Rome, and in all fairness he owed nothing to Hannibal; he posted guards round his guest's villa. Realising that this time he could not escape, Hannibal, now an old man of sixty-four called for a cup of wine and took poison rather than be taken alive. Livy has given us what he professes to be Hannibal's last words: 'Let me free the Roman people from their long anxiety, since they think it tedious to wait for an old man's death. Flaminius will gain no great or famous victory over a helpless victim of treachery. The Roman character has changed: they send an ambassador to suggest to Prusias the crime of murdering a guest'. Even in death Hannibal had defeated his enemies.

Chapter 15

Sequel—*Delenda est Carthago*

Hannibal died in 185 BC and his great opponent, Scipio Africanus, followed him to the grave the same year. With their passing the eyes of little men in the Senate returned to Carthage. With her finances revitalised by Hannibal's innovations, the merchant city had proved able even with her now limited resources, to pay off the crushing war indemnity faster than the peace treaty had called for, and though her military power was all but non-existent, economically she had reached new heights. In doing so she was monopolising markets which Roman merchants believed should belong to them, and their representatives in the Senate sought for any underhand means by which to undermine her.

Carthage had kept faithfully to the terms of the peace treaty of 201, despite a constant stream of annoying pinpricks inflicted by Rome's ally, Masinissa. The Numidian king, established by Rome's victory as a powerful ruler, was determined to turn Numidia into a civilised, modern state on the pattern of Rome and Carthage, and in the course of doing so to expand his boundaries at the expense of Carthage. In 193, taking advantage of the fact that Carthage, following Hannibal's flight, was in bad odour with Rome, he seized some territory in the neighbourhood of Emporiae, and when Carthage appealed to Rome no action was taken to eject him. Ten years later the situation was repeated, and in fact on seven separate occasions Carthage was forced to appeal to Rome for redress against Numidia. Although on some of these occasions Rome did act to restrain her client king, on none of them was he forced to disgorge his ill-gotten gains.

Finally, in 155, Carthage in desperation took up arms against Masinissa, who was now claiming the Great Plains area, and two years later yet another Roman delegation came to Africa to settle the dispute. It was headed by Cato the Elder, a remarkable old man of eighty-one who had served in the Hannibalic war but who was tied heavily to the trading party. What he saw in Carthage frightened him: some writers have tried to show him as an honourable man who genuinely saw Carthage as a continuing menace to Rome, but this seems unlikely, for it is impossible to conceive that at this stage, with the power of both Macedonia and Syria broken, that Carthage could pose any military menace to Rome. Commercially, however, she was indeed a threat, and Cato cleverly used the current situation against her. From the time of his return to Rome, every speech he made in the Senate was ended with the words *'Delenda est Carthago'*—Carthage must be destroyed. He was not without opposition, which came mainly from the Scipionic party, but, like a dripping tap, he steadily wore down his opponents.

In 151-150 there was again war between Carthage and Masinissa, in which the former was defeated. Terrified at what might happen, the city government executed those responsible for the hostilities, and sent embassies to Rome to explain what had happened. They met with a hostile reception, and were told ambiguously that 'Carthage must satisfy the Roman people'. Rome was in fact preparing for war, and was determined to follow through, quite regardless of any injustice involved. Cato had succeeded in convincing the Senate that Carthage was still a threat: and Rome's very successes had led her into a policy of consistent brutality against anyone regarded as such. Recent massacres in both Liguria and Spain had shown a horrifying contempt for the lives of those who opposed her directives, and now the same treatment was to be meted out to the old enemy.

Without more ado Rome declared war on Carthage and despatched a fleet and army to Africa under the Consuls Manilius and Censorinus; when the Consuls landed at Utica they were at once met by Carthaginian envoys begging for peace at any price. They were told that peace could be had, but that Carthage must first give up three hundred hostages, and hand over all arms of any kind within the city. Since resistance seemed pointless, Carthage agreed. The hostages were duly given up, and some 200,000 sets of arms and two thousand catapults are said to have been delivered to the Romans. Then, with Carthage as they thought completely helpless, the Consuls delivered the final blow: the citizens, they said, must quit the city. Carthage was to be utterly destroyed, but the inhabitants could build a new dwelling place wherever they liked, provided it was no less than ten miles from the sea.

For once, however, Rome had overplayed her hand. When the news reached the city, the populace erupted into violence: those who had counselled peace and handing over the arms and hostages were torn to pieces in the streets by angry mobs, and the government was forced into attempting the defence of the city. With great enthusiasm, the whole populace set about replacing the vanished weapons: houses and buildings were despoiled to use their metal, and the stacks of wood on the waterfront were used for the construction of ships and engines of war. Within an incredibly short time the city was put in a state of defence, and messengers had been sent into the hinterland to raise a relief force.

Carthage was naturally strong, situated as it was on a peninsula. It was girdled by a stone wall, forty-six feet high and thirty-four feet thick, studded with towers which rose a further storey above it. In addition, on the landward side, ie at the neck of the peninsula, the city was actually guarded by a triple wall: the main city wall forming the inner defence, with beyond it a deep ditch guarded by a lower, less substantial wall, and beyond that again another ditch with a wooden palisade. The harbour of Carthage was double, the outer being the mercantile port, while the inner or Cothon, circular in shape, was the naval harbour. Its only approach was through the mercantile port, and the narrow entrance was closed off by heavy iron chains.

Nevertheless, the Romans hardly expected any serious resistance and they were quite unprepared for the fanatical fury with which the city was defended. Manlius attacked the land wall, but was driven off with heavy loss; Censorinus with the fleet attempted an attack by way of the lagoon which covered the north-western side, and also failed to make any impression. He then set to work to fill in part of the lagoon, and when this was done succeeded in breaching part

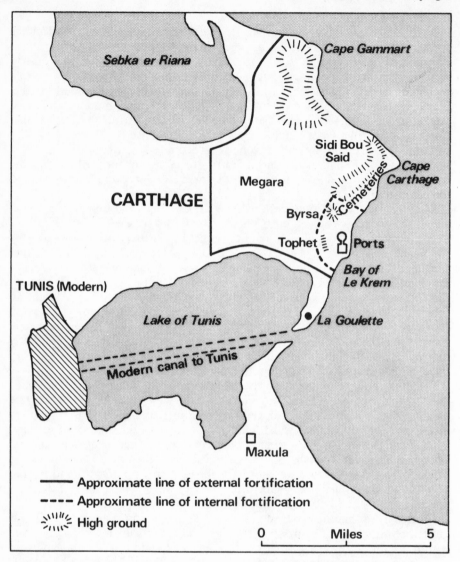

of the walls, but the subsequent assault was beaten back with loss. Not content with this, the defenders made constant damaging sallies, and the Romans were also faced with a new enemy, as disease decimated their crews in the unhealthy area of the lagoon. The year drew to a close and Carthage remained unconquered.

During the winter the position of the besiegers worsened, as an army of relief arrived and encamped outside the city. In 148 the new Consuls, Piso and Mancinus, made no progress, handling affairs with gross incompetence, and being saved from disaster only by the efforts of a military Tribune, Scipio Aemilius, the grandson of Scipio Africanus. The following winter, however, the young Scipio returned to Rome and was there elected Consul with the specific task of the reduction of Carthage; and upon his return to Africa the whole aspect of affairs changed.

Upon his arrival Scipio set about raising the morale and efficiency of his troops and pressing the siege with vigour. His first move was to attack the suburb of Megaera; he succeeded in forcing an entrance with some four thousand men, but later prudently withdrew to avoid getting himself bogged down in an area which was cut up by hedges, watercourses and gardens. However, the operation had an unexpected bonus, for Hasdrubal, the commander of the army outside the walls, thinking the city in danger of falling, drew his troops within the walls to reinforce the garrison, and Scipio was now able to cut the peninsula off from the hinterland. He then proceeded methodically to reduce the interior, thus cutting off any source of supply and reinforcement, before finally turning back upon Carthage itself.

The citizens, however, still fought on with the courage of despair, partly because Hasdrubal, to ensure their resistance, had deliberately paraded all his Roman prisoners across the seaward front of the city and there put them to death with considerable brutality; an action with naturally quelled any possibility of surrender terms. Scipio then set about the building of a massive wall across the harbour mouth further to seal off the city; but the citizens, pouring forth in their thousands, succeeded in tearing down the work before it could be completed, and sending out a force of fifty ships to attack the Roman fleet. Though some successes were at first gained, however, the Carthaginian ships were finally defeated and bottled up in the harbour.

At last, in 146 Scipio was ready to launch the final assault. By now, the shortage of food had taken its toll in the city, and when the Romans assaulted the harbour defences they fell after a brief resistance. Scipio led his army into the city, penetrating without much difficulty to the market-place; but Hasdrubal had withdrawn into the Byrsa, the fortified citadel, and here the last desperate remnant held out for a further six days while the city below them burnt and resounded to the shouts of the victors as they looted and pillaged, and the pitiful cries of the townspeople. Finally the last remnant, some fifty thousand souls it is said threw themselves on Scipio's mercy, including Hasdrubal himself; his wife, of sterner metal, first killed their children and then threw herself into a burning building rather than surrender. Nine hundred deserters from the Roman army who could expect no mercy, also barricaded themselves into a temple and were burned to death.

The city itself burned unchecked for ten days while the Romans looted and pillaged freely, all gold and silver being reserved for the coffers of the State but all other valuables being left to the legionaires. The surviving citizens were all sold into slavery, and then the city was systematically demolished, building by building, until not a stone was left standing. Finally and symbolically the plough was driven across the area and the ground was deliberately salted to show that it was to remain barren for evermore.

So, almost forty years after the death of its greatest son, perished Carthage, once the proud mistress of the Mediterranean. Now, at last, Rome could sleep in peace.

Chapter 16

Summing up

It is always difficult correctly to assess the stature of a General who is defeated in the end; historians tend to assume that he is inevitably inferior to the General who defeated him, forgetting the circumstances which may have brought about that defeat. Of all the great Generals, only Napoleon has risen above this criticism: he, too, was defeated in the last battle of his career—and, indeed, lost a battle or two along the way—yet no-one seriously considers him as anything but the supreme commander of his age. In some ways, of course, it is a measure of the fear in which a seemingly unbeatable General is held that, when he at last goes down in defeat, it is assumed that his conqueror is an even greater soldier. Thus, after the American Civil War, Grant enjoyed, and still does enjoy in many circles, a superior fame to Lee: yet an analysis of their records must inevitably show that Lee was a better man in almost every respect. It is, therefore, not surprising that we find a consensus behind the statement that at Zama, as Polybius says, Hannibal met a better man.

In order to decide just how good Hannibal was, it is necessary to look at the qualities which go together to make up the top-flight commander. The first two are obvious enough—he must be a good strategist and tactician. These abilities do not necessarily go together: there have been many good strategists who failed to win battles, and many excellent battlefield tacticians who had no grasp of strategy. But apart from these, the great General must have many other qualities. He must be a good administrator, otherwise his army will fail for lack of supplies—an ability probably more important in ancient times, when he lacked the backing of a quartermaster's department which today takes the main burden off him. Even today, however, he may well still have to make the right decisions about the allocation of vital supplies: a case in point is in late 1944 when Eisenhower, with limited supplies of petrol and transport, had to base his strategy on their allocation. In all cases except those of a quick, decisive war your General must be capable of long term overall planning so that he does not lose sight of his true objective; yet at the same time he must be capable of improvisation, so that, as Wellington put it, when something goes wrong you tie a knot and carry on. Above all, he must possess the faculty of leadership, that charisma which inspires men to follow and, if necessary, to die for you—something which no truly great General has lacked. Finally, he needs two other abilities: audacity, by which I do not mean rashness, but the ability to know when to be bold, and opportunism, the instinctive grasp of the need of the moment, the hesitation of the enemy which must be instantly exploited.

Let us therefore see how Hannibal matches up to these qualifications. No-one, surely, can doubt his superlative ability as a strategist. The conception of the invasion of Italy by itself is a breath-taking achievement, which completely outwitted the Romans. Rome had assumed that the Second Punic War would follow much the same course as the first, with Carthage essentially on the defensive and Rome dictating the play. No Roman statesman had ever considered the possibility of a Carthaginian invasion of Italy, and when it suddenly dawned on the Senate that this was what was happening, it completely upset their carefully laid plans and forced them to abandon all thought of an invasion of Africa. It is very possible that, but for the inspiration of the elder Scipio, it might well have caused the abandonment also of the invasion of Spain, with incalculable results.

Hannibal's reputation as a strategist does not, however, stand on this feat alone. Some people tend to misinterpret the differences between strategy and tactics; the easiest definition, though it is probably a simplification, is that strategy is the art of luring your opponent into battle under circumstances favourable to you, while tactics is the art of beating him once you have got him there. Taking this definition, then Hannibal's reputation as a strategist would be high enough if it was only based on his three great successes of Trebbia, Trasimene and Cannae, in each of which he manoeuvred to such purpose that the issue was more than half decided before the armies even joined battle. Yet Hannibal was almost certainly to be seen at his best later during the war, in the period after Cannae when many historians have either ignored his achievements or suggested that he was declining in power. With his army steadily dwindling in numbers while that of his opponents grew in strength, he nevertheless marched through much of Italy very much as he pleased, never being caught at a disadvantage himself yet continually springing upon and destroying some unfortunate Roman force. This in itself was strategic ability of the highest order, certainly equal to and probably surpassing Napoleon's conduct of the campaign of 1814—for while Napoleon was operating in friendly country within reach of his capital, Hannibal was marching and counter-marching for much of the time in country which was either dubiously neutral or downright hostile.

Tactically, of course, Hannibal was superb. Cannae was undoubtedly his finest achievement and as such ensures him a place in the Hall of Fame. What other General could turn an open plain into a gigantic trap in full sight of his opponent? It is easy to dismiss the Roman commanders as fools, but as already argued earlier in this book, a true analysis of the situation shows that they were not inexperienced at war and against the normal run of opponents would have been adequate enough. It is true that Hannibal probably would not have caught Scipio Africanus in such a trap—but then he would not have tried to, for one of Hannibal's best traits was that he adapted his tactics and strategy to the character of his opponents, using their own strengths and weaknesses to entrap them. Similarly, the ambush at Trasimene was a supreme use of local conditions carried out with beautiful precision in what must rank as one of the greatest ambushes in all time, while at the Trebbia the way in which the Roman army was drawn across the icy river and into battle on empty stomachs was another masterpiece. These tactical innovations were repeated again and again on a smaller scale during his later years in Italy.

'Ah', I can hear you saying, 'but what about Zama? He got beaten there, didn't he?' True: but an examination of the battle shows clearly that he was beaten, not by a better man but by a better army. His handling of the tactical situation at Zama was probably, under the circumstances, the best that could be done. He certainly outsmarted Scipio by his deployment in three lines and the retaining of his best troops as a reserve, and had the return of the Roman cavalry been delayed much longer the result could easily have gone the other way. He has been harshly criticised for his use of the elephants in this battle, but in fact with eighty of them at his disposal—albeit young and inadequately trained—it was certainly a justifiable tactic to try launching them in one huge shock-wave. It might have succeeded: if it had, those same critics would be hailing Hannibal as a genius. Moreover, all the evidence is that, though the elephants were not as successful as had been hoped, they did in fact inflict casualties on the Roman Velites, who seem to have played little further part in the action, and those which were turned back do not seem to have had much, if any, effect on Hannibal's infantry line. It is true that they do seem to have disordered his cavalry somewhat and contributed to their defeat, but this was inevitable anyway in face of the Roman superiority, even if we do not accept the suggestion that the Carthaginian cavalry had been deliberately ordered to draw that of Scipio off the field.

The very fact that Hannibal's troops survived for years in what was often hostile territory, and lived for other years in friendly but still alien country without alienating the local population by proving an intolerable burden economically, shows that he rates good marks as an administrator. In fact, throughout his years in Italy he tailored his marches admirably to the need for supplies of food for his men and fodder for his horses, and made Rome provide the great bulk of both. Moreover, he contrived, even when cut off from his sources of money in Spain and Carthage, to keep his troops paid and able to refrain from taking supplies from friendly countryside without paying for it—again a major achievement which was attained only by careful economy and using money obtained from the sale of prisoners and booty. He was to prove later, in Carthage after the war, that he had a complete grasp of financial affairs and the ability to see the faults in a corrupt administration and adequately reform them, transforming Carthage from a state of virtual bankruptcy to one of economic stability in only a year or two.

His grasp of overall planning and long term strategy was complete. Few historians have given him credit for the far-seeing plans he had drawn up before ever he began the march to Italy. We will discuss these in more detail later in this chapter; at this stage it is perhaps sufficient to say that he laid down an overall strategy at the beginning and stuck to this through thick and thin, never losing sight of his main objective, which was the voluntary disbanding of the Roman Confederacy and the establishment of a loose organisation of Mediterranean countries in its place—an organisation in which Carthage would play the leading but not necessarily the dominating part. On the smaller scale, his planning of the march from New Carthage to the Po was a feat which has not often been duplicated in military annals. Not only was it a march of great length, but a good deal of it was through territory which he knew only from the reports of his agents and of passing merchants, over two mighty mountain ranges and one major and many lesser rivers. He had to allow for contact with all the various peoples along the route, and wherever possible to induce them to help rather than hinder him, and to pace his march so that he could rely on living off the country most of the time. Even today, to carry a force of that size through a trackless wilderness in face of potentially hostile inhabitants would not be an easy task; yet Hannibal performed it without the help of all the trained staff and mechanical devices which would be at the disposal of today's commander.

When we come to the matter of leadership, again Hannibal can rank with the best. He was never in command of a truly national army, but regularly led one which was made up from men of various races and creeds—native Carthaginians, Africans from the hinterland, Numidians, Spaniards of differing tribes, Gauls and Celts from Cisalpine Gaul and Liguria, Italians from Campania, Lucania and Bruttium, and probably Moors, Greeks and other races in a minor degree. Yet we never read of any quarrelling between these nationalities, and very rarely of any disloyalty or desertion, despite the long years spent in circumstances which grew steadily more strained as the advantage swung toward Rome at the end of the war. Hannibal does not seem to have achieved this in the manner of Napoleon, or even perhaps Alexander or Marlborough, all of whom were gifted with silver tongues and the ability to mingle with the common herd and trade jest for jest. Although in his youth in Spain there is evidence that he got on well with the Celtiberian tribesmen, he was never a convivial man, and by the time he left Spain he seems to have become a somewhat austere figure. Yet, like all great men, he had the ability to inspire trust and loyalty, even affection, and he retained throughout his long life a dry sense of humour which from time to time inspired such remarks as the exchange with Gisco before Cannae. Of all his officers only one, Masinissa, left him; and in the case of the Numidian prince it was a decision of purely political origin where self-interest was stronger than any friendship or respect Masinissa may have felt for Hannibal. It is noticeable, however, that Hannibal was able thus to influence the simple warrior peoples and fighting men more than the statesmen and the aristocrats. He had less success with the rulers of Carthage, and when he fled to Syria there was an almost total lack of communication with the decadent court of Antiochus III. It was probably the simple strengths of the man himself which called out to those same qualities in the common soldier—plus, of course, the confidence and trust in his leadership which could be born only of experience. Hannibal's veterans knew that when he committed them to battle he had done everything humanly possible to ensure victory, and that the rest was up to them; and in return they did their best for him.

Audacity and an instinctive grasp of the moment to act, Hannibal had in plenty. He was always producing something new, and compared to the plodding workhorse Generals of Rome he was the purebred stallion. Time and again his enemies thought they had him trapped, and time and again he broke out by simple audacity or by ingenious use of their own mistakes. His escape from the Falernian Plain when Fabius thought he had him penned is a case in point, but there are plenty of others. The tactical use of the mist at Trasimene and the icy waters of the Trebbia spring naturally to mind, and the baiting of Minucius was a brilliant indication of how he used the characters of his opponents against them.

Thus we find that in all these essentials Hannibal scores very high marks indeed. What were his main strengths? I think his greatest strength was his ability to handle every part of his army in unity so that each part fulfilled its complete potential. He is, of course, renowned for his use of cavalry—though some uninformed individuals have claimed that Maharbal was the great cavalry leader. Cavalry played a large part in all Hannibal's victories, but it was not just a battlefield strength. Hannibal knew that cavalry is at its showiest on the battlefield, but it really earns its corn by scouting, feeling for the enemy in advance, covering the rear in retreat, obtaining knowledge for its commander while denying knowledge to the enemy. For all these latter duties, of course, Hannibal's Numidian light horse was ideal, and he used it superbly. In addition, when the time came for battle the light horse was again used naturally; not for them the shock action of the heavy Spanish and African cavalry, but holding actions designed to tie down the enemy until the heavy cavalry could deliver the *coup de grâce*. After an action, the Numidians could be unleashed for pursuit of the fugitives; but always in any event, they were under perfect control, always capable of carrying out further tasks.

Similarly the heavy cavalry were used for their principal purpose of shock action, but again were kept on a very tight rein. In Napoleonic times the British heavy cavalry could usually defeat their French counterparts in a charge, but once committed it was almost impossible to control them. At Cannae, the Carthaginian heavy horse charged and broke the cavalry opposing them, rallied, rode round the Roman army, charged and broke the Italian horse opposing the Numidians, rallied again and charged into the rear of the Roman infantry: evidence of a very high standard of control indeed, and of the superb co-ordination by Hannibal.

However, though he used his cavalry as a battle-winner, Hannibal knew the true worth of his infantry too, and used it to perfection in every situation. In almost every case one part of his army consisted of Gallic tribal levies, excellent fighters but not as well trained and disciplined as his African and Spanish veterans. While it is true that the tribes of Cisalpine Gaul did defeat a couple of Roman armies, in both cases these were probably fairly second-rate troops without much experience. Normally Roman armies, with their excellent training and discipline, had little difficulty in defeating much larger numbers of Gauls who were probably more than a match for them man-to-man, but could not match them in the mass. Yet under Hannibal's guidance the Gauls fought with a fair amount of skill and precision, as witness their fighting retreat at Cannae which was so important to Hannibal's plan. Somehow he inspired them with confidence and the ability to find a staying power unusual to the volatile barbarian. His Spaniards and Africans were, of course, very good infantry indeed, and once fitted out with Roman equipment were equal to the best Roman troops. They were therefore given the tasks that needed manoeuvreability and shock power, and proved themselves fully capable of it. Yet the same type of troops failed in Spain under different commanders—a further proof of how Hannibal could raise his troops above themselves.

Hannibal could also use his light infantry with finesse, and they always acquitted themselves well. The escape from the Falernian Plain, though due to Hannibal's improvisation and cunning, would have been impossible but for the work of the light infantry, who showed themselves capable of operating on their own and using a high degree of initiative and enterprise. But more important than any of these individual skills was the way Hannibal wove them together into a coherent whole, as the conductor links together the instruments in his orchestra; when Hannibal conducted, everyone played in tune.

Probably his other greatest strength was his unfailing eye for terrain. Hannibal always made the terrain fight for him, and he chose his battlefields with great care: with the single exception of Zama, where circumstances allowed him little choice, he dictated the choice of terrain and refused battle until the ground suited him. To this was allied the ability to think his way round difficulties, and he was never too proud to give ground if he thought it necessary. Hannibal was never one to bull his way through by a frontal attack when he could find his way in by the back door, and above all he was careful of his men's lives—something which is always apparent to the man in the ranks and is valued highly by him.

Did Hannibal have any weaknesses? Strategically, it is hard to put a finger on a weak point in his career. Many writers have criticised him for not marching on Rome after Cannae, but we have already been through the arguments for and against such a move which, to my mind, show that he made the correct decision. In fact, the real mistake Hannibal made may well have been much earlier, when he chose not to give battle to Scipio the Elder on the Rhône. As discussed earlier, at the time this was a very logical decision: why risk a battle at this point, with the possibility of unprofitable losses, when the action could be fought more profitably later in Italy? As it turned out, however, the decision may well have been wrong. If Hannibal had fought Scipio on the Rhône, all the evidence shows that the result would have been the destruction of Scipio's army, with the consequences that there would have been no invasion of Spain that year. With Hannibal loose in Italy, it seems very likely that no Roman army would have sailed for Spain the next year either, or the year after that—years in which Hasdrubal could have tightened his control over the Iberian Peninsula and sent reinforcements to his brother. Who knows what the results might have been? It could be, indeed, that the whole fate of the Second Punic War was decided by Hannibal's decision not to fight on the Rhône, and Scipio's complementary decision to send his army on to Spain.

Hannibal has also been accused of lacking in siegecraft. This may well be true to an extent, but if so it was a failing shared by almost every commander of an age where the defence, as typified by fortified cities, was stronger than the attack. With the single exception of New Carthage which was inadequately garrisoned and taken by a *coup de main*, no major city fell quickly during this period of history, and most showed a capability of holding out for years at a time. This was to be largely the case until gunpowder was introduced to counter the strength of stone walls, and even then the engineers were not slow to introduce new and ingenious touches to make fortifications almost impervious to attack. If a city was held stoutly enough, it could only be taken by assault by an army which was prepared to buy it with blood, and that was never Hannibal's way. Strangely enough, many of the other great commanders of history have been deficient in siegecraft: Napoleon's only experience of it was at Toulon—where admittedly he showed an eye for ground in siting his guns—Alexander ran into grave difficulties at Tyre. Wellington's capture of Ciudad Rodrigo and Badajoz were unbelievably bloody affairs and he was stopped dead at Burgos; while Marlborough at the great siege of Lille wisely handed it over to his colleague Eugene and commanded the covering army. So if Hannibal had a weakness here, he was in good company.

Possibly a more important failing on Hannibal's part was his lack of interest in naval affairs. He was, like Napoleon, essentially a land animal, and until given a squadron of ships by Antiochus seems to have had little dealings with the sea. As we have discussed earlier, he was probably unimpressed by the record of the Carthaginian fleet in the First Punic War, and felt that little reliance could be placed upon it—a judgement that was, also, to prove only too true. It is debatable whether, in fact, he could have done much to make an impact on naval affairs; there was a squadron of warships stationed in Spain which were presumably at his disposal, but there is no evidence that he was ever in a position to influence the conduct of the main Carthaginian fleet. After taking over most of southern Italy, however, he seems to have made no attempt to use the Tarentine fleet to his advantage; though small, it seems to have been reasonably efficient. Here again of course, he may have been influenced by his policy of never seeming to interfere in the affairs of his Italian allies, but overall one cannot escape the feeling that he underestimated the importance of control of the sea.

To decide just where Hannibal stands as a General it is necessary to compare him with his contemporaries and with other commanders. Of the general run of both Roman and Carthaginian commanders we need say little: as a rule, they were competent but uninspired, pedestrian Generals who did things by the book and were incapable of original thought. On the Roman side, Marcellus comes through as perhaps the Roman Blucher, full of fighting spirit if lacking in great tactical skill, and his death was an undoubted blow to Rome. Claudius Nero showed during the Metaurus campaign that he had a sound grasp of both strategy and tactics, and it would have been interesting to see him in action elsewhere: it is hard to rate a General on the strength of one campaign. Fabius showed sound common sense and it is arguable that his policy saved Rome by giving her time to recover from the blow of Trasimene; on the other hand it may well be that his policy was in fact too supine and led irrevocably to the disaster of Cannae. It cannot be denied that he was a man of great moral courage, but he does not seem to have been possessed of much tactical or strategical skill. Scipio the Elder, as we have already mentioned, showed sound judgement in sending his army on to Spain instead of carrying it back to Italy, but tactically he does not impress. It is quite clear that, despite the claims of Livy, Hannibal was never defeated or even in danger of defeat during his years in Italy, and that he was in fact a pike among minnows.

Which brings us to Scipio Africanus, and the claims that he was a better man than Hannibal. Let us, therefore, examine Scipio's achievements. In his first campaign in Spain he showed great strategical insight and considerable tactical dash in his seizure of New Carthage, though it must be admitted that the situation was made to measure for just such an enterprise by the lack of co-operation between the three Carthaginian commanders. After this, however, his performance in Spain, though capable, is not completely impressive. At Baecula he defeated Hasdrubal but allowed him to get away the better part of his army and slip off to Italy unchallenged, after which he seems to have spent the next campaigning season doing very little indeed. His best battle was probably Ilipa, where he showed great tactical skill: though here we cannot judge completely owing to the storm which brought the battle to a premature close. Certainly the pursuit and destruction of Hasdrubal's army after Ilipa was a masterly performance. None of these feats, however, can reasonably be contrasted with Hannibal's performance in Italy under far more trying circumstances.

So we come to the invasion of Africa. Scipio's strategy here was by no means a new one, for he was merely following in the footsteps of Agathocles and Regulus, and indeed, but for Hannibal, Rome would have launched such an invasion in 218 BC. His conduct of the actual invasion seems, compared with

Hannibal's invasion of Italy, hesitant and over-cautious, though it is easy to be critical and Scipio's methods payed off in the end. Finally we come to Zama itself. We cannot fault Scipio's strategy in drawing Hannibal inland away from his base, or the ravaging of the Bagradas area which probably forced Hannibal into battle before he was ready. But at Zama itself Scipio showed little or no tactical originality: his army was deployed very much in the standard Roman fashion, with the one exception of the elephant lanes, and the battle was won purely by the excellence of his infantry and the numerical superiority of his cavalry. While, therefore, there can be no doubt that Scipio was the best Roman General of his day, I would not hesitate to pronounce Hannibal the better all-round soldier.

If we search further for comparisons, the obvious one is with Alexander the Great. No-one denies Alexander his place among the best Generals in history, yet when one compares his achievements with those of Hannibal, one cannot help being struck by the advantages Alexander possessed. He inherited from his father the best army in the world, and he never faced one of similar worth: the fact that he was usually heavily outnumbered does not offset this, for numbers do not make up for quality, as has been proved time and time again. Similarly, he faced a succession of fairly mediocre Generals: so did Hannibal, but Alexander's opponents did not include a Scipio Africanus with an army to match. But Alexander's great advantage was that he was not only General but ruler as well, with control of the state at his fingertips; he decided the strategy of the war as a whole, not just his part of it. While not in any way belittling Alexander's achievements, they were accomplished in circumstances far more favourable than those of Hannibal. If you weight the great Carthaginian in the balance against the Macedonian, the scales must be pretty level.

Finally, how does Hannibal compare with later protagonists such as Marlborough, Frederick the Great, or Napoleon? In the case of the last two, again we note the same advantage as with Alexander, in that they were masters of their fate where Hannibal was not. Marlborough was not completely so, but at least he had a say in the grand strategy of the alliance and did not spend years cut off in a hostile country. It is a strange fact that all of these Generals seemed to deteriorate tactically in the latter part of their careers, tending to discard the tactical innovations and rapier like thrusts of their earlier days in favour of brutal, bloody frontal attacks—though it could be argued that in Marlborough's case Malplaquet was not fought in the manner he intended it—whereas Hannibal seemed to improve with the years in Italy; and it must be remembered that he fought far longer than any of the other Generals in question. Probably a much fairer comparison is with another great commander who failed in the end—Rober E. Lee. The two shared a number of characteristics, one being a chivalrous attitude toward the enemy, as evidenced in Hannibal's case by his treatment of dead Roman Generals; but here again, Lee held the fort against superior resources for a mere four years, Hannibal for four times that length.

The conclusion is therefore inescapable: Hannibal, on all counts, ranks with the greatest Generals in history.

It would be foolish to close this summary without posing the question: could Carthage have won? On the face of it, looking at the resources of the two protagonists, the answer would appear to be, emphatically, no. As we have seen, Rome's resources in manpower were far greater than those of Carthage, and politically her dominions were far more stable. This latter fact was in part because her main conquests had been in areas which had already been colonised and civilised by the Greeks, or had contained civilisations older than that of Rome, such as Etruria and Samnium, while the Carthaginian empire in Spain and Africa consisted of comparatively uncivilised tribal areas which could not be readily absorbed into a political whole. It must be admitted, moreover, that in Italy the Roman conquest had been carried out with more humanity than was to mark Roman expansion over the rest of the world, and that by the time in question large areas of Italy had accepted Roman domination without resentment. Carthage's advantages lay in her maritime trade and her control of Spanish silver, but both of these were inevitably at risk in time of war and were likely to be eroded away. Spain was both her strength and her weakness: she drew much of her wealth and many of her troops from the area, but her occupation had been too short for her to attain any real integration of the tribes, with the result that when the Romans invaded, the tribes were only too ready to play off one side against the other to their own advantage. Fully as many Spaniards fought for Rome in the Second Punic War as fought for Carthage.

However, it is necessary to look deeper below the surface to see whether Rome's victory was in fact inevitable. When Hannibal first drew up his plans for carrying a war with Rome into Italy, his design went far beyond the mere fact of fighting on enemy soil rather than his own: he had, in fact, a grand design which aimed at altering the whole balance of power in the Mediterranean. Hannibal was, first and foremost, the servant of Carthage and, as he saw it, there would be no safety for Carthage as long as Rome controlled Italy; her successful expansion into Sicily and Sardinia would only be the prelude to a further clash of interests in which Carthage by herself would be heavily outweighed. Hannibal, as was to be proved later when he intervened in Carthaginian politics after the war, was at heart a democrat rather than an aristocrat; his political ideas were related far more to those of tribal Spain and Gaul or democratic Greece than to the aristocratic domination of both Rome and his own Carthage. What he seems to have envisaged was a Mediterranean world in which the free peoples of Spain, Gaul, Italy and Greece all gathered together in a great confederation under the leadership of Carthage.

The idea may sound preposterous to us, but it was based on certain solid facts. Hannibal had already made a good start in Spain, where he had increased the independence of some tribal leaders in the area he had taken over from Hasdrubal the Splendid, and had endeavoured to persuade rather than coerce the tribes north of the Ebro. It is quite possible that, without a Roman invasion to spark off tribal discontent, Spain might have gradually evolved into an autonomous state within the Carthaginian sphere. Hannibal had made friends with the majority of the Gallic tribes both north and south of the Alps, and it is possible that, given time, they too could have been brought into the loose confederation Hannibal envisaged. But the corner-stone of the edifice was the cities of southern Italy—Magna Graecia—and, to a slightly lesser extent, Samnium and Etruria. The industrial potential of Campania, plus Capua's very real jealousy of Rome, the old stirrings of democracy to be found in any Greek-founded city, made this a possibility indeed. Break the power of Rome in the field, and Magna Graecia could regain its independence.

It was, perhaps, a dream, but it was a dream founded on reality. It is interesting to speculate on what would have happened to the world if it had succeeded. Certainly Carthage itself would have had to change, and it is doubtful if this would have been acceptable to the ruling aristocracy. Yet a Hannibal with all the aura of success behind him would have been strong enough, one imagines, to have brought democracy to his native city. Greece, too, would almost inevitably have been drawn into the fold, probably Macedonia too. Whether the dream would have survived Hannibal, though, seems doubtful: the alliance was perhaps too volatile, the chances of the individual members wanting supreme power too great.

In the end, as we have seen, the dream foundered, mainly because Hannibal over-estimated the spirit of rebellion against Rome. He was perhaps fifty years too late; to the citizen of Samnium or Etruria, and to many in Campania and other parts of the south, there was more reason now to identify with rather than against Rome, and it was Hannibal and his soldiers who were the aliens; while the Latins themselves never wavered in their support of Rome. Yet, even so, if Spain had held and reinforcements had come from that quarter, or if Carthage had stretched herself to contest the control of the sea and support Hannibal from that direction: even if the invasion of Sicily in support of Syracuse had been handled with real efficiency, Roman power might have been weakened to the extent that her hold over Italy might have faltered. We cannot say for sure: all we can say is that, after Hannibal, Rome was never again in serious danger of failing to become mistress of the world. Certainly she never forgot Hannibal, and perhaps that is epitaph enough.

Bibliography

The most important sources for any study of Hannibal or the Punic Wars are of course, Polybius and Livy. Unfortunately the complete work of Polybius has not survived, so that his coverage is at times patchy compared with that of Livy. Polybius may not compare with Livy for style of writing, but he has the inestimable virtue of sticking to facts rather than using imagination, and one can surely do without the tedious, interminable speeches which Livy inevitably invents for the main characters in any action. Livy, nevertheless, has his uses as long as one treats him with suspicion.

Among other ancient writers, Plutarch, Appian and Cassius Dio are the most helpful, and for our purposes, in what is intended as a work of military history rather than a political one, Appian probably contributes the most. Here again, however, one cannot necessarily take everything he says on trust.

Besides the ancients, there are a number of standard works dating to this century which are of considerable interest; the ones I have used to any extent are listed below:

Arnold, Dr G.: *The Second Punic War*.
Barker, P.: *Armies of the Macedonian & Punic Wars*.
Beer, Sir Gavin de: *Hannibal's March*.
Bosworth Smith, R.: *Rome and Carthage*.
Church, A.J.: *Carthage*.
Connolly, P.: *The Roman Army*.
Connolly, P.: *Hannibal and the Enemies of Rome*.
Cottrell, L.: *Enemy of Rome*.
Creasey, Sir Edward: *Decisive Battles of the World*.
Denison, G.T.: *History of Cavalry*.
Dodge, T.A.: *Hannibal*.
Dorey, T.H. & Dudley, D. H.: *Rome Against Carthage*.
Fuller, J.F.C.: *Decisive Battles of the Western World*
Lamb, H. *Hannibal*.
Lazenby, J.F.: *Hannibal's War*.
Picard, G.C. & C.: *Life and Death of Carthage*.
Scullard, H.H.: *Scipio Africanus*.
Warmington, B.H.: *Carthage*.